Canadian Short Stories
FIFTH SERIES

D1258596

Canadian Short Stories
FIFTH SERIES

Selected by
ROBERT WEAVER

TORONTO
Oxford University Press
1991

Oxford University Press, 70 Wynford Drive, Don Mills, Ontario M3C 1J9

Toronto Oxford New York
Delhi Bombay Calcutta Madras Karachi Petaling Jaya
Singapore Hong Kong Tokyo Nairobi Dar es Salaam
Cape Town Melbourne Auckland

and associated companies in
Berlin Ibadan

CANADIAN CATALOGUING IN PUBLICATION DATA
Weaver, Robert, 1921—
Canadian short stories, fifth series

ISBN 0-19-540738-5

1. Short stories, Canadian (English).*
2. Canadian fiction (English) - 20th century.* I. Title

PS8319.C355 1991 C813' 0108054 C91-093780-X PR9197.32.C355 1991

Cover painting photographed by See Spot Run Inc., Toronto

In memory of
MORLEY CALLAGHAN
1903-1990

Contents

Preface

This is the fifth short-story anthology I've edited for Oxford University Press in an occasional series called *Canadian Short Stories*. The first collection was published in 1960, and as I wrote at the time, it was 'designed to give a very general impression of the development of the short story in Canada'. It began with stories by E.W. Thomson, Sir Charles G.D. Roberts, and Duncan Campbell Scott and ended with two young writers who were not yet in their thirties, Alice Munro and Mordecai Richler—all anthologists should have that good luck.

The 1950s in Canada were for the most part a period of economic expansion and political blandness when the arts struggled to survive in thin soil. But there were some favourable developments as well. The CBC and the National Film Board had come out of the war with admirable reputations and were still enjoying good times. When the Canada Council was founded in 1957 it quickly had an influence on all the arts and for a number of years was remarkably little criticized.

As for the short story, in 1947 Desmond Pacey had been able to put together a substantial collection, *A Book of Canadian Stories*, and this anthology went through four editions by 1967. But short-story collections by individual writers certainly weren't common in the 1950s; by the standards of recent years their numbers were pathetic. However, three significant collections were published in the latter half of the decade: Mavis Gallant's *The Other Paris* in 1956, and in 1959 both *Morley Callaghan's Stories* and Thomas Raddall's *At the Tide's Turn and Other Stories.* Even so, at the end of the 1950s poetry was flourishing in Canada, the novel's status was respectable, but the literary orphan was still the short story.

There was no thought in 1960 that the first *Canadian Short Stories* might have a successor. But there *was* a successor in 1968 that concentrated on stories from the 1950s and early 1960s and included Hugh Hood, Margaret Laurence, Dave Godfrey, and Shirley Faessler. Two indications in this period that the short story was at least gaining official respect were a Governor General's Award to Hugh Garner for *Hugh Garner's Best Stories* in 1963 and to Alice Munro for her first collection, *Dance of the Happy Shades*, in 1968.

The *Third Series* of *Canadian Short Stories* was published in 1978 and contained short fiction from the late sixties and the seventies. Among its contributors were Norman Levine, Margaret Atwood, Jack Hodgins, John Metcalf, Audrey Thomas, and Rudy Wiebe. A Fourth Series (in 1985) of stories from the early eighties included Sandra Birdsell, Leon Rooke, Joyce Marshall, Guy Vanderhaeghe, and Helen Weinzweig.

This *Fifth Series* concentrates on the second half of the 1980s. Thirty years after the first *Canadian Short Stories* appeared, the problem of selection was of course much more difficult. The number of writers whose work must be considered had increased dramatically. Collections of short fiction come from McClelland & Stewart, Penguin, Macmillan, and other publishers in Toronto, but also from Oolichan and Sono Nis on Vancouver Island, Talon in Vancouver, Coteau in Regina, and Turnstone in Winnipeg—to name a few of the regional publishers that distribute their literary books nationally. Yet anthologies have to deal with constraints in size and budget. To the writers we would have liked to publish here but could not, we offer our regrets.

The stories in this book take place in various parts of Canada and abroad. Many of the writers were born and have always lived here; others have come from all corners of the world. The mixture of origins and preoccupations found now in Canadian fiction is surely one of its most attractive qualities. On the one hand the writers here explore, as do writers in other countries, their own backyard, a region or community. In this book there are stories that take place in Toronto and Vancouver, in a cottage in Saskatchewan, and in one of Alice Munro's fictional towns in southwestern Ontario. On the other hand, many of these stories take place outside the country—in France, Scotland, and the United States, in Iceland and the Caribbean. In two of the stories there is even a curious linkage of home and abroad, local and international: Timothy Findley's 'Stones' is a Toronto story, while Norman Levine's 'Something Happened Here' takes place in northern France; but pivotal to both stories is the tragic assault by Canadian troops on Dieppe in the Second World War. As long ago as the twenties and thirties Morley Callaghan—to whose memory this book is dedicated—found no difficulty placing his stories in Paris or New York, as well as in Toronto and the small Ontario towns beside Georgian Bay. There then developed a preference for stories set in the regions of Canada. Now, the battle over regionalism versus internationalism seems barely relevant.

Only two writers have appeared in all five of these anthologies: Mavis Gallant and Alice Munro. Women writers were in a minority in Canada when Gallant and Munro first began publishing, but there have been remarkable changes since that time, which this collection bears witness to: women contributors outnumber the men.

The arts may have had to survive in thin soil in the 1950s, but as I remember the time there was a stubborn belief in the idea of progress. As we enter the 1990s the situation is in some ways more depressing. In attempting to continue to fulfil their mandates, organizations such as the CBC and the Canada Council are suffering from exhaustion. The dramatic collapse early in 1991 of the Toronto publisher Lester & Orpen Dennys was bad news for writers and readers alike. The economy is soft, and of the present government in Ottawa it must be said that if it has an arts policy, that policy is unsympathetic. Now, more than ever before, it is clear that the government support that has assisted the production of a large body of distinguished works by creative Canadians in all the arts—which we continue to take for granted and enjoy, and some of which have made their way internationally—must not be diminished, and certainly never withdrawn.

I want to thank Oxford University Press for giving me such a long run. I owe special thanks to my longtime editor and friend, William Toye, and to Phyllis Wilson.

ROBERT WEAVER

Toronto
March 1991

Acknowledgements

MARGARET ATWOOD. 'Age of Lead' reprinted by permission of Margaret Atwood, © 1989, to be published in the collection *Wilderness Tips* in Canada by McClelland and Stewart.

NEIL BISSOONDATH. 'Security', originally published as part of the short story collection *On the Eve of Uncertain Tomorrows*, Lester & Orpen Dennys 1990. Copyright © Neil Bissoondath.

DIONNE BRAND. 'St Mary's Estate' from *San Souci and Other Stories*. Published by Williams-Wallace Publishers, Toronto. Reprinted with permission.

BONNIE BURNARD. 'Moon Watcher' from *Women of Influence* (Regina: Coteau Books, 1988). Reprinted with permission of the author and publisher.

TIMOTHY FINDLEY. 'Stones' from *Stones* by Timothy Findley. Copyright © Pebble Productions, Inc., 1988. Reprinted by permission of Penguin Books Canada Limited.

CYNTHIA FLOOD. 'The Young Girl Typist . . .' from *Animals in Their Elements* © 1987, Cynthia Flood, Talon Books Ltd, Vancouver.

MAVIS GALLANT. 'Lena' from *Overhead in a Balloon* by Mavis Gallant © 1985. Reprinted by permission of Macmillan of Canada, a Division of Canada Publishing Corporation.

KATHERINE GOVIER. 'The King of Siam' from *Before and After*. Copyright © Katherine Govier, 1989. Reprinted by permission of Penguin Books Canada Limited.

JANICE KULYK KEEFER. 'A Really Good Hotel' from *Travelling Ladies*, copyright Janice Kulyk Keefer. Reprinted by permission of Random House Canada Limited.

NORMAN LEVINE. 'Something Happened Here' by Norman Levine, from *Something Happened Here*, published in Canada by Viking Canada. © Norman Levine 1991. Reprinted by arrangement with the author.

DANIEL DAVID MOSES. 'King of the Raft' copyright © Daniel David Moses. Reprinted by permission of the author.

ALICE MUNRO. 'Meneseteung' from *Friends of My Youth* by Alice Munro. Used by permission of the Canadian Publishers, McClelland and Stewart, Toronto.

CAROL SHIELDS. 'Milk Bread Beer Ice' from *The Orange Fish*, copyright © 1990 by Carol Shields. Reprinted by permission of Random House Canada Limited.

DIANE SCHOEMPERLEN. 'The Red Plaid Shirt' from *Man of My Dreams* © 1990. Reprinted by permission of Macmillan of Canada, a Division of Canada Publishing Corporation.

AUDREY THOMAS. 'Blue Spanish Eyes' from *The Wild Blue Yonder*. Copyright © Audrey Thomas, 1990. Reprinted by permission of Penguin Books Canada Limited.

W.D. VALGARDSON. 'The Cave' from *What Can't Be Changed Shouldn't Be Mourned* by W.D. Valgardson. Reprinted by permission of the publisher, Douglas & McIntyre.

RUDY WIEBE. 'A Night in Fort Pit or (if you prefer) The Only Perfect Communists in the World' from *Alberta Rebound*. © Rudy Wiebe 1989. By permission of the author.

MARGARET ATWOOD

The Age of Lead

The man has been buried for a hundred and fifty years. They dug a hole in the frozen gravel, deep into the permafrost, and put him down there so the wolves couldn't get to him. Or that is the speculation.

When they dug the hole the permafrost was exposed to the air, which was warmer. This made the permafrost melt. But it froze again after the man was covered up, so that when he was brought to the surface he was completed enclosed in ice. They took the lid off the coffin and it was like those maraschino cherries you used to freeze in ice-cube trays for fancy tropical drinks: a vague shape, looming through a solid cloud.

Then they melted the ice and he came to light. He is almost the same as when he was buried. The freezing water has pushed his lips away from his teeth into an astonished snarl, and he's a beige colour, like a gravy stain on linen, instead of pink, but everything is still there. He even has eyeballs, except that they aren't white but the light brown of milky tea. With these tea-stained eyes he regards Jane: an indecipherable gaze, innocent, ferocious, amazed, but contemplative, like a werewolf meditating, caught in a flash of lightning at the exact split second of his tumultuous change.

Jane doesn't watch very much television. She used to watch it more. She used to watch comedy series, in the evenings, and when she was a student at university she would watch afternoon soaps about hospitals and rich people, as a way of procrastinating. For a while, not so long ago, she would watch the evening news, taking in the disasters with her feet tucked up on the chesterfield, a throw rug over her legs, drinking a hot milk and rum to relax before bed. It was all a form of escape.

But what you can see on the television, at whatever time of day, is edging too close to her own life; though in her life, nothing stays put in those tidy compartments, comedy here, seedy romance and sentimental tears there, accidents and violent deaths in thirty-second clips they call *bites*, as if they are chocolate bars. In her life, everything is mixed together. *Laugh, I thought I'd die*, Vincent used to say, a very long time ago, in a voice imitating the banality of mothers; and that's how it's getting to be. So when she flicks on the television these days, she flicks it off again soon enough. Even the commercials, with their surreal dailiness, are beginning to look sinister, to suggest meanings behind themselves, behind their façade of cleanliness, lusciousness, health, power, and speed.

Tonight she leaves the television on, because what she is seeing is so unlike what she usually sees. There is nothing sinister behind this image of the frozen man. It is entirely itself. *What you sees is what you gets*, as Vincent also used to say, crossing his eyes, baring his teeth at one side, pushing his nose into a horror-movie snout. Although it never was, with him.

The man they've dug up and melted was a young man. Or still is: it's difficult to know what tense should be applied to him, he is so insistently present. Despite the distortions caused by the ice and the emaciation of his illness, you can see his youthfulness, the absence of toughening, of wear. According to the dates painted carefully onto his nameplate, he was only twenty years old. His name was John Torrington. He was, or is, a sailor, a seaman. He wasn't an able-bodied seaman though; he was a petty officer, one of those marginally in command. Being in command has little to do with the ableness of the body.

He was one of the first to die. This is why he got a coffin and a metal nameplate, and a deep hole in the permafrost—because they still had the energy, and the piety, for such things, that early. There would have been a burial service read over him, and prayers. As time went on and became nebulous and things did not get better, they must have kept the energy for themselves; and also the prayers. The prayers would have ceased to be routine and become desperate, and then hopeless. The later dead ones got cairns of piled stones, and the much later ones not even that. They ended up as bones, and as the soles of boots and the occasional button, sprinkled over the frozen stony treeless relentless ground in a trail heading south. It was like the trails in fairy tales, of bread crumbs or seeds or white stones. But in this case nothing had sprouted or lit up in the moonlight, forming a miraculous pathway to life; no rescuers had followed. It took ten years before anyone knew even the barest beginnings of what had been happening to them.

All of them together were the Franklin Expedition. Jane has seldom paid much attention to history except when it has overlapped with her knowledge of antique furniture and real estate— '19th C. pine harvest table', or 'prime location Georgian centre hall, impeccable reno'—but she knows what the Franklin Expedition was. The two ships with their bad-luck names have been on stamps—the *Terror*, the *Erebus*. Also she took it in school, along with a lot of other doomed expeditions. Not many of those explorers seemed to have come out of it very well. They were always getting scurvy, or lost.

What the Franklin Expedition was looking for was the Northwest Passage, an open seaway across the top of the Arctic, so people, merchants, could get to India from England without going all the way around South America. They wanted to go that way because it would cost less, and increase their profits. This was much less exotic than Marco Polo or the headwaters of the Nile; nevertheless, the idea of exploration appealed to her then: to get onto a boat and just go somewhere, somewhere mapless, off into the unknown. To launch yourself into fright; to find things out. There was something daring and noble about it, despite all of the losses and failures, or perhaps because of them. It was like having sex, in high school, in those days before the Pill, even if you took precautions. If you were a girl, that is. If you were a boy, for whom such a risk was fairly minimal, you had to do other things: things with weapons or large amounts of alcohol, or high-speed vehicles, which at her suburban Toronto high school, back then at the beginning of the sixties, meant switchblades, beer, and drag races down the main streets on Saturday nights.

Now, gazing at the television as the lozenge of ice gradually melts and the outline of the young sailor's body clears and sharpens, Jane remembers Vincent, sixteen and with more hair then, quirking one eyebrow and lifting his lip in a mock sneer and saying, 'Franklin, my dear, I don't give a damn.' He said it loud enough to be heard, but the history teacher ignored him, not knowing what else to do. It was hard for the teachers to keep Vincent in line, because he never seemed to be afraid of anything that might happen to him.

He was hollow-eyed even then; he frequently looked as if he'd been up all night. Even then he resembled a very young old man, or else a dissipated child. The dark circles under his eyes were the ancient part, but when he smiled he had lovely small white teeth, like the magazine ads for baby foods. He made fun of everything, and was adored. He wasn't adored the way other boys were adored, those boys with surly lower lips and greased hair and a studied air of smouldering menace. He was adored like a pet. Not a dog, but a cat. He went where he liked, and nobody owned him. Nobody called him *Vince*.

Strangely enough, Jane's mother approved of him. She didn't usually approve of the boys Jane went out with. Maybe she approved of him because it was obvious to her that no bad results would follow from Jane's going out with him: no heartaches, no heaviness, nothing burdensome. None of what she called *conse-*

quences. Consequences: the weightiness of the body, the growing flesh hauled around like a bundle, the tiny frill-framed goblin head in the carriage. Babies and marriage, in that order. This was how she understood men and their furtive, fumbling, threatening desires, because Jane herself had been a consequence. She had been a mistake, she had been a war baby. She had been a crime that had needed to be paid for, over and over.

By the time she was sixteen, Jane had heard enough about this to last her several lifetimes. In her mother's account of the way things were, you were young briefly and then you fell. You plummeted downwards like a ripe apple and hit the ground with a squash; you fell, and everything about you fell too. You got fallen arches and a fallen womb, and your hair and teeth fell out. That's what having a baby did to you. It subjected you to the force of gravity.

This is how she remembers her mother, still: in terms of a pendulous, drooping, wilting motion. Her sagging breasts, the downturned lines around her mouth. Jane conjures her up: there she is, as usual, sitting at the kitchen table with a cup of cooling tea, exhausted after her job clerking at Eaton's department store, standing upright all day behind the jewellery counter with her bum stuffed into a girdle and her swelling feet crammed into the mandatory medium-heeled shoes, smiling her envious, disapproving smile at the spoiled customers who turned up their noses at pieces of glittering junk she herself could never afford to buy. Jane's mother sighs, picks at the canned spaghetti Jane has heated up for her. Silent words waft out of her like stale talcum powder: *What can you expect*, always a statement, never a question. Jane tries at this distance for pity, but comes up with none.

As for Jane's father, he'd run away from home when Jane was five, leaving her mother in the lurch. That's what her mother called it—'running away from home'—as if he'd been an irresponsible child. Money arrived from time to time, but that was the sum total of his contribution to family life. Jane resented him for it, but she didn't blame him. Her mother inspired in almost everyone who encountered her a vicious desire for escape.

Jane and Vincent would sit out in the cramped backyard of Jane's house, which was one of the squinty-windowed little stuccoed wartime bungalows at the bottom of the hill. At the top of the hill were the richer houses, and the richer people: the girls who owned cashmere sweaters, at least one of them, instead of the Orlon and lamb's wool so familiar to Jane. Vincent lived about halfway up the hill. He still had a father, in theory.

They would sit against the back fence, near the spindly cosmos flowers that passed for a garden, as far away from the house itself as they could get. They would drink gin, decanted by Vincent from his father's liquor hoard and smuggled in an old military pocket flask he'd picked up somewhere. They would imitate their mothers.

'I pinch and I scrape and I work my fingers to the bone, and what thanks do I get?' Vincent would say peevishly. 'No help from you, Sonny Boy. You're just like your father. Free as the birds, out all night, do as you like and you don't care one pin about anyone else's feelings. Now take out that garbage.'

'It's love that does it to you,' Jane would reply, in the resigned, ponderous voice of her mother. 'You wait and see, my girl. One of these days you'll come down off your devil-may-care high horse.' As Jane said this, and even though she was making fun, she could picture Love, with a capital L, descending out of the sky towards her like a huge foot. Her mother's life had been a disaster, but in her own view an inevitable disaster, as in songs and movies. It was Love that was responsible, and in the face of Love, what could be done? Love was like a steamroller. There was no avoiding it, it went over you and you came out flat.

Jane's mother waited, fearfully and uttering warnings but with a sort of gloating relish, for the same thing to happen to Jane. Every time Jane went out with a new boy her mother inspected him as a potential agent of downfall. She distrusted most of these boys; she distrusted their sulky, pulpy mouths, their eyes half-closed in the up-drifting smoke of their cigarettes, their slow, sauntering manner of walking, their clothing that was too tight, too full, too full of their bodies. They looked this way even when they weren't putting on the sulks and swaggers, when they were trying to appear bright-eyed and industrious and polite for Jane's mother's benefit, saying goodbye at the front door, dressed in their shirts and ties and their pressed heavy-date suits. They couldn't help the way they looked, the way they were. They were helpless; one kiss in a dark corner would reduce them to speechlessness, they were sleepwalkers in their own liquid bodies. Jane on the other hand was wide awake.

Jane and Vincent did not exactly go out together. Instead they made fun of going out. When the coast was clear and Jane's mother wasn't home, Vincent would appear at the door with his face painted bright yellow, and Jane would put her bathrobe on back to front and they would order Chinese food and alarm the delivery boy and eat sitting cross-legged on the floor, clumsily, with chopsticks. Or Vincent would turn up in a threadbare thirty-year-old suit and a bowler hat and a cane, and Jane would rummage around in the cupboard for a discarded church-going hat of her mother's, with smashed cloth violets and a veil, and they would go downtown and walk around, making loud remarks about the passers-by, pretending to be old, or poor, or crazy. It was thoughtless and in bad taste, which was what they both liked about it.

Vincent took Jane to the graduation formal, and they picked out her dress together at one of the second-hand clothing shops Vincent frequented, giggling at the shock and admiration they hoped to cause. They hesitated between a flame-red with falling-off sequins and a backless hip-hugging black with a plunge front, and chose the black, to go with Jane's hair. Vincent sent a poisonous-looking lime-green orchid, the colour of her eyes he said, and Jane painted her eyelids and fingernails to match. Vincent wore white tie and tails, and a top hat, all frayed

Sally-Ann issue, and ludicrously too large for him. They tangoed around the gymnasium, even though the music was not a tango, under the tissue-paper flowers, cutting a black swath through the sea of pastel tulle, unsmiling, projecting a corny sexual menace, Vincent with Jane's long pearl necklace clenched between his teeth.

The applause was mostly for him, because of the way he was adored. Though mostly by the girls, thinks Jane. But he seemed to be popular enough among the boys as well. Probably he told them dirty jokes, in the proverbial locker room. He knew enough of them.

As he dipped Jane backwards, he dropped the pearls and whispered into her ear, 'No belts, no pins, no pads, no chafing.' It was from an ad for tampons, but it was also their leitmotif. It was what they both wanted: freedom from the world of mothers, the world of precautions, the world of burdens and fate and heavy female constraints upon the flesh. They wanted a life without consequences. Until recently, they'd managed it.

The scientists have melted the entire length of the young sailor now, at least the upper layer of him. They've been pouring warm water over him, gently and patiently; they don't want to thaw him too abruptly. It's as if John Torrington is asleep and they don't want to startle him.

Now his feet have been revealed. They're bare, and white rather than beige; they look like the feet of someone who's been walking on a cold floor, on a winter day. That is the quality of the light that they reflect: winter sunlight, in early morning. There is something intensely painful to Jane about the absence of socks. They could have left him his socks. But maybe the others needed them. His big toes are tied together with a strip of cloth; the man talking says this was to keep the body tidily packaged for burial, but Jane is not convinced. His arms are tied to his body, his ankles are tied together. You do that when you don't want a person walking around.

This part is almost too much for Jane, it is too reminiscent. She reaches for the channel switcher, but luckily the show (it is only a show, it's only another show) changes to two of the historical experts, analysing the clothing. There's a closeup of John Torrington's shirt, a simple, high-collared, pin-striped white-and-blue cotton, with mother-of-pearl buttons. The stripes are a printed pattern, rather than a woven one; woven would have been more expensive. The trousers are grey linen. Ah, thinks Jane. Wardrobe. She feels better: this is something she knows about. She loves the solemnity, the reverence, with which the stripes and buttons are discussed. An interest in the clothing of the present is frivolity, an interest in the clothing of the past is archaeology; a point Vincent would have appreciated.

After high school, Jane and Vincent both got scholarships to university, although Vincent had appeared to study less, and did better. That summer they did everything together. They got summer jobs at the same hamburger heaven, they went to movies together after work, although Vincent never paid for Jane. They still occasionally dressed up in clothes and went downtown and pretended to be a weird couple, but it no longer felt careless and filled with absurd invention. It was beginning to occur to them that they might conceivably end up looking like that.

In her first year at university Jane stopped going out with other boys: she needed a part-time job to help pay her way, and that and the schoolwork and Vincent took up all her time. She thought she might be in love with Vincent. She thought that maybe they should make love, to find out. She had never done such a thing, entirely; she had been too afraid of the untrustworthiness of men, of the gravity of love, too afraid of consequences. She thought however that she might trust Vincent.

But things didn't go that way. They held hands, but they didn't hug; they hugged, but they didn't pet; they kissed, but they didn't neck. Vincent liked looking at her, but he liked it so much he would never close his eyes. She would close hers and then open them, and there would be Vincent, his own eyes shining in the light from the streetlamp or the moon, peering at her inquisitively as if waiting to see what odd female thing she would do next, for his delighted amusement. Making love with Vincent did not seem altogether possible.

(Later, after she had flung herself into the current of opinion that had swollen to a river by the late sixties, she no longer said 'making love'; she said 'having sex'. But it amounted to the same thing. You had sex, and love got made out of it whether you liked it or not. You woke up in a bed or more likely on a mattress, with an arm around you, and found yourself wondering what it might be like to keep on doing it. At that point Jane would start looking at her watch. She had no intention of being left in any lurches. She would do the leaving herself. And she did.)

Jane and Vincent wandered off to different cities. They wrote each other postcards. Jane did this and that. She ran a co-op food store in Vancouver, did the financial stuff for a diminutive theatre in Montreal, acted as managing editor for a small publisher, ran the publicity for a dance company. She had a head for details and for adding up small sums—having to scrape her way through university had been instructive—and such jobs were often available if you didn't demand much money for doing them. Jane could see no reason to tie herself down, to make any sort of soul-stunting commitment, to anything or anyone. It was the early seventies; the old heavy women's world of girdles and precautions and consequences had been swept away. There were a lot of windows opening, a lot of doors: you could look in, then you could go in, then you could come out again.

She lived with several men, but in each of the apartments there were always cardboard boxes, belonging to her, that she never got around to unpacking; just as well, because it was that much easier to move out. When she got past thirty she decided it might be nice to have a child, sometime, later. She tried to figure out a way of doing this without becoming a mother. Her own mother had moved to Florida, and sent rambling, grumbling letters, to which Jane did not often reply.

Jane moved back to Toronto, and found it ten times more interesting than when she'd left it. Vincent was already there. He'd come back from Europe, where he'd been studying film; he'd opened a design studio. He and Jane met for lunch, and it was the same: the same air of conspiracy between them, the same sense of their own potential for outrageousness. They might still have been sitting in Jane's garden, beside the cosmos flowers, drinking forbidden gin and making fun.

Jane found herself moving in Vincent's circles, or were they orbits? Vincent knew a great many people, people of all kinds; some were artists and some wanted to be, and some wanted to know the ones who were. Some had money to begin with, some made money; they all spent it. There was a lot more talk about money, these days, or among these people. Few of them knew how to manage it, and Jane found herself helping them out. She developed a small business among them, handling their money. She would gather it in, put it away safely for them, tell them what they could spend, dole out an allowance. She would note with interest the things they bought, filing their receipted bills: what furniture, what clothing, which *objets*. They were delighted with their money, enchanted with it. It was like milk and cookies for them, after school. Watching them play with their money, Jane felt responsible and indulgent, and a little matronly. She stored her own money carefully away, and eventually bought a townhouse with it.

All this time she was with Vincent, more or less. They'd tried being lovers but had not made a success of it. Vincent had gone along with this scheme because Jane had wanted it, but he was elusive, he would not make declarations. What worked with other men did not work with him: appeals to his protective instincts, pretenses at jealousy, requests to remove stuck lids from jars. Sex with him was more like a musical workout. He couldn't take it seriously, and accused her of being too solemn about it. She thought he might be gay, but was afraid to ask him; she dreaded feeling irrelevant to him, excluded. It took them months to get back to normal.

He was older now, they both were. He had thinning temples and a widow's peak, and his bright inquisitive eyes had receded even further into his head. What went on between them continued to look like a courtship, but was not one. He was always bringing her things: a new, peculiar food to eat, a new grotesquerie to see, a new piece of gossip, which he would present to her with a sense of occasion, like a flower. She in her turn appreciated him. It was like a yogic exercise, appreciating Vincent; it was like appreciating an anchovy, or a stone. He was not everyone's taste.

There's a black-and-white print on the television, then another: the nineteenth century's version of itself, in etchings. Sir John Franklin, older and fatter than Jane had supposed; the *Terror* and the *Erebus*, locked fast in the crush of the ice. In the high Arctic, a hundred and fifty years ago, it's the dead of winter. There is no sun at all, no moon; only the rustling northern lights, like electronic music, and the hard little stars.

What did they do for love, on such a ship, at such a time? Furtive solitary gropings, confused and mournful dreams, the sublimation of novels. The usual, among those who have become solitary.

Down in the hold, surrounded by the creaking of the wooden hull and the stale odours of men far too long enclosed, John Torrington lies dying. He must have know it; you can see it on his face. He turns towards Jane his tea-coloured look of puzzled reproach.

Who held his hand, who read to him, who brought him water? Who if anyone loved him? And what did they tell him, about whatever it was that was killing him? Consumption, brain fever, Original Sin. All those Victorian reasons, which meant nothing and were the wrong ones. But they must have been comforting. If you are dying, you want to know why.

In the eighties, things started to slide. Toronto was not so much fun any more. There were too many people, too many poor people. You could see them begging on the streets, which were clogged with fumes and cars. The cheap artist's studios were torn down or converted to coy and upscale office space, the artists had migrated elsewhere. Whole streets were torn up or knocked down. The air was full of windblown grit.

People were dying. They were dying too early. One of Jane's clients, a man who owned an antique store, died almost overnight of bone cancer. Another, a woman who was an entertainment lawyer, was trying on a dress in a boutique and had a heart attack. She fell over and they called the ambulance, and she was dead on arrival. A theatrical producer died of AIDS, and a photographer; the lover of the photographer shot himself, either out of grief or because he knew he was next. A friend of a friend died of emphysema, another of viral pneumonia, another of hepatitis picked up on a tropical vacation, another of spinal meningitis. It was as if they had been weakened by some mysterious agent, a thing like a colourless gas, scentless and invisible, so that any germ that happened along could invade their bodies, take them over.

Jane began to notice news items of the kind she'd once skimmed over. Maple groves dying of acid rain, hormones in the beef, mercury in the fish, pesticides in the vegetables, poison sprayed on the fruit, God knows what in the drinking water. She subscribed to a bottled springwater service and felt better for a few weeks, then read in the paper that it wouldn't do her much good, because whatever it was had been seeping into everything. Each time you took a breath, you breathed some of it in. She thought about moving out of the city, then read about toxic dumps, radioactive waste, concealed here and there in the countryside and masked by the lush, deceitful green of waving trees.

Vincent has been dead for less than a year. He was not put into the permafrost or frozen in ice. He went into the Necropolis, the only Toronto cemetery of whose general ambience he approved;

he got flower bulbs planted on top of him, by Jane and others. Mostly by Jane. Right now John Torrington, recently thawed after a hundred and fifty years, probably looks better than Vincent.

A week before Vincent's forty-third birthday, Jane went to see him in the hospital. He was in for tests. Like fun he was. He was in for the unspeakable, the unknown. He was in for a mutated virus that didn't even have a name yet. It was creeping up his spine, and when it reached his brain it would kill him. It was not, as they said, responding to treatment. He was in for the duration.

It was white in his room, wintry. He lay packed in ice, for the pain. A white sheet wrapped him, his white thin feet poked out the bottom of it. They were so pale and cold. Jane took one look at him, laid out on ice like a salmon, and began to cry.

'Oh Vincent,' she said. 'What will I do without you?' This sounded awful. It sounded like Jane and Vincent making fun, of obsolete books, obsolete movies, their obsolete mothers. It also sounded selfish: here she was, worrying about herself and her future, when Vincent was the one who was sick. But it was true. There would be a lot less to do, altogether, without Vincent.

Vincent gazed up at her; the shadows under his eyes were cavernous. 'Lighten up,' he said, not very loudly, because he could not speak very loudly now. By this time she was sitting down, leaning forward; she was holding one of his hands. It was thin as the claw of a bird. 'Who says I'm going to die?' He spent a moment considering this, revised it. 'You're right,' he said. 'They got me. It was the Pod People from outer space. They said, "All I want is your poddy."'

Jane cried more. It was worse because he was trying to be funny. 'But what *is* it?' she said. 'Have they found out yet?'

Vincent smiled his ancient, jaunty smile, his smile of detachment, of amusement. There were his beautiful teeth, juvenile as ever. 'Who knows?' he said. 'It must have been something I ate.'

Jane sat with the tears running down her face. She felt desolate: left behind, stranded. Their mothers had finally caught up to them and been proven right. There were consequences after all; but they were the consequences to things you didn't even know you'd done.

The scientists are back on the screen. They are excited, their earnest mouths are twitching, you could almost call them joyful. They know why John Torrington died; they know, at last, why the Franklin Expedition went so terribly wrong. They've snipped off pieces of John Torrington, a fingernail, a lock of hair, they've run them through machines and come out with the answers.

There is a shot of an old tin can, pulled open to show the seam. It looks like a bomb casing. A finger points: it was the tin cans that did it, a new invention back then, a new technology, the ultimate defence against starvation and scurvy. The Franklin Expedition was excellently provisioned with tin cans, stuffed full of meat and soup and soldered together with lead. The whole expedition got lead poisoning. Nobody knew it. Nobody could taste it. It invaded their bones, their lungs, their brains, weakening them and confusing their thinking, so that at the end those that had not yet died in the ships set out in an idiotic trek across the stony, icy ground, pulling a lifeboat laden down with toothbrushes, soap, handkerchiefs, and slippers, useless pieces of junk. When they were found (ten years later, skeletons in tattered coats, lying where they'd collapsed) they were headed back toward the ships. It was what they'd been eating that had killed them.

Jane switches off the television and goes into her kitchen—all white, done over the year before last, the outmoded butcher-block counters from the seventies torn out and carted away—to make herself some hot milk and rum. Then she decides against it; she won't sleep anyway. Everything in here looks ownerless. Her toaster oven, so perfect for solo dining, her microwave for the vegetables, her espresso maker—they're sitting around waiting for her departure, for this evening or forever, in order to assume their final, real appearances of purposeless objects adrift in the physical world. They might as well be pieces of an exploded spaceship orbiting the moon.

She thinks about Vincent's apartment, so carefully arranged, filled with the beautiful or deliberately ugly possessions he once loved. She thinks about his closet, with its quirky particular outfits, empty now of his arms and legs. It has all been broken up now, sold, given away.

Increasingly the sidewalk that runs past her house is cluttered with plastic drinking cups, crumpled soft-drink cans, used take-out plates. She picks them up, clears them away, but they appear again overnight, like a trail left by an army on the march or by the fleeing residents of a city under bombardment, discarding the objects that were once thought essential but are now too heavy to carry.

NEIL BISSOONDATH

Security

Alistair Ramgoolam stretched himself carefully out on the sofa in the living room, the cushion under his head oozing a newness powerful enough to efface, at least momentarily, the thicker, sweeter scents of the incense sticks he had lit in the corner behind him. He clasped his hands on his paunch—the stomach medicine was slow in acting on his ulcer—and sighed. The smell, of plastic and newly milled material, distressed him; it conjured an unfamiliarity and a sense of dislocation he had never really believed would come to him. To his children and his grandchildren, yes, but not to him or to his wife of so many years. He mumbled, in a voice of grumbling complaint, 'I knew we were insecure in that place.'

But only the television responded: *Althea Wilson, come on down!* And Althea Wilson, convulsed with nerves gone epileptic, bounded ecstatically from the audience, careened down the stairs, her heavy breasts leaping and swaying as if alive under her blouse, to the podium at the front.

Mr Ramgoolam thought: Fool, why are you making such a spectacle of yourself? On national television, yet? But a part of him envied her, coveted this opportunity for wealth that had so easily bartered itself for her dignity.

Althea Wilson, on the verge of drooling, yelped and squealed and squirmed before the microphone, as if called by nature and not permitted to answer. The television audience applauded, roared its approval of Althea Wilson, of her fellow competitors, of the silver-haired host recoiling into his own dignity with a febrile guardedness. Mr Ramgoolam could not push away the man's silver hair, his wrinkled face, the plasticized smile, and the eyes appalled by, disbelieving of, the thirsts he had un-leashed.

Mr Ramgoolam shifted onto his side, away from the bright television, banishing from sight this vision of himself as he might be, as—he was uncomfortably aware—he had partly become. But he could not fully escape Althea Wilson, knew too well the dynamics of the emotion and the manipulated greed, needed too deeply the vicarious thrill of her excitement. His gaze drifted to the balcony doors, a geometry of black aluminum frame and double-glazed glass, windows and wiremesh screens. He could see the narrow balcony, his back yard now, and the sky grey and unfriendly beyond. These clouds, this deepening greyness; the sky seemed to weigh on him, like the heavy blankets in which he still felt encased.

His wife had removed the drapes before going to work that morning, lifting with them a sense of cloister, baring the living room to the sky and the clouds and the tops of taller buildings. Earlier that morning, peering through the dusty panes and squared wiremesh, he had been able to see, as if for the first time because so long unseen, the solid, upward rush of the dense downtown, the trees still stripped to forlorn brown in the—at last!—fading winter, the distant lake a grey horizontal smudge almost indistinct from the sky. It had been an enervating sight, and he could not prevent a rush of resentment against his wife, against the missing drapes, against the city itself.

Mr Ramgoolam thought with unease of the hours of television that lay ahead, the game shows and the movies and the discus-sions of beauty and sex. The weekdays were long for him. He had not, even after many months, grown accustomed to the endless stretches of being alone. Someone had always been there: his mother, his wife, a maid. But now—curious thought—his wife went out to work. His eldest son—after years of residence here, Canadian to the point of strangeness—was at his desk in a big, black office tower downtown, a telephone receiver plastered to one ear, a computer terminal sitting luminescent on his desk. Vijay, his second son, having taken to life in the new country more avidly than his father would have guessed after the unhappiness of his university years, was out there somewhere, working on the deals that he mentioned only vaguely, keeping details to himself with a calculated display of irritation. His youngest son was at the university, studying a subject—something to do with electrical impulses in crabs legs—that Mr Ramgoolam would have thought foolishness were it not for the lucrative job offers his son, not even close to graduation, was already receiving.

He closed his eyes, felt his consciousness slip. A deep male voice boomed orgasmic over a set of new luggage. His awareness grew listless, and he sensed with nebulous pleasure the tentative encroachment of submerged images.

Images of bustle and fear. Of darkness buzzing with a confusion of rumours. Of shortened breath and the acidic seething of his ulcer.

Vijay, grown mysteriously from a wild-eyed teenager into a gloomy young man, a little extra skin on him now—he looked no longer simply like a rake, but like a rake draped loosely in a flesh-coloured garment—had quietly taken charge. Vijay had surprised his father with his cool efficiency, the effect, Mr Ramgoolam speculated, of the business degree he had paid so dearly for and which had seemed, in the years following Vijay's return to the island from Toronto, to have been utterly useless. But, the boy had done well in the multiplying chaos. Had somehow, through whispered telephone calls and furtive car trips into the night, made what he called 'arrangements'.

'Arrangement?' Mr Ramgoolam had said. 'Arrangements for what?'

And he had put it well, the boy, with a subtlety Mr Ramgoolam appreciated even at the time, even as his wife crumpled tearfully into her handkerchief. Vijay had said, 'To go, Pa. To Toronto.' Not, Mr Ramgoolam noted, to *leave* but *to go*: The boy was forward-looking.

'When?'

'In two hours.'

'Two hours!'

'Two hours or nothing.'

'How?'

'By plane.'

'What plane? No planes comin' in these days.'

But Vijay had not replied, had simply gazed back at him with a look that was tired of questions.

Mrs Ramgoolam had said, 'Two hours? But, son, is not enough time to pack, we have too much—'

'Ma.' Vijay's voice was merciless. 'One person, one suitcase.'

Her mouth fell slowly open. 'One person, one suitcase?'

'But you jokin', son.' Mr Ramgoolam reached out a hand to support his wife. 'We live here all our lives, Vijay. How we going to put a lifetime in one suitcase?'

'Pack tight.' Vijay spun on his heel, headed for his bedroom.

Mr Ramgoolam was stunned. But he was, at the same time, pleased to note that his son had made his 'arrangements' as he himself had always conducted his business, deftly, with skill but without fanfare, knowing through experience slyly acquired which string to pull, which button to press. And presenting, then, a *fait accompli*. For the first time, he felt pride in Vijay, felt him to be his son in ways beyond the physical. It made the packing—a discarding of the sentimental in favour of the financial—easier on him.

Vijay, silent, tension channelled into activity of quiet bustle, loaded family and baggage into his Mercedes convertible. He remained indifferent to his mother's sobbing, seemed himself unmoved by considerations other than those of flight: so what if this was the house he'd grown up in? so what if his parents were leaving behind significant parts of themselves? Vijay's gloominess had nothing of the sentimental about it. Mr Ramgoolam knew this about his son, appreciated it, understood that much of his strength—the strength here displayed—came from this bloodless practicality. But it disturbed him, nevertheless. He wished he could have seen in his son the merest hint of regret, the briefest glance backwards. But Vijay would make no concession, concentrated on the task at hand: the easing of the car from the driveway, the chaining of the gate that had to it the feel of unreasoned ritual, senseless but comforting.

They seemed such a little group, Mr Ramgoolam thought, feeling suddenly vulnerable as they rushed through the quiet night, through its deceptions and its camouflaged perils. He sat in the front seat beside his son while his wife sat sniffling in the back seat beside their hand luggage, Vijay driving in his usual anarchic way, the darkness a spur to his recklessness. Mr Ramgoolam shut his eyes, the lids heavy and stinging against the lower rims.

Vijay had not put on the headlights. He didn't want to draw attention, pointed out he would spot the lights of oncoming vehicles before they saw him, would be able to avoid them with ease. Mr Ramgoolam wondered what would happen if the other driver had had the same ideas as his son but he said nothing— Vijay was in charge—and settled for not staring into the nocturnal void ahead. He opened his eyes only occasionally during the drive through the deserted streets, and it was the sight of blackened vehicles and smouldering ruins, the frantic dishevelment of wilful urban disorder, that caused his ulcer to seethe. Only then did he realize that, in the haste of departure, he had neglected to bring along his bottle of stomach medicine.

The airplane flight—a powered surge through the black, starless night, offering in its first minutes a distant glimpse of the city below aglow with dim electricity and angry flame, followed quickly by visions of another, deeper, more encompassing void—was an agony of pain and uncertainty. It was then, as Mr Ramgoolam writhed in discomfort and Vijay, function fulfilled, responsibility relieved, lapsed into a reverie of alcohol and pills furtively consumed, that his wife seemed suddenly seized by a vein of energy he had thought long exhausted. A clearness appeared in her eyes, a sureness in her touch and her words, that made him think of youth. But it took him a while—days, weeks even, so much did he take her personality for granted, so certain was he that he knew the most intimate detail of her—to realize that the change in her went much deeper; that she had shucked off a timidity he had always believed innate, as if leaving the island had unclipped her constraints and revealed a self concealed by the demands and expectations of family and of an island small enough to gossip into scandal the slightest deviation from the social code. And it was there, on the airplane, even as she did what little she could to ease his discomfort, that he sensed the shuffling of intangibles that was her taking possession of herself. That was—and he saw this only later, when he'd understood more clearly what had happened—her taking leave of him.

Their sons were waiting for them at the airport, smiles creasing through the strain on their faces. The eldest—the thoughtful boy!—held a bottle of stomach medicine in his hand, not his usual brand, that wasn't available here, but an effective one nevertheless. After the embraces and the tears and the murmurs of reassurance, Mr Ramgoolam noticed that his sons had failed to bring coats and, having visited Toronto only in winter, having last seen the city in the aftermath of a blizzard, he began upbraiding them for the oversight: why, they would freeze to death without coats in this devil of a country, they should think of their poor mother, their brother, not to mention their long-suffering father, and— What's this? Laughing? Such insolence! You too, Vijay? You going to freeze, too, you know—

But it was the middle of July and outside, away from the air-conditioned comfort of the terminal, the day was as hot and as humid as in the island they'd just left. Even his wife, patting at the her forehead and neck with a perfumed handkerchief, twittered at him as they wended their way through the parking garage, the air seeming to suck perspiration from their pores.

When Vijay saw his elder brother's car, he was horrified. A Honda? Didn't he have any shame? Top of the line? So what? It wasn't a Mercedes, was it? He got in nevertheless, with an unbecoming delicacy, while his younger brother squeezed into the back seat between their parents. Mr Ramgoolam, ulcer going dormant, suddenly felt like kicking Vijay. Mercedes? What nonsense was the boy talking? All that was gone now, didn't he realize that? But he said nothing. He, too, had his regrets to deal with, his losses to mourn. They all did.

Applause exploded. The blond assistant, smiling determinedly through heavy makeup, a human mannequin appealing in her vacuity to Mr Ramgoolam held a camera up to the contestants. Althea Wilson stared hard, listened with puzzlement to the ecstatically voiced description. Thirty-five millimetre. Automatic focus. Automatic flash. Black, solid, compact. A brand-name that meant nothing to her. Great for their vacation shots! How much was it worth? Her brow crinkled into thick parallel cords, perspiration, bright and fresh in the television lights, laminating her skin.

'Two-fifty, you chupid woman,' Mr Ramgoolam muttered. 'Anybody know that.'

Althea Wilson hazarded five hundred.

Mr Ramgoolam sucked his teeth in disgust: Point a television camera at people and they go *bazody*, as if the lens suck out their brains.

A brace of pigeons fluttered onto the balcony railing. Mr Ramgoolam knew he should get up and shoo them away—given half a chance, they would cake the balcony in excrement that dried to the consistency of cement—but he couldn't, just then, be bothered. Pigeons, pigeon feathers, pigeon shit. His eldest son got very exercised over them running onto the balcony flapping his arms and shouting when they threatened to alight; but Mr Ramgoolam figured that everybody—even birds—needed a safe place to land, a comfortable corner to crap. He wouldn't go as far as the woman on the fifth floor who for years littered her balcony with bread and seed for them—it had taken two workmen a week of concentrated labour to chip away the layered excrement—but he couldn't condone his son's almost phobic hatred of them either. Surely their wings would tire, he thought. Surely even pigeons, with their innate sense of direction, occasionally needed a point of reference from which they could reassure themselves of their place in the world. Mr Ramgoolam could deny them such a temporary respite only with difficulty; and then, mainly to keep the peace when his eldest son was around. He watched as the pigeons strutted stiffly on the rail, their round, red-rimmed, manic eyes darting around, orienting themselves, then, one after the other, plunged off as if diving to the earth. He sighed, noticing only then that he had held his breath throughout their presence, that he had managed in the tension of the long moment—looking for the little shot of excrement that he would have to clean up or risk the wrath of this eldest son—to ignore the abrasive fretting of his ulcer.

This bareness open to a greater barrenness: It was, he knew, his fault in the end. He was the one who had insisted on celebrating *Divali* in as traditional a manner as possible. He was the one who had ignored the infidel groans of this youngest son, the fatigued pleas of his wife, the cautions of his eldest son. He was the one who had appealed to an unresponsive Vijay and interpreted his silence as support. He, too, who had gone yesterday to the supermarket to buy the two dozen aluminum muffin cups (In this pagan society you couldn't find *deeyas*, the little earthenware oil lamps that flickered an air of mystery over the alter. He'd had to make do with aluminum muffin cups instead, but that was the price of safety, and progress too, he consoled himself). It was he who had rolled the cottonwool wicks; who had distributed the cups filled with ghee around the living room, making sure that the wicks were adequately soaked and well placed.

While his wife stirred and fried at various pots in the small kitchen; while his youngest son picked at the plates of sweets and appetizers laid out on the table; while Vijay sat hunched in a corner of the sofa smoking a cigarette of vaguely familiar scent; while his eldest son—deliberately, the father thought—worked late at the office, Mr Ramgoolam girded his loins in a *dhoti* and meandered around the living room with a box of matches lighting his modern *deeyas*. The room blazed in the brilliance of the two dozen little flames. Mr Ramgoolam was pleased, was put in mind of his parents' house on *Divali* evening when much of their meagre financial solvency was dissolved in hundreds of the little lights, unbroken lines of them on windowsills, beside pathways, throughout the yard of hardened clay, even along the branches of the mango tree. Spectacle for the gods: the way lit, the house exalted.

Mr Ramgoolam stuck twenty incense sticks into a brass cuspidor filled with potting soil and lit them. 'Ma! Ma!' He called to his wife. 'Come look.'

Mrs Ramgoolam emerged from the kitchen, perspiring, eyes dull with fatigue, wringing her hands in a towel. She looked around, smiled thinly, said, 'It nice, Pa. Very nice. They lookin' like the real thing.' Then she paused, her eyes blinking. 'But—'

Mr Ramgoolam's glow of achievement converted to irritation. 'But what?' he demanded.

But she didn't have to tell him: already the living room was hazy with the smoke of the burning ghee.

His youngest son suggested opening the balcony door to let out some of the smoke. Vijay remarked dreamily that it was a cold night. Instead, Mr Ramgoolam opened the door to the corridor.

His eldest son arrived not two minutes later. He was alarmed. 'What's going on here? The corridor's thick with smoke—'

'We just airin' out the place, son,' Mr Ramgoolam said. 'Look at the *deeyas*, you don't find they pretty—'

'Jesus Christ, Pa, you can hardly breathe in here.'

'Is just temporary, son'—

His son, dropping his briefcase to the floor, swept his hands around the living room. 'We've got to put some of these lights out, Pa. Before someone calls the fire department.'

Mrs Ramgoolam, suppressing a smile of relief, moved to the closest *deeya*.

'No, no!' Mr Ramgoolam snatched at his wife's reaching arm. 'Is bad luck to out a *deeya*, Ma, you don't know that? Don't—'

But he couldn't finish. His words were cut off by the hammering wail of the fire alarm.

His eldest son covered his face with his hands.

His wife and youngest son whipped around the room extinguishing the little fires.

Vijay smiling happily, remained where he was.

When the *deeyas* were all out, when the alarm had been turned off and the firemen sent away with apologies, when the neighbours had all returned to their dinners and their television sets, Mr Ramgoolam stood in the middle of the living room surveying the damage. The incense sticks continued their slow burn in the cuspidor, but his aluminum *deeyas* had all gone cold and dark. The bad luck acquired was incalculable. And in the air cleared of smoke, he saw that the white walls and ceiling now swirled with elegant grey patterns; saw that the white drapes and his shirt and *dhoti*, and his wife's skirt, had greyed. Tissues were splattered black when he blew his nose, the water ran grey when he washed his face.

So it had been his fault when, this morning, his wife stood on a chair and unhooked the drapes for washing, when she unwittingly revealed this world to him, and him to this world. But still, he couldn't help feeling that she should have known better, that she should have had a bit more consideration for his bruised feelings and the imminence of their bad luck. He couldn't, despite himself and because of himself, restrain his resentment.

On the television, Althea Wilson pondered a trade: the camera for the hatbox.

'Take the box,' Mr Ramgoolam muttered. 'Take the box, you stupid woman.'

Mr Ramgoolam wasted no time in attempting to create gainful employment, but he was hindered by the way in which his plans, so well laid, had failed to materialize. It had begun years before, with his eldest son's insistence on spending the Toronto nestegg on a nest, as his son, with the metropolitan sense of humour, had taken to calling the house. The healthy bank account, to Mr Ramgoolam's distress, went suddenly anorexic. He had had to become doubly creative in finding ways of smuggling money out of the island to make the monthly mortgage payments. His son, still at school at the time, had been too busy being independent at plays and operas and European 'films' to find a part-time job. Who the hell was this Bergman—surely not Ingrid—that his son kept writing about in his letters home? Mr Ramgoolam remembered wondering more than once.

As the years passed, the value of the house rose almost dizzily, leaping and jumping with no apparent reason except greed in an overheated market. Mr Ramgoolam's initial anxiety eased, his confidence in his eldest son rising with each new quote received, with each new unsolicited offer to buy the house.

But then, one day out of the blue, his son decided to sell the house, informing his father only after the deal had been finalized. Mr Ramgoolam would have preferred to hold on to it—the property seemed not only a phenomenal investment, but reflected too the traditional virtues of independence, stability and self-reliance that Mr Ramgoolam had learnt from his father—but his son had declared it too much trouble; the house was not new, there was always something that needed repairing, it claimed too much of his time. So he'd sold it to a Yuppie—he had to explain the word to his father as someone young, rich and foolish, someone, his father thought, rather like his son himself—and immediately rolled most of the substantial profit into a condominium, less room but less trouble, paying for it in cash.

So when the family arrived, unexpectedly, little planning possible in the sudden cartwheeling of politics and fear, there was a place for them to go to, but little money available for them to live on. Mr Ramgoolam had hoped to use the excess from the sale to begin a humble business along the lines he knew best, import-export. But the money, a modest if not insignificant sum, was locked into a term deposit. There was nothing for him to work with.

He turned to the newspapers, discovering there, for the first time in the life, his lack of qualification and the limitations of a high school education that had ended almost half a century before. The employment requirements, long lines of incomprehensible terms linked by strings of undefined letters, bewildered him. He gravitated to the simpler jobs, to salaries progressively more modest buttressed by claims progressively more fantastical.

His first job had promised *Progressive Working Conditions. Friendly Supportive Environment. Five Hundred to a Thousand Dollars a Week.* 'Canadians are thirsting for education!' the advertisement had assured, painting a picture of millions of Canadians, crazed by educational deprivation, scrambling and fighting to place encyclopedia orders. He had trudged from door to unfriendly door for a week, encountering not a single person who lit up with relief and delight at his well-rehearsed opening gambit. Only one woman had invited him in, and that only because she had mistaken him for a fellow Jehovah's witness.

His second job—*Join Our Family! Generous Commissions! Twelve Hundred to Fifteen Hundred dollars Per Week! Free Transportation!*—had lasted for two weeks. Few people, he quickly discovered, were interested in owning an industrial strength vacuum cleaner, especially once he had washed and groomed their rugs in demonstration. Surprising himself, he actually managed to sell one to a retired janitor, but it quickly came clear to him that most of the people who made demonstration appointments did so because of age and retirement and a need of company; they usually could not afford the machine, or had failed to understand that this was a sales demonstration and resented learning the sad truth. And, yes, the company provided free transportation—the machine was heavy, and none of the salespeople he had met earned enough to acquire a car—but there were long waits for pickup, anywhere from a half-hour to two hours. Sometimes he was served coffee and cookies by sympathetic, always talkative clients; more often than not he was politely but firmly ushered out to wait on the sidewalk. He quit in a huff the day the company van was an hour late, giving enough time for a storm to break, the rain soaking through his suit and through the box of his demonstration machine. The driver, a young man, himself a salesman, a believer in the school of hardsell and irritated by his own recent failures, had greeted Mr Ramgoolam's complaints with a distinct lack of sympathy.

At home later that evening, having changed out of his wet clothes and into his pyjamas, Mr Ramgoolam ran his hands through his damp hair, long silvered and now thinning as his father's had done in his final years, and told himself he was too old for such nonsense. He deserved a position of greater dignity and ease, had earned the right to be treated with respect, especially by pushy, half-educated, impolite, foul-mouthed puppies like the van driver.

He was up half the night nursing his burning ulcer, while his wife, solicitous but somehow too methodical, her touch and her words governed by a curious dispatch, ministered to him. When, in the silent hours of the early morning, he bemoaned their losses, when he spoke with pain of their jettisoned houses and cars, the abandonment of the accumulations of a lifetime, she sucked her teeth softly, brushed his hair back from his sweat-slicked forehead with her hand and said, 'Shh, shh, is not a time to cry, we ain't have time to cry, we have to think 'bout tomorrow.'

And it was the next day, as he remained in bed with a raw throat and soaring temperature, that she went out without saying a word to him and applied for the job as a cook at the Indian restaurant on Bloor Street.

Mr Ramgoolam was infuriated at the thought of his wife's working. She had never held a job before, had depended on him for money, she the homemaker, he the provider. And now suddenly, he was the one who remained at home, she the one who dressed and went out. It was shameful, it was scandalous. And, when he had had a chance to think about it, it was extraordinary.

Mr Ramgoolam, left to his own devices, could not deal with the ensuing silence, could not fill the empty spaces by himself. He was grateful for the raucous intervention of the television. It offered company of a sort, helped hold back the deeper silence beyond. And it provided, too, the soothing even if ephemeral and vicarious fantasies of easy answers.

'A brand new . . . washing machine!'

The audience gasped as if the curtains had slid back to reveal the British Crown Jewels.

Althea Wilson was stunned. Her hands clapped onto her shining cheeks, her mouth fell open.

Mr Ramgoolam was disappointed. A washing machine: it was like finding a tie under the tree on Christmas morning, or unwrapping a bottle of after-shave lotion at your birthday. Oh well, he thought, at least she could sell it, pocket the cash. But he found her reaction overdone. It was embarrassing. The sum involved—six, seven hundred dollars, no more—was barely significant, it hardly justified a further diminution of dignity. He would have shown greater coolness, a take-it-or-leave-it attitude. But then, he realized, he had never done the wash; that had always been his wife's responsibility. He had no idea of the passions—yes, that was the word, judging by Althea Wilson's reaction—that a washing machine could arouse in a woman. He was pleased for her when, with a flashing of lights and a clanging of bells, the machine was hers; but he could not bear the sight, captured in close-up, of her voluminous buttocks tightly encased in slacks and jiggling in jubilation. He averted his gaze, embarrassed.

Outside, the day remained unfriendly. From time to time, flurries, crazed by unexpected gusts of wind, lurched down out of the sky. The clouds thickening, lost luminosity. A clutch of balloons—red, blue, white, green—lurched drunkenly across the sky.

Mr Ramgoolam thought, with distress, of his wife's going out into this day, into this weather that battered in subtle ways at her body, evoking aches and pains and new abrasions of rheumatism. He thought of her, wrapped in a white apron, cutting and chopping and stirring pots not her own. This vision of her, and of the deep fatigue she brought home every evening, ripped at him, confronted him with failures and inadequacies he had always, in his success, attributed only to other people. She had never complained, his wife, had not once accused him of dereliction of husbandly duty. But she didn't have to. His silent self-accusation sufficed.

Althea Wilson stared glassy-eyed at a projected slide of a blue sea and a crescent of white sand loomed over by a hotel of mammoth proportions. It was a beach such as Mr Ramgoolam had never seen: built up, industrialized. The orgasmic male voice tripped, giggling, over exotic foreign names. The audience caught its collective breath on cue.

Mr Ramgoolam thought of the beaches left behind, thought of plunging into warm, salty water, of playing cricket on the sand with his three sons, these boys whose lives he had so carefully nurtured, whose well-being he had so intensely fretted over. He had long known his sons to be distant from him, the major consequence of travel and education and lives led in foreign lands. The discovery years before had been a blow—his ulcer had grated for days, he had sipped at bottles of stomach medicine as at bottles of soft drink—but he had gradually grown to accept the distancing, even in his mellower moments to view it as a sign, distressing it may have been, of his success as a father.

Now his wife too had grown distant, not through her own fault but through force of circumstance. Yet, he could learn to live with even that.

Most frightening of all, though, was the realization that he too had grown distant, not just from his sons, not just from his wife, but from himself as well. He no longer recognized himself, no longer knew who Alistair Ramgoolam was. Was he the independent businessman, proud of his self-sufficiency and success? No, not any more. Was he this man who spent more time than was healthy in front of a television set while his wife and sons went out to earn a living? No, he would not accept that, refused to believe it. But if he was neither of these, then just what—who—was he? More and more, it seemed, he was the Alistair Ramgoolam of the sofa, the Alistair Ramgoolam who found haven in televised thrills of easy acquisition and in childhood memories, ever sharper, cleansed of ringworm and scorpion stings and vicious parental beatings. It was an Alistair Ramgoolam he did not like. He was becoming the kind of man he had spent much of his life railing against, a man for whom he would have once used the word *parasitic*. But now, watching Althea Wilson sweat under the television lights, seeing her screw up her face in concentrated thought, acknowledging his own longing to be in her place, he thought it an odious word.

Mr Ramgoolam had begun dreaming his own fantasies of easy money, of untold, unearned riches. Every week, he threw out handfuls of lottery tickets and horse race stubs, stepping back from the sense of hope evaporated to the renewed possibilities of fresh numbers and fresh horses. Yet he had earned the right, he thought, had worked hard all his life and did not deserve to find himself returned, in the twilight of his life, to the moneyless uncertainties of his youth.

His luck, it occurred to him, required a measure of divine intervention. He set about erecting, in the tiny den of the condominium apartment, an altar for his morning devotions. He hung various pictures of deities on the wall—the females fair and pink-cheeked, the males black to the point of blueness—constructing below them an altar of stacked milk crates smothered in a length of heavy drapery material.

He located most of the necessary implements in the little Indian-owned stores on Yonge Street, crowded enterprises of glutinous atmosphere and ingratiating service. He had not lingered. The turbanned men and saried women, people so obviously of India in their dress, in their smells, had unsettled him, for while he resembled them, was welcomed as one of them in a language familiar only in a religious context, he felt himself to be different, found himself distrustful of them and wishing to flee.

But he had acquired enough of the brass vases and plates and idols and muffin cups to suit his needs, to more or less reconstruct the altar he had had at home. The result, a delicate blending of piety and glitz necessary to the full exercise of his devotion, pleased him. There was no longer a dew-smothered garden in which to pick fresh flowers, but a daily trip to the convenience store provided the necessary. There was no longer a large yard in which to plant the *jhandi*, the little flags that fluttered at the top of towering bamboo stalks signalling the completion of devotional duty, but he had found an acceptable compromise in a package of wooden chopsticks and a plant-pot of soil tucked into a corner of the balcony.

Mr Ramgoolam was a religious man, but not a philosophical one. He was punctilious in his performance of ritual, but in obedience only to the talismanic, Whatif school of thought: Whatif they—and *they* could be anyone with anything to say on religion, even contradictory information finding a home in his fears and uncertainties and yet powerful childhood sense of mystery—whatif they were right? Whatif opening an umbrella in the house really brought bad luck? Whatif failure to propitiate the gods really attracted their anger? Whatif moving into a house on the astrologically wrong date really led to collapse and personal ruin, even death? Why take the chance? Why not do it all? Why not fulfil all the requirements, only occasionally onerous, and assure a maximum of protection?

He had little adjustments in his life. Beef was banned from the condominium, as was pork. No flesh—no fish, no chicken—was eaten on Fridays. Footwear was left at the door, incense sticks burnt every morning.

His wife paid little attention to his deepening devotions. She was just pleased that he was keeping himself occupied. His sons, less tolerant, protested mildly, but backed down before his adamant rules.

'You always did your *pooja*, Pa,' his youngest son said to him one evening after being upbraided for wearing his shoes in the living room, 'but how come you never get into this incense and beef-banning and all this other shit before? How come now, here, of all places?'

But that was the point, Mr Ramgoolam pointed out with glee, wondering in an aside to his wife what all this education was doing to their children's brains: if they were all here now, in this foreign land, with insufficient money, with his mother slaving away in the kitchen of a Bloor Street restaurant, with his father having to put up with indignity after indignity in the little jobs he had tried, it was all because they had led improper lives before. They had not prayed enough, they had eaten beef and pork, they had failed to consult the gods adequately. This—and Mr Ramgoolam strode to the window, gestured grandiloquently at the sweep of the city, at the soaring buildings, the dense greenery, the placid blue of the distant lake—this, all this, was their punishment.

His son grinned mischievously. 'If that's so, beat me more,' he said.

Mr Ramgoolam was not amused.

In bed that night, he lamented the inadequate upbringing his sons had received. 'We didn't bring them up as good Hindus,

Ma, we didn't give them no culture. And now we payin' for it. Look at them, Ma, look at our sons. Barbarians, every one of them. Stuffin' themselves in restaurants with steak and hotdogs and hamburgers and—' But she was already asleep, head turned away from him, mouth opened in a gentle, rifling snore. Mr Ramgoolam felt abandoned.

It was once more his youngest son—the scientist, as Mr Ramgoolam began sarcastically referring to him—who precipitated a minor theological crisis by pointing out that all of his father's shoes and belts were made of leather: *dead cow skin.* An hour of meditation brought the answer, however: plastic around his waist and running shoes, leatherless, on his feet. His attempt to discard his wife's shoes—she had discovered him in the garbage room attempting to stuff a bag of her footwear into the chute—had met him a hard-eyed rejection.

And she had been less than sympathetic—her response was to twirl her index finger at her temple—when he admitted his growing resentment of the vacuum cleaner and the broom. He objected to the noise of the one, to the stiff man-made fibres of the other. He wished he could lay his hands on a *cocoyea* broom instead, he said, the implement made from the leaves of a dried coconut-tree branch, spines stripped and bound into a crude broom. It was a sweet, soft sound, a soothing swish that evoked in its trail the clucking of chickens and the distant bleat of a grazing goat. And, he claimed, it did a far better job than either vacuum cleaners or these unnatural, new-fangled gizmos. His wife was somewhat less than convinced, reminding him that his mother had used the *cocoyea* broom only to sweep the yard. Inside, she had used a regular, modern broom. Mr Ramgoolam was displeased, resorted in his irritation to sullying his mother's memory by declaring that her house had never really sparkled. 'And the yard was shinin' bright, I suppose?' his wife retorted. 'You coulda eat off it!' he hissed, locking himself away in the bathroom with his sense of his own foolishness.

Mr Ramgoolam began feeling, after a while, that in this

unexpected deprivation was singlehandedly fighting a war of domestic skirmishes to uphold traditions which, he acknowledged, had meant little to him before but which, suddenly, inexplicably, loomed in importance. He could not, when challenged by his sons, explain them; could not, when confronted by his wife's weary hesitation, justify his renewed reliance on them; just knew that in this alien land, far from all that had created him, far from all that he had created, they were vital.

On Saturday mornings, Mr Ramgoolam would tune the radio to a program of popular Indian music, turning the volume up until the sounds reached into every corner of the apartment. Sunday mornings brought a program of popular music and dance on the television, the saried hostess chattering in Hindi between numbers. Mr Ramgoolam would sit in the living room, paying full attention to the programs, not understanding a word that was said or sung, not even really wishing to, simply letting the sounds wash over him, honing his sense of self, taking him back decades to the mystery and hubbub of his parents' religious gatherings: to huge cauldrons of food bubbling spicy aromas at blazing fires, to toothless old women singing and chattering as they stirred and sweated in the flickering light, to grizzled men drinking and arguing as they played cards and smoked marijuana cigarettes late into the night. It was always a disappointment when the programs ended and reality came full-force back at him in the form of a jingled advertisement for a hamburger chain or an unfamiliar airline. Then he would feel an ache just under his ribcage, and his ulcer would begin a gentle burn.

And he felt battered the Saturday morning that his eldest son, awaking with a hangover to the insistent strains of Bombay film music—Indian female singers, he had once remarked, all sounded as if they suffered from permanent nasal congestion—propelled him out to the balcony, pointed to the slash of blue lake in the distance and said in a voice rasped with anger, 'You see that, Pa? That is not the Caribbean. You understand? That is *not* the Caribbean you're seeing there.'

It was from this loneliness, this sense of abandonment, that emerged Mr Ramgoolam deepest worry: Would his sons do for him after his death all that he had done for his parents after theirs? Would they—and, beyond this, *could* they, in this country—fulfil their cremation duties, feed his hungry and wandering soul, have themselves ritually shaved beside a river, dispatch his soul to wherever with the final farewell ceremony? He feared they would not, feared they had grown too far from him and from the past that was his. That they knew none of the reasons the ceremonies had to be performed did not disturb him—neither, after all, did he—but their remaining almost wilfully ignorant of even the simplest of the protective and supplicatory gestures conjured paralyzing visions of his soul abandoned to the vagaries of an alien and forbidding void. Mr Ramgoolam had never credited his imagination with much power; movies, whether in the cinema or on television, had never engaged him, usually lulled him into somnolence after ten or fifteen minutes; books could never hold his attention past the first four or five pages. The images sat dull in his mind, his imagination incapable of sharpening their vagueness into a reality deserving of serious consideration. But now, for the first time in his life, he could imagine only too well the fate that he feared awaited him: could feel himself floating free, out of control in a chilled darkness; could feel his mouth opening and closing in soundless appeals for rescue.

Althea Wilson and a friend would be going to Hawaii. And she was going to have a new camera to take her photographs with. And a set of new luggage to put her new designer wardrobe into. And a thousand dollars spending money. US, Mr Ramgoolam thought, quickly and automatically working out the exchange into Canadian dollars.

His ulcer crabbed at him, its heated pinch spreading and tightening from his belly to under his ribcage and beyond.

Althea Wilson jumped and jumped and jumped. She hugged

the host, never noticing the momentary look of distaste that crossed his smiling face.

Mr Ramgoolam felt the vise-like grip of Althea Wilson fasten itself around his chest.

The host extricated himself, self-consciously straightening his jacket and tie. His expression verged now on the aghast.

Althea Wilson turned in thoughtless exuberance to the blond vacancy, froze momentarily, recoiled, flung herself into the arms of a beaming relative.

Mr Ramgoolam was puzzled when he felt his breath leave him.

The television screen glowed brightly. The images grew indistinct, edges erasing themselves, light eating rapidly into Althea Wilson, the relatives who had run to join her, the host.

Mr Ramgoolam thought: The tube has blown. Tried to sit up on the sofa. Couldn't. His arms would not rise. Legs would not obey. Lungs would not expand.

Applause filled his head.

Alistair Ramgoolam, come on down!

He thought: But I'm not going down, it's up, I'm going up.

And he was blinded by the lights.

DIONNE BRAND

St Mary's Estate

St Mary's Estate was further on. Past the two rum and grocery shops, past Miss Dots', past the savannah, past Miss Jeanne's parlour—paradise plums in large bottle jars. Then a piece of bush. Then St Mary's.

Most of it is still there I notice, as the jeep misses the St Mary's entrance and drives a little way on to Schoener's Road, the dried-out river bed in which duennes used to play all night, or so the story goes. I tell my sister this is where the spirits of dead unchristened children used to live, duennes, calling children in the evening to come and play. Our friend, driving the jeep, asks if I want to write down the correct spelling of the name of the road. I tell him it does not matter. I have known that road and that dry river bed for thirty-four years with a mixture of fear and curiosity, though I've only ever stood this distance from it. The story might still be true. The trees and the stones have been preserved in my head with their sign of silence, yellowness and eerie emptiness. When we look toward the river bed, the three of us, we look as if we're watching something or someone. Not emigration, not schooling, not brightly lit cities have managed to remove the shapes of duennes in the river bed by Schoener's Road. Not even Schoener, probably a dutch privateer, with all his greed and wickedness, debauchery and women-burning, not even he could remove the shapes of duennes in this river bed, by putting his strange name to it. It is still quiet, waiting for dusk to come out calling to play whoop.

The jeep turns around. The two male passengers of a truck

leaving Schoener's Road stare at us as vehicles negotiate passage. Then the jeep turns right into the gravelled entrance of St Mary's. There is still a white sign board on a post, now leaning into the ditch at the entrance, now woodlice eaten. The letters are worn, but officious and distant; painted a long time ago, they survive like the post. A vigilant reminder and a current record of ownership and property. At this point you can see the sea straight ahead, in back of the house where I was born. This entrance gives you a sense of coming home, the same sense I've always had upon seeing it. The eyes light on the completeness of the scene it guards. There are two long barracks, one on each side of the gravel road. In front of the right barracks there is a great tamarind tree, now a little shrivelled but still protecting the place underneath, dirt swept clean, where people, mostly men, used to gather and play cards, drink rum and talk. Of the two barracks this one still houses people. All that is left of the other are the nine to twelve thick white pillars which it stood on once and the triangular moving roof under which copra is put to dry. Bush has overgrown the floors and the walls have been removed, perhaps from fire, or perhaps from ancient wear, sunk into the ground. That's where Cousin Johnny used to live. He was deaf and did not speak. He made beautiful soups and mouth-watering coconut bakes and saltfish. The whole compound would smell sweetly of his bakes on a Saturday evening.

The jeep eases along for another fifty yards; my eyes rest on the place, old and familiar like watching the past, feeling comfortable and awestruck at once. Then too, resentful and sad. A boy atop the left barracks stops raking the copra to watch us. No one else is about. The air is very still, yet breathing, a breeze, quiet and fresh, blowing from the sea. The sea here too, is still. A country beach, a beach for scavenging children, thinking women, fishermen. The sea is not rough or fantastic, nothing more stupendous than an ordinary beauty, ever rolling, ever present. The kind of sea to raise your eyes to from labour. This must have been the look toward the sea that slaves saw as they pulled oxen, cut and shelled coconut, dug provisions from the black soil on the north side of the road. This must have been a look of envy.

There used to be a big well near the tamarind tree. Plait Hair and Tamasine used to live over there, in the third place of the back row of the right barracks. She had seventeen children; he plaited his hair, refusing to cut it. He worked hard, always in silence, his cheeks sucked in. Tamasine was a big red woman, as big as Plait Hair was slight and wiry. The walls separating each quarter of the barracks from the other did not go up to the roof, so everyone could hear what was going on in the other. Each quarter was one room. People used to wonder how Plait Hair and Tamasine had seventeen children, since it was difficult to be private. Maybe they'd wait till everyone was asleep, including their children. Even now, I find myself speculating.

There used to be a lagoon on the left, past the barracks, off into the bush . . .

The gravel road slows the jeep, as it edges toward the small wood house where I was born. Set in the centre to observe the two barracks, its back is toward the sea, its legs standing halfway in sand, halfway in dirt. It's the same house, thirty-four years later. The jeep moves even more slowly because of the silence of the place. As it passes the barracks there is no sign or sound of life except the boy on the copra house gone back to his work.

'It's the same house,' I say; and to my sister, 'Do you remember it?'

'No,' she says, 'I wasn't born yet.'

Two men come out of the house as the jeep pulls to a stop near the front steps. I recognize one of them as the man who took over after my grandfather was fired as overseer of St Mary's Estate. An emotion like resentfulness rises in me. It is only a memory of my grandfather, in his sixties; after twenty years, he was to be let go and, from what I could pick up at three or four years old, this new man was the cause. The new man, the overseer, is now an old man. His youth had been thrown in my grandfather's face and his ability to husband cocoa. I'm amused that something learned such a long time ago can still call upon the same emotion and have it come, fresh and sharp like this. I put on a smile and walk up the steps, my hand outstretched, saying, 'Hi, I was born in this house. I just want to look around.' He cracks a smile in his stern face, as recognition passes over his eyes and confirms, 'Oh you is a Jordann,' saying my last name as it has always sounded—like the name of a tribe, a set of characteristics ranging criminal to saint, axe women to shango priestess, obeah woman. My grandfather's life put the sound into my last name. My grandmother's life put the silence after it. Jordann, like a bearing, like a drum.

My grandfather had children and outside women and outside children. He could read and he could write, which made him valuable. He was the overseer for twenty years at St Mary's. He had an ornate hand and was such a strict parent that all his children wrote exactly like him. He rode two horses, Noble and Buddha. Noble was white and Buddha was black. Noble for show and Buddha for faithfulness. He drank rum at the first shop and the second shop, drinking and gambling out the pittance that he made tending St Mary's for a white man. He wrote letters and took care of everyone else's business. He gave advice freely, he took only advice which could ruin him. He always walked straight up and stiff, the length of his six feet. Until the last years which he spent here, he lived a life of grace, depending on what was not possible, riches, and escaping payment of the debts he incurred dreaming about it. Grace only lasts forever with God, not with white men, so papa was disposed of when age was tired of holding out on his face and when he was unable to create a vision of acres of rich purple cocoa trees for the estate owner. Then everything caught up with him, mostly his debts and we all went to live in town, except he.

He first went to live in a house up a steep cliff which he could not mount because of a sore foot and then settled into a shack near the road where he sold ground provisions, callaloo bush, okra and pepper. Finally he got a job as an agricultural officer, walking miles into the bush to talk to farmers. The last entries in his diary, the ones before he died, only said, optimistically, 'can't go to work, sick today.'

The dirt around the house is mixed with sand and broken bits of shells. During neep tide, the sea comes in as far as the front yard, lashing against the pillow tree trunks which the house stands atop. We get the okay from the new man and head toward the beach. My sister and our friend follow me as I tell them,

'There used to be a lagoon over there; once it caught on fire. This is where we used to put garbage. See the shells are better here. This is a place for a kid to hunt shells and stones. This is where I used to play.'

They follow me, looking at me a little strangely or perhaps trying to see what I see. My childhood—hunting up and down the beach for shells, bits of bottles, snails, things washed up by the sea, lagan; the blue red transparent shine of 'garlent'; seeing how far you could walk; pointing to Point Galeoto; swearing we could see Venezuela; digging into crab holes.

'This is a place for a kid,' I say. 'Every Good Friday, a tree would appear in the lagoon. Mama said it was a sign of Christ.'

We move away toward the lagoon. It is the dry season. The lagoon is still there despite the years of garbage throwing. Then we walk back toward the house, along the beach, and I point toward a river's mouth rippling into the sea, two hundred yards to the right of the wooden house.

'It was hard to cross there, the tide was too strong sometimes.'

And then I see it, and I feel something in me hesitate to walk toward that side. It is a huge green house, hidden from the wood house by trees but visible on the sea side. It used to be yellow, it seems to me; but I could be mistaken. Rust, brought on by the spray of the sea, swells on its sides. It is empty and it is closed. I turn to my sister,

'That fucking house. Do you see that fucking house!'

My sister looks at me, understanding. I cannot bring myself to move toward the house or that part of the beach.

'That goddamned house. It's still there.'

I feel such anger and yet, still, my feet do not move toward it. So angry, I feel nauseous. 'Fuckers!' I yell, but the wind and the sound of the sea lift the word and balloon it into a feeble scream. The uselessness of that sound stops me and I explain to our friend who looks perturbed, 'That's where they used to live.'

In fact, they didn't live there. They came with their children every July. Then we had to be reverential toward them; we could not walk to that side, especially if they were on the beach. They left at the end of August and then, we kids would rush, with my mama who went to clean the house, to see what they had left. Even what they had left we could not touch, thank God, because mama wouldn't allow us. Mostly, we children envied the real doll's head that lay here or there and the shoes discarded. Their children always wore shoes and socks. We ran about like mad things in bare feet and washed-out clothing.

For two months, this wasn't our place. For two months papa bowed and scraped, visibly. And mama warned us grandchildren not to misbehave or embarrass the family.

And still after this long, the imperative of habit and station causes my legs to stand where they are. Do not go near the house. It is the white people's house. It is their place and we are 'niggers'. Reaching back into me, thirty-four years, a command, visceral, fresh as the first day it was given. It still had the power of starvation, whip and . . . blood. I turn and we walk back toward the wood house and the stern-faced new man.

This is where I was born. This is the white people's house. This is the overseer's shack. Those are the estate workers' barracks. This is where I was born. That is the white people's house, this is the overseer's shack those are the slave barracks. That is the slave owner's house this is the overseer's shack those are the slave barracks.

This estate has been here for hundreds of years. Papa was the overseer. It is the end of the twentieth century and the slave barracks are still standing; one, with people living in it; the other refusing to drop into the earth, even though it has no walls. Tamasine and Plait Hair used to live in the barracks, Uncle Johnny used to live in the one that's half gone. The walls were thin cardboard and the daily gazette was used as wallpaper.

To sleep beneath the raw stench of copra, night after night, for two hundred years is not easy; to hear tired breathing, breathless fucking, children screaming, for five hundred years is not easy. And the big house was always empty, except for two months of the year. The slave barracks whose layers of gazette paper stretched for hundreds of years, was packed with Black humanity, rolling over and over and over without end, and still. This is where I was born. This is how I know struggle, know it like a landscaper. An artist could not have drawn it better.

'Fuckers. Fuckers. Fuckers.' I hear myself muttering, under my breath. 'Fu-u-ck, they're still there.'

I go up the steps of the wood house, asking the new man,

'Sir, who owns this place?'

'Hackens and them, nah,' he replies, leaning his now grey head as if I should know or remember, 'They always own it.'

'Always?'

'Yes.' The new man nods as he speaks, 'You know, them is big shot.'

I must not have remembered about the house; because now, I can see it from the front of the wood house, too. Twenty of us were born in the two rooms of this wood house, while that other one stood empty, locked. I'm looking to where I had instinctively not looked before. The house is still there, green, the windows locked, rust bleeding from its joints.

We climb into the jeep saying good-bye to the new man.

Always.

The jeep hobbles up the gravel road past the quiet barracks. The boy on the roof doesn't stop his work this time to look at us. We get to the sign post. 'St Mary's Estate,' it says once again, judiciously. Red-eyed, I have a picture of the green house in my head, ablaze.

BONNIE BURNARD

Moon Watcher

Marg gripped the cottage hammer, a heavy old claw, and swung again at the locks. They were badly rusted and misshapen from the hammer blows of other seasons. Though winter was over, the shutters still held tight against the wind off the lake; they waited, pale green and chipped and slightly warped, for release. She braced her back on the thick trunk of the front maple, the one whose branches she likes to hear thumping on the screen porch roof. Any thief could have had the contents of the cottage, such as they were, with a well placed boot against the door; the locks were meant to protect against natural elements and, though rusted and bent, they did that, quite dependably.

Marg had counted the jobs before she started and she guessed it would take more than double the usual time to get settled. The things her husband normally did would consume a lot of figuring-out time because she'd never paid much attention to them. She counselled herself, half-seriously, to give this fact some weight when she was deciding, after the jobs were done, whether or not to continue to have a husband.

When the shutters were all opened and fastened back, she moved away to assess her work. The early evening breeze off the lake caught the stiff porch screens and the screens returned the push. She saluted the porch with the hammer. She walked around to the lean-to shed behind the cottage and exchanged the hammer for the axe, moving to the wood pile where she chose a chunk of wood. Last fall, when the driver dumped the wood on a newly seeded patch of grass, Alec had ranted with dismay, had worked late into the night sorting and stacking it on a gravelly spot near the pump in his precise, deliberate way. She could still hear his dismay and she could hear the echo of his clear hard choppings. She wondered which of her noises would come, unsought, to him.

The axe felt heavy in Marg's hand, pulled on her arm. She had always been attracted to loud work noises, but making them was something else. She wanted to excuse herself to anyone who might be within earshot.

She missed and cursed the first piece of wood more than a few times before she connected with it. The noise was less than she had anticipated, but more surprising was the simple joy she felt in actually splitting the thing. She lined up another chunk and swung again. She felt someone behind her just as the axe connected the second time.

'Could you use a hand?' Marg turned toward a tall lumpy man. He wore baggy jeans and a peach-coloured golf shirt. Black curly hair filled the gap at the neck of his shirt and a beard, more white than black, grew around a small, narrow mouth. His eyes were round and frank and friendly. He offered his hand. 'Rob,' he said. 'Rob Carrigan.'

'Hello.' Marg wiped her hands on her rear end and offered one. 'Marg MacPhail.'

'We heard some activity over here. We're in the Kemp place.' His small mouth opened into a smile. 'Rebecca is just making a new pot of coffee.' He nodded at the wood pile. 'I could finish a few of these.'

'Is Mr Kemp dead then?' Mr Kemp had been their neighbour since they'd bought the place, ten years before. Marg had looked forward to watching him skim the sand of the nearby public beach with his metal finder this summer. He said he did it to collect enough silver to buy the light beer he favoured but Marg knew the contraption for what it was: company, a replacement for a wife who had died while napping in the Kemp front porch three summers before. She'd thought maybe this summer she'd walk with Mr Kemp, maybe get her own metal finder.

Rob Carrigan withdrew a little. 'The real estate woman said he died last fall. His kids didn't want the bother of the cottage.'

'Sorry. I just liked him a lot.' Marg picked up the axe. 'The wood's fine, thanks anyway. I'll do a few more. Maybe I could have that coffee in the morning?' She laughed. 'If I can move.' Rob nodded again and said that would be fine and that they had some liniment if she found she needed it. He left.

It had always been the tradition among the cottagers that friendship was kept to a minimum. Everyone depended on a summer of effortless privacy; that's what made the place so peaceful. Marg did not relish the idea of teaching this tradition to the new people. She thought about strategy as she swung, with less energy now, at the wood.

She carried the wood in small loads into the living room and dumped it beside the fireplace. She found some faded funny papers and built a fire around a bunched-up pile of them. This, at least, had always been her job, and she knew the idiosyncrasies of the fireplace well. When the wood had taken, she gave herself a sponge bath and changed into her new red polo pyjamas, stopping in the tiny galley kitchen to pour herself a light scotch, without ice. She sank into her corner of the old maroon couch that faced the fireplace, letting the fatigue move around inside her, feeling it settle finally in her shoulders. The scotch and the fire lifted the chill from her and from the room, and as she listened to the snapping wood she imagined she heard her husband's voice, from his corner of the couch. But he was in the city, maybe in their bed, maybe not. He had an option. Since last October he'd been welcome in another bed.

Marg looked at her watch. She gave herself ten minutes to think about Alec. She had refused to think at all during the first few weeks she had known, told herself she didn't know at all, then she thought about the two of them together for days and nights running and then she stopped. It had begun when the dead leaves covered the lawns, with his missing just a few nights beside her; then he stayed home for a while and then he was gone nine nights in a row and then, quietly, home again. It was a pattern she couldn't read. She expected every piece of mail to be for her, from his lawyer.

When the delicate first snow began to fall she'd told him she could use an explanation and he gave her one: the woman had come to him, at him, from nowhere. He hadn't been looking for anything particularly, had been happy sometimes, a lot of times. But everything had changed once she was there in front of him, and he thought he had a right to something. Marg was dumbfounded and weak from thinking and not thinking; she told him she understood, she agreed, he did have a right.

She didn't know if this decency was achieved by some perverse Christian love or by her stunned inability to jump in and play the game to win, but she depended on it for as long as she could. When grief and rage began to overtake the decency, she signed up with a psychiatrist. He suggested that perhaps she wasn't as decent as she was in the habit of believing and sure enough, it turned out she wasn't. Given a little air, a little nurturing, the grief and rage thrived. Alec sensed the thriving. One night in bed he touched her elbow, said he wouldn't be leaving her but he needed time. Marg told him he could have time and she called the lawyer her brother had been urging her to call. Together they got Alec out of the house.

Now that Alec wanted the winter to be forgiven, to be put in the past, Marg had to make a decision. His wanting to come back was only his decision. She needed to picture him the way he was before he'd had a right to something, but all she could summon was his sorry, sorry face and the self-loathing which he wore like a complexion. She should have brought a photograph with her, the one of him bare-chested on the boat, leaning against the windshield, half-asleep. He didn't know she'd taken that picture, and she'd kept it for herself, in her panty-hose drawer. Even in her worst state of rage she hadn't thought of ripping it in half.

It had been too long a winter. She felt disdain now for everyone involved, herself included. Often, alone in bed, she wished someone would come to her and slice her back open, lift her spinal cord away from her flesh like the backbone of a well cooked lake trout, and leave her free of nerve endings. Her doctor said nothing about her problem was unusual, that many people found themselves in the same situation, that patterns were recognizable. She'd told him to put it in his ear.

The erratic shadows in the room brought Marg's attention back to the fire. She checked her watch. Too much time had passed, again.

She poured herself another, lighter scotch and walked outside, switching the porch light on as she passed. The grass was already wet, and her sneakers were soon soaked, so when she came to the hip-high fieldstone wall that separated the grass from the beach she sat on it, outside the half-circle of light thrown by the porch bulb. The lake water lapped harmlessly against the sand. The sky, much farther away and dark as anything could ever be, was lit with stars and the full summer moon. Always the moon. A cloud she hadn't seen drifted across the face of it, but the cloud was inconsequential, moved in a haphazard, trivial way and was soon gone, made invisible again by the darkness. It hadn't changed the moon; the moon could withstand anything. She damned Alec for not being beside her on the wall. If he were with her he would have made the ice, and when she moved her glass around, as she was in the habit of doing, she would have had the comfort of the sound of the ice.

Perhaps because of the silence, Marg felt someone out there with her, not close, but close enough. She turned toward a dark shape in front of the Kemp cottage, twenty yards away.

'Couldn't ask for a better moon.' Rob Carrigan leaned against a maple trunk, just outside his own half-circle of light.

'Very dependable, that moon,' she answered.

'I watched you walk out and sit down,' he said. 'I'm going in now and I want you to watch me.'

Marg made a quirky face to herself in the dark, but she watched him anyway. This man Rob wore red polo pyjamas, identical to hers though a good deal sloppier, with the same pretentious label on the ass. As he swung the screen door open he assumed a quick model's stance, and she laughed louder than she might have on such a quiet night.

Her sleep in the middle of the sagging mattress was nearly dreamless. In the morning, still in her pyjamas, she hauled the chaise longue from the porch to the grass, beat the dust and cobwebs from it and went inside to make herself a tray of cereal and instant coffee. She was just back and settled when the wife came bouncing over in a bikini. It was pea green with dozens of tiny orange fish, some whole, some in bits where the bathing suit ended and flesh began. She walked in strides rather than steps and extended her hand to Marg long before it was necessary. This was not a woman Marg wanted to know.

'Hi,' she said. 'I'm Rebecca. I've heard all about you.'

Marg found herself putting the tray carefully on the grass and heaving herself up out of the chaise. She asked herself if she had brushed her teeth.

'Nice to meet you.' They shook hands, as at a conference.

'I won't stay to talk now, just going in for a dip. Catch you later.' And the woman strode away, leaping over the fieldstone wall rather than taking the decrepit wooden steps that led to the beach, as any self-respecting forty-year-old woman would have.

Yes, you likely will, Marg thought, as she lowered herself into the chaise and set the tray on her thighs again. She didn't watch the woman swim. She kept her head bent over her mug, sipping her coffee. Her Raisin Bran was half gone before she felt Rob Carrigan this time.

'Morning,' he said.

'And to you,' she answered.

He sat in Mr Kemp's old chaise with his back to her, eating breakfast in his red polo pyjamas. 'What kind of cereal are you eating over there?'

Marg decided she didn't want to count coincidences all summer. She scouted her mind for an unlikely cereal, just in case.

'Cream of Wheat. How about you?'

'Too bad,' he said. 'Raisin Bran.'

Marg eyed the flakes of bran in her spoon.

'Do you play this game with everyone?' she asked.

'No,' he laughed. 'Never happened before. I've always wanted a double. Thought maybe you were mine.'

'You feel the need of one?'

'Yup.' He put his cereal bowl on the grass beside him. 'Would you show me your cereal if I walked over there now?'

'It's gone,' Marg lied.

'How about that cup of coffee when Becky comes back up?'

'Thanks no. I'm on a kind of retreat. Sorry if that sounds rude and I'm sorry about the cream of wheat.'

'Understood,' he said, and he took on an aura of permanent silence, and Marg wanted to say thank you but she held back. When Becky returned from her swim, Marg heard him mumble something to her and saw Becky shrug her shoulders. She leaned back and closed her eyes to avoid the woman's coming glance.

Well, that much had been accomplished. After a respectable time she went into the cottage, changed into a T-shirt and cut-offs and drove over to the point to talk to Jack. Jack was the handyman, mechanic and willing false idiot for all the summer people. She asked him if he could come over to show her how to get the boat down from its suspended moorings in the boathouse; he told her sure and right now seems as good a time as any, and he followed her back to the cottage in his blue half-ton. After he showed Marg how to work the pulleys and cranks and the boat sat rocking in the water, he got the motor from the back porch and put it on. He said he'd better run the boat over to his shop and give it a good servicing. She suspected he just wanted to take the thing for a macho spin across the lake, but then she thought no, that's just what he wants me to think; he's working on his summer personality. He roared off to the point.

Marg changed into her bathing suit and returned to the chaise longue, turning it a bit, away from the Kemp cottage and into the sun. She'd found a mildewed homemaker's magazine in the cottage and she leafed through it. A still-bright lead page with bold yellow letters caught her eye. Cooking for one, it said. She read the first recipe. It was a small elegant dish, with obscure ingredients. She closed the book and opened her arms and legs to the sun. The yellow phrase reappeared in the darkness of each blank eye. She adapted the phrase. Paying the heat bill for one. Listening to jazz for one. Calling your seventy-year-old mother for one. Of course there would be friends, there damned well better be. Friends for one. Not so unnatural. She thought about the peripheral people, the ones who would have just enough interest in her to make small judgements over coffee. Alec liked to avoid divorced people, said divorced people tended to forget how to be private, assumed empathy when it wasn't necessarily there. Marg knew how wrong he was. Even just here, on the edge of divorce, she knew more about privacy than she had ever wanted to know, and nothing was assumed. Her thoughts wandered to some of Alec's other philosophies, and she didn't realize she'd fallen asleep until the homemaker's magazine slid from her belly and startled her awake. She had been dreaming. She knew she had because she could feel the edge of a sob caught in her throat. She looked over at the Kemp place, but no-one was there, not outside anyway. There could have been a movement from the porch to the inside of the cottage, but her eyes were dazed from the sun and she couldn't be sure.

The sound of the boat approaching and Jack's uncivilized yell took care of the dream. Marg walked, dizzy, over to the water. 'Shipshape,' Jack said. 'Shipshape.' He gave her the key. 'You come in and settle up the next time you're over for groceries.' She thanked him and walked him to his truck at the back of the cottage. As he was pulling away he leaned out the window. 'Where's your old man?'

'Not here,' she said.

'Well don't run her too hard the first few times out.'

Marg leaned against the wood pile, watching him disappear around the bend in the road. After a time a grub tried to slip itself onto the back of her shoulder; she winced away and rubbed her skin hard. She went into the cottage to make some ice and—the pump, she remembered the pump. It should have been checked and flushed with Javex. She had used the water without thinking. Alec always muttered about mice when he worked on the pump at the beginning of the season. She'd have to go to the store for Javex if she wanted ice later.

She drove through the dust to the store. Jack's wife collected for his morning's work and Marg gathered up a few things she hadn't brought from home along with a bottle of bleach. Rob Carrigan leaned on her arm at the till.

'That for your pump or are you going to drink it?' His smile was not at all sure of itself or of Marg, and the peak of his Labatt's cap was at two o'clock.

'Pump,' Marg said.

'Let me do it for you. Then I swear I'll never speak to you again.' He grinned then; the grin was the kind that is good to see.

'Yes,' Marg said.

He followed her back to the cottage, and each time she took a bend in the road Marg slowed until she could see him again in her rearview mirror. He drove steadily and sensibly, and she wondered if he knew his hat was on crooked.

He worked on the pump without a word. When he was finished and gone, Marg made two trays of ice cubes.

She leaned her head against the fridge, checked her watch. The trouble with the doctor was that he had no opinions. Every damned suggestion he made was countered with another, alternate ones. She didn't need alternatives; she needed guidance. He said he wouldn't feel comfortable telling another human being what to do. 'Who cares how you feel?' Marg had asked him. He answered this with his professional smile, and offered her more coffee.

It had been years since Marg had had a supercilious friend, not since university. She'd give something to have one now. She did have two fine ordinary friends who touched her more than was usual for them, and who made sure she had all the intimate lunches anyone could eat, but they, too, had no opinions. 'Give it time,' they said, separately. 'Then you'll know.'

She was almost used to missing Alec, the smell of him and his grunts and his sharp shoulders. Over the months she had assembled and arranged all the bits of him that came to her, like a patchwork quilt she could warp around her shoulders when she felt chilled. The harder thing was the plain hurt. It was as if he had fouled the air that enclosed them, their own rich stale air, had opened some valve and allowed an unnatural odour to seep in when he should have kept that valve tight, as she did. Maybe if she'd tried harder to have kids; maybe if they'd adopted. Alec had wanted to. Kids might have helped.

Maybe if she flipped a coin. She could rest a coin on the ridge of her middle finger, flick it high and vow as she watched it sail up that she would live the rest of her life with the coin's decision and never look back, never. She could grab what she needed from the air, slap it against the back of her hand. It was preposterous to depend on time.

She'd known from the beginning that none of them could help her; her doctor, her friends, even Alec would have if it were possible.

But she couldn't do it alone, couldn't push hard enough to stop the balancing act she'd perfected. Something extra had to happen.

Marg's eyes moved to the window, an ordinary square of light and shade, and just in the instant before she would have looked away, Rob Carrigan placed himself exactly in the centre of what she saw. He was looking up at the branches of an old tree, dragging a wooden ladder under one arm and holding a red birdhouse in the other hand. He wore a carpenter's apron, bulky with hammer and nails, tied over his bathing suit.

She turned from him, to clear her head. She walked to the front of the cottage, down the beach to where the boat sat nudged against the sand by the water. She pushed it out into the lake and climbed over the side. The key was still on its hook in the cottage, the oars in the boathouse. She stayed there, thirty feet from shore, rocking. With her back to the shore she could see the point, dark and small and hazy, and that was all. There were no other boats on the water, just the end of the water at the horizon and a thin white line dividing one blue from the other. She turned to the cottages, saw how strange they were, how exposed in their clearing and how alike. The structure, the positioning, the idea of them, was identical; only paint and vines and a certain leaning here and there made them separate. The waves moved her to the shore. The answer would come tonight; she had no idea how but she knew there was no stopping it.

She went back into the cottage, to the fridge. The shrimp she'd brought from home had thawed, so she stir-fried it, adding onion and garlic and peppers and mushrooms. She stuck her nose into the steam. She'd cooked enough for two and she ate every bite of it. It had been a long time since she'd felt full-blown hunger; a long time since she'd felt satisfied. She cleaned up the dishes and drove over to the point to buy a book. It would have to be something good to get her through the next few hours. She almost wished she had brought some books with her, but then half the fun of the summers had always been letting Jack and his wife serve as literary guides. Their squeaky carousel offered Harlequins and obscure mysteries and lots of smut, and once in a while, at least a couple of times each summer, some colourful, renowned, paperback turned up that both she and Alec told themselves they'd been wanting to read for years. She chose a thin, dark blue book. On the cover, someone's idea of a heroine sat on a stump. Marg liked her hat.

Back in the cottage she changed into her pyjamas and started a fire in the fireplace. The ice was slushy hard; she dumped a tray into the sink, threw a couple of cubes into her glass and eased some scotch around them. She set the drink on the three-legged table beside her corner of the couch and settled into the book. She knew how things would go half-way into the first chapter, but she kept on, remembered what everyone looked like, what everyone said, offered far-fetched empathy to the far-fetched characters. Chapter by chapter, the time passed. She kept the fire high and hot.

When it was finally late enough she closed the book and tossed it on the cushion beside her. It slipped to the floor, and as she picked it up she noticed a moon behind the heroine, a fingernail moon, a quarter moon. She held the book tight in her hands. The moon did change, was diminished, was, now and then, according to the dictates of orbits and seasons, obliterated. She rubbed the moon with her thumb and she told herself it would be possible to give up her full strong moon out there over the water and believe finally in nothing much at all. It might make all the difference. She wouldn't have to feel any more than the moon feels. She could continue then, with Alec, wouldn't have to live through years of missing him, regretting things she couldn't even remember.

She put the book on the mantel, poured a second scotch and walked carefully out of the cottage, switching the porch light on as she passed. She walked through the light to the fieldstone wall and perched herself on it. She was shivering and thought about going back for a sweater, but no, everything should be the same. She felt him very close. He didn't speak.

'Have you got your pyjamas on?' she asked.

'Yup.' She could hear him chuckling just over the sound of the small waves on the sand.

'I'm glad,' she said.

'That's not what you want to ask me though, is it?'

Marg rattled the ice around in her glass. 'What do you mean?'

'Just ask,' he said.

She took off her runners and threw both legs over the fieldstone wall, easing herself down onto the sand. It was surprisingly cold.

If she could have looked anywhere, deliberately, it would have been to him, but she didn't, she kept her eyes on her own cold bare feet in the cold bare sand, commanding him, with no sign, to follow her. He did. He came to walk with her.

They walked toward the boat and then around it and down the beach. He hiked his red pyjama legs up to his knees and waded, tentatively, into the lake water. Marg kept to the sand, and they had moved well down the beach when he offered his hand. He didn't move out of the water toward her; she was to come to him. She hiked up her own pyjama legs. Just as her hand went into his bigger, stronger hand, he kicked a footload of water at her, soaking her, chilling her immediately, startling her more than a slap on the face could have. He stood poised, ready to run. Marg look at his face and she knew it could go either way, she had a choice; she could cry and wheel around, run back to the cottage where she could strip down and warm herself in front of the fire, or she could soak him. She wondered how fast she could move, that had to be part of the decision; she wanted a fair fight. She missed and half-fell on the first try, but on the second she got him, turned the bright red of his crotch dark. She took off back toward the cottage, running hard through the moonlit sand, and she nearly made it, nearly escaped, but he followed her, panting, finally catching the arm she had flung behind her in flight and whoosh, her rear was soaked. She laughed then, a loud rude eruption, and she scooped her arms down into the lake and soaked him again, hesitating before taking off, thinking it might be over, watching his face for the sign. He was bent over double with laughter, his hands on his knees, catching his breath in short hard puffs. He looked up to Marg for the sign.

The voice came to them from the fieldstone wall. It was Becky's.

'Fun?' she wanted to know.

She stood with one of Rob's sweaters pulled over her nightgown, exposed by the light from the moon. Marg felt her cold wet arm go up in welcome, waving her down, inviting her to join them, as if what they were having was fun. Becky's head moved just enough to indicate refusal. Rob had stopped grinning, stood with his back to his wife, and Marg recognized on his face the hard old need she had been so long without. He's helping me, she thought. He's doing what he can. Then she saw Becky vault the fieldstone wall, land upright in the sand. She was pulling Rob's sweater up over her head; her nightgown was pale blue satin. Marg tried, in that split second of privacy, to acknowledge Rob's gift. A hug was out of the question, but there was time for a slight quickening of her lower lip and she watched his eyes to make sure he'd seen it. She wasn't convinced that she had faked the quickening or that it mattered if she had.

She turned her back on them then and stripped down to her goose-pimpled flesh, leaving her pyjamas in a heap on the sand. She lined herself up with the ancient path laid by the moon and ran through the water until it was high on her legs. She swam hard, visible to anyone who might be watching the iridescence on the face of the water.

TIMOTHY FINDLEY

Stones

We lived on the outskirts of Rosedale, over on the wrong side of Yonge Street. This was the impression we had, at any rate. Crossing the streetcar tracks put you in another world.

One September, my sister, Rita, asked a girl from Rosedale over to our house after school. Her name was Allison Pritchard and she lived on Cluny Drive. When my mother telephoned to see if Allison Pritchard could stay for supper, Mrs Pritchard said she didn't think it would be appropriate. That was the way they talked in Rosedale: very polite; oblique and cruel.

Over on our side—the west side—of Yonge Street, there were merchants—and this, apparently, made the difference to those whose houses were in Rosedale. People of class were not meant to live in the midst of commerce.

Our house was on Gibson Avenue, a cul-de-sac with a park across the road. My bedroom window faced a hockey rink in winter and a football field in summer. Cy, my brother, was a star in either venue. I was not. My forte, then, was the tricycle.

Up at the corner, there was an antique store on one side and a variety shop on the other. In the variety shop, you could spend your allowance on penny candy, Eskimo pies, and an orange drink I favoured then called *Stubby*. *Stubby* came in short, fat bottles and aside from everything else—the thick orange flavour and the ginger in the bubbles—there was something wonderfully satisfying in the fact that it took both hands to hold it up to your lips and tip it down your throat.

Turning up Yonge Street, beyond the antique store, you came

to The Women's Bakery, Adam's Grocery, Oskar Schickel, the butcher, and Max's Flowers. We were Max's Flowers. My mother and my father wore green aprons when they stood behind the counter or went back into the cold room where they made up wreaths for funerals, bouquets for weddings, and corsages for dances at the Kind Edward Hotel. Colonel Matheson, retired, would come in every morning on his way downtown and pick out a boutonnière from the jar of carnations my mother kept on the counter near the register. Once, when I was four, I caused my parents untold embarrassment by pointing out that Colonel Matheson had a large red growth on the end of his nose. The 'growth' was nothing of the sort, of course, but merely the result of Colonel Matheson's predilection for gin.

Of the pre-war years, my overall memory is one of perfect winters, heavy with snow and the smell of coal- and wood-smoke mingling with the smell of bread and cookies rising from The Women's Bakery. The coal-smoke came from our furnaces and the wood-smoke—mostly birch and maple—came to us from the chimneys of Rosedale, where it seemed that every house must have a fireplace in every room.

Summers all smelled of grass being cut in the park and burning tar from the road crews endlessly patching the potholes in Yonge Street. The heat of these summers was heroic and the cause of many legends. Mister Schickel, the butcher, I recall once cooked an egg on the sidewalk outside his store. My father, who was fond of Mister Schickel, made him a bet of roses it could not be done. I think Mister Schickel's part of the bet was pork chops trimmed of excess fat. When the egg began to sizzle, my father slapped his thigh and whistled and he sent my sister, Rita, in to get the flowers. Mister Schickel, however, was a graceful man and when he placed his winnings in the window of his butcher shop, he also placed a card that read: *Thanks to Max's Flowers one dozen roses.*

The Great Depression held us all in thrall, but its effects on those of us who were used to relative poverty—living on the west side of Yonge Street—were not so debilitating as they were on the far side in Rosedale. The people living there regarded money as something you had—as opposed to something you went out and got—and they were slower to adjust to what, for them, was the unique experience of deprivation.

I remember, too, that there always seemed to be a tramp at the door: itinerants asking if—for the price of a meal, or the meal itself—they could carry out the ashes, sweep the walks, or pile the baskets and pails in which my father brought his flowers from the market and the greenhouse.

Our lives continued in this way until about the time I was five—in August of 1939. Everyone's life, I suppose, has its demarcation lines—its latitudes and longitudes passing through time. Some of these lines define events that everyone shares—others are confined to personal, even to secret lives. But the end of summer 1939 is a line drawn down through the memory of everyone who was then alive. We were all about to be pitched together into a melting pot of violence from which a few of us would emerge intact and the rest of us would perish.

My father joined the army even before the war had started. He went downtown one day and didn't come back till after supper-time. I noticed that he hadn't taken the truck but had ridden off on the streetcar. I asked my mother why he had worn his suit on a weekday and she replied *because today is special*. But that was all she said.

At the table, eating soufflé and salad, my brother Cy—who was nine years old that summer—talked about the World's Fair in New York City and pictures he'd seen of the future in magazines. The Great World's Fair was a subject that had caught all our imaginations with its demonstrations of new appliances, aeroplanes, and motor cars. Everything was 'streamlined' in 1939; everything designed with swept-back lines as if we were all preparing to shoot off into space. Earlier that summer, the King and Queen of England had come to Canada, riding on a streamlined train whose blue-painted engine was sleek and slim as something in a silver glove. In fact, the King and Queen had arrived in Toronto just up Yonge Street from where we lived. We got permission from the Darrow family, who lived over Max's Flowers, to stand on the roof and watch the parade with its Mounties in scarlet and its Black Watch Band and the King and Queen, all blue and white and smiling, sitting in an open Buick called a *McLaughlin—built*, according to Cy, *right here in Canada!* For one brief moment, while all these symbols of who we were went marching past, the two communities—one on either side of Yonge Street—were united in a surge of cheering and applause. But after the King and Queen were gone, the ribbon of Yonge Street divided us again. It rained.

Now Cy and Rita were arguing over the remnants in the soufflé dish. Cy held the classic belief that what was in the dish was his by virtue of his being the eldest child. He also held the classic belief that girls were meant to be second in everything. Rita, who was always hungry but never seemed to gain an ounce, held none of these beliefs and was capable of fighting Cy for hours on end when our parents weren't present. With Mother at the table, however, the argument was silenced by her announcement that the soufflé dish and all the delicious bits of cheese and egg that clung to its sides would be set aside for our father.

Then—or shortly thereafter—our father did indeed arrive, but he said he wasn't hungry and he wanted to be left alone with Mother.

In half an hour the children were called from the kitchen where we had been doing the dishes and scooping up the remains of the meal. I—the child my mother called *The Rabbit*—had been emptying the salad bowl, stuffing my mouth with lettuce, tomatoes, and onion shards and nearly choking in the process. We all went into the sitting-room with food on our lips and tea towels in our hands: Father's three little Maxes—Cy and Rita and Ben. He looked at us then, as he always did, with a measure of pride he could never hide and a false composure that kept his lips from smiling, but not his eyes. I look back now on that moment with some alarm when I realize my father was only twenty-seven years old—an age I have long survived and doubled.

'Children, I have joined the army,' he said—in his formal way, as if we were his customers. 'I am going to be a soldier.'

Our mother had been weeping before we entered the room, but she had dried her eyes because she never allowed us to witness her tears. Now she was smiling and silent. After a moment she left the room and went out through the kitchen into the garden where, in the twilight, she found her favourite place and sat in a deck-chair amidst the flowers.

Cy, for his part, crowed with delight and yelled with excitement. He wanted to know if the war would last until he was a man and could join our father at the front.

Father, I remember, told him the war had not yet begun and the reason for his own enlistment was precisely so that Cy and I could not be soldiers. 'There will be no need for that,' he said.

Cy was immensely disappointed. He begged our father to make the war go on till 1948, when he would be eighteen.

Our father only laughed at that.

'The war,' he said, 'will be over in 1940.'

I went out then and found our mother in the garden.

'What will happen to us while he's away?' I asked.

'Nothing,' she said. And then she said: 'Come here.'

I went and leaned against her thigh and she put her arm around my shoulder and I could smell the roses somewhere behind us. It was getting dark.

'Look up there,' she said. 'The stars are coming out. Why don't you count them?'

This was her way of distracting me whenever my questions got out of hand. Either she told me to count the stars or go outside and dig for China. *There's a shovel in the shed*, she would tell me. *You get started and I will join you.* Just as if we would be in China and back by suppertime.

But that night in August 1939, I wasn't prepared to bite. I didn't want to dig for China and I didn't want to count the stars. I'd dug for China so many times and had so many holes in the yard that I knew I would never arrive; it was much too far and, somehow, she was making a fool of me. As for the stars: 'I counted them last night,' I told her. 'And the night before.'

'Oh?' she said—and I felt her body tense, though she went on trying to inject a sense of ease when she spoke. 'So tell me,' she said. 'How many are there?'

'Twelve,' I said.

'Ah,' she said. And sighed. 'Just twelve. I thought there might be more than twelve.'

'I mean twelve zillion,' I said with great authority.

'Oh,' she said. 'I see. And you counted them all?'

'Unh-hunh.'

For a moment she was quiet. And then she said: 'What about that one there?'

One week later, the war began. But my father had already gone.

On the 14th of February 1943 my father was returned. He came back home from the war. He did this on a Sunday and I recall the hush that fell upon the house, as indeed it seemed to have fallen over all the city. Only the sparrows out in the trees made sound.

We had gone downtown to the Exhibition Grounds to meet him. The journey on the streetcar took us over an hour, but Mother had splurged and hired a car and driver to take us all home. The car, I remember, embarrassed me. I was afraid some friend would see me being driven—sitting up behind a chauffeur.

A notice had come that told us the families of all returning soldiers would be permitted to witness their arrival. I suspect the building they used for this was the one now used to house the Royal Winter Fair and other equestrian events. I don't remember what it was called and I'm not inclined to inquire. It was enough that I was there that once—and once remains enough.

We sat in the bleachers, Cy and Rita and Mother and me, and there was a railing holding us back. There must have been over a thousand people waiting to catch a glimpse of someone they loved—all of them parents, children, or wives of the men returning. I was eight years old that February—almost nine and feeling I would never get there. Time was like a field of clay and all the other children I knew appeared to have cleared it in a single bound while I was stuck in the mud and barely able to lift my feet. I hated being eight and dreaded being nine. I wanted to be ten—the only dignified age a child could be, it seemed to me. Cy, at ten, had found a kind of silence I admired to the point of worship. Rita, who in fact was ten that year and soon to be eleven, had also found a world of silence in which she kept herself secreted—often behind closed doors. Silence was a sign of valour.

The occasion was barely one for public rejoicing. The men who were coming home were mostly casualties whose wounds, we had been warned, could be distressing and whose spirit, we had equally been warned, had been damaged in long months of painful recuperation. Plainly, it was our job to lift their spirits and to deny the severity of their wounds. Above all else, they must not be allowed to feel they could not rejoin society at large. A man with no face must not be stared at.

Our father's wounds were greater by far than we had been told. There was not a mark on his body, but—far inside—he had been destroyed. His mind had been severely damaged and his spirit had been broken. No one had told me what this might have made of him. No one had said *he may never be kind again.* No one had said *he will never sleep again without the aid of alcohol.* No one had said *he will try to kill your mother.* No one had said *you will not be sure it's him when you see him.* Yet all these things were true.

I had never seen a military parade without a band. The effect was eerie and upsetting. Two or three officers came forward into the centre of the oval. Somebody started shouting commands and a sergeant-major, who could not yet be seen, was heard outside the building counting off the steps.

I wanted drums. I wanted bugles. Surely this ghostly, implacable sound of marching feet in the deadening sand was just a prelude to everyone's standing up and cheering and the music blaring forth. But, no. We all stood up, it is true, the minute the first of the columns rounded the wooden corner of the bleachers and came into sight. But no one uttered a sound. One or two people threw their hands up over their mouths—as if to stifle cries—but most of us simply stood there—staring in disbelief.

Nurses came with some of the men, supporting them. Everyone was pale in the awful light—and the colours of their wounds and bruises were garish and quite unreal. There was a predominance of yellow flesh and dark maroon scars and of purple welts and blackened scabs. Some men wore bandages—some wore casts and slings. Others used canes and crutches to support themselves. A few had been the victims of fire, and these wore tight, blue skull-caps and collarless shirts and their faces and other areas of uncovered skin were bright with shining ointments and dressings.

It took a very great while for all these men and women—perhaps as many as two hundred of them—to arrive inside the building and make their way into the oval. They were being lined up in order of columns—several long lines, and each line punctuated here and there with attendant nurses. The voices of the sergeant-major and of the adjutant who was taking the parade were swallowed up in the dead acoustics, and—far above us— pigeons and sparrows moved among the girders and beams that supported the roof. I still had not seen Father.

At last, because my panic was spreading out of control, I tugged my mother's elbow and whispered that I couldn't see him. Had there been a mistake and he wasn't coming at all?

'No,' she told me—looking down at my sideways and turning my head with her ungloved fingers. 'There he is, there,' she said.

'But don't say anything, yet. He may not know we're here.'

My father's figure could only be told because of his remarkable height. He was six feet four and had always been, to me, a giant. But now his height seemed barely greater than the height of half a dozen other men who were gathered out in the sand. His head was bowed, though once or twice he lifted his chin when he heard the commands. His shoulders, no longer squared, were rounded forward and dipping towards his centre. His neck was so thin I thought that someone or something must have cut over half of it away. I studied him solemnly and then looked up at my mother.

She had closed her eyes against him because she could not bear to look.

Later on that night, when everyone had gone to bed but none of us had gone to sleep, I said to Cy: 'What is it?'
    'What?'
    'That's happened to Dad. . . .'
    Cy didn't answer for a moment and then he said: 'Dieppe.'
    I didn't understand. I thought it was a new disease.

We were told the next day not to mention at school that our father had come back home. Nothing was said about why it must be kept a secret. That was a bitter disappointment. Other children whose fathers had returned from overseas were always the centre of attention. Teachers, beaming smiles and patting heads, would congratulate them just as if they had won a prize. Classmates pestered them with questions: *What does he look like? Have you seen his wounds? How many Germans did he kill?* But we had none of this. All we got was: *What did you do on the weekend?*
    Nothing.
    All day Monday, Father remained upstairs. Our parents' bedroom was on the second floor directly over the sitting-room. Also, directly underneath the bedroom occupied by Cy and me. We had heard our mother's voice long into the night, apparently

soothing him, telling him over and over again that everything was going to be all right.

We could not make out her words, but the tone of her voice was familiar. Over time, she had sat with each of us, deploying her comforts in all the same cadences and phrases, assuring us that pains and aches and sicknesses would pass.

Because we could not afford to lose the sale of even one flower, neither the single rose bought once a week by Edna Holmes to cheer her ailing sister, nor the daily boutonnière of Colonel Matheson—our mother had persuaded Mrs Adams, the grocer's wife, to tend the store while she 'nipped home' once every hour to see to Father's needs. It was only later that we children realized what those needs entailed. He was drinking more or less constantly in every waking hour, and our mother's purpose was first to tempt him with food—which he refused—and then to make certain that his matches and cigarettes did not set fire to the house.

On the Wednesday, Father emerged from his shell around two o'clock in the afternoon. We were all at school, of course, and I have only the account of what follows from my mother. When she returned at two, Mother found that Father had come down into the hallway, fully dressed in civilian clothes. He had already donned his greatcoat when she arrived. She told me that, at first, he had seemed to be remarkably sober. He told her he wanted to go outside and walk in the street. He wanted to go and see the store, he said.

'But you can't wear your greatcoat, David,' she told him.

'Why?'

'Because you're in civilian dress. You know that's not allowed. A man was arrested just last week.'

'I wasn't here last week,' said my father.

'Nevertheless,' my mother told him, 'this man was arrested because it is not allowed.'

'But I'm a soldier!' my father yelled.

My mother had to play this scene with all the care and cunning she could muster. The man who had been arrested had been a deserter. All that winter, desertions had been increasing and there had been demonstrations of overt disloyalty. People had shouted *Down with the King!* and had booed the Union Jack. There were street gangs of youths who called themselves *Zombies* and they hung around the Masonic Temple on Yonge Street and the Palais Royale at Sunnyside. Some of these young men were in uniform, members of the Home Guard: reserves who had been promised, on joining up, they would not be sent overseas. They may have disapproved of the war, but they did not disapprove of fighting. They waited outside the dancehalls, excessively defensive of their manhood, challenging the servicemen who were dancing inside to *come out fighting and show us your guts!* Men had been killed in such encounters and the encounters had been increasing. The government was absolutely determined to stamp these incidents out before they spread across the country. These were the darkest hours of the war, and morale, both in and out of the Forces, was at its lowest ebb. If my father had appeared on the street with his military greatcoat worn over his civilian clothes, it would have been assumed he was a *Zombie* or a deserter and he would have been arrested instantly. Our neighbours would have turned him in, no matter who he was. Our patriotism had come to that.

'I don't have a civilian overcoat,' my father said. 'And don't suggest that I put on my uniform, because I won't. My uniform stinks of sweat and I hate it.'

'Well, you aren't going out like that,' my mother said. 'That's all there is to it. Why not come to the kitchen and I'll fix you a sandwich. . . .'

'I don't want a goddamned sandwich,' my father yelled at her. 'I want to see the store!'

At this point he tore off his greatcoat and flung it onto the stairs. And then, before my mother could prevent him, he was out the door and running down the steps.

My mother—dressed in her green shop apron and nothing but

a scarf to warm her—raced out after him.

What would the neighbours think? What would the neighbours say? How could she possibly explain?

By the time she had reached the sidewalk, my father had almost reached the corner. But when she got to Yonge Street, her fears were somewhat allayed. My father had not gone into Max's Flowers but was standing one door shy of it, staring into the butcher's window.

'What's going on here?' he said, as my mother came abreast of him.

Mother did not know what he meant.

'Where is Mister Schickel, Lily?' he asked her.

She had forgotten that, as well.

'Mister Schickel has left,' she told him—trying to be calm—trying to steer my father wide of the butcher's window and in towards their own front stoop.

'Left?' my father shouted. 'He's only just managed to pay off his mortgage! And who the hell is this imposter, Reilly?'

'Reilly?'

'Arthur Reilly the bloody butcher!' My father pointed at and read the sign that had replaced *Oskar Schickel, Butcher* in the window.

'Mister Reilly has been there most of the winter, David. Didn't I write and tell you that?' She knew very well she hadn't.

My father blinked at the meagre cuts of rationed meat displayed beyond the glass and said: 'What happened to Oskar, Lily? Tell me.'

And so, she had to tell him, like it or not.

Mister Schickel's name was disagreeable—stuck up there on Yonge Street across from Rosedale—and someone from Park Road had thrown a stone through the window.

There. It was said.

'But Oskar wasn't a German,' my father whispered. 'He was a Canadian.'

'But his name was German, David.'

My father put his fingers against the glass and did not appear to respond to what my mother had said.

At last my mother pulled at his arm. 'Why not come back home?' she said. 'You can come and see the shop tomorrow.'

My father, while my mother watched him, concentrated very hard and moved his finger over the dusty glass of Oskar Schickel's store.

'What are you doing, David?'

'Nothing,' said my father. 'Setting things right, that's all.'

Then he stepped back and said to her: 'Now—we'll go home.'

What he had written was:

Oskar Schickel: Proprietor in absentia.

Mother said that Mrs Reilly rushed outside as soon as they had reached the corner and she washed the window clean.

This was the only remaining decent thing my father did until the day he died.

The rest was all a nightmare.

I had never seen Dieppe. I had seen its face in photographs. I had read all the books and heard all the stories. The battle, of which my father had been a victim, had taken place in August of 1942—roughly six months before he was returned to us. Long since then, in my adult years, I have seen that battle, or seen its parts, through the medium of documentary film. It was only after Cy and Rita had vetted these films that I was able to watch. Till then, I had been afraid I would catch my father's image un-awares—fearful that somehow our eyes would meet in the worst of moments. I couldn't bear the thought of seeing him destroyed. So, I had seen all this—the photographs, the books, the films—but I had never seen the town of Dieppe itself until that day in March of 1987 when I took my father's ashes there to scatter them.

Before I can begin this ending, I have to make it clear that the last thing I want to provoke is the sentimental image of a wind-blown stretch of rocky beach with a rainbow of ashes arching over the stones and blowing out to sea. If you want that image, let me tell you that had been the way it was when Cy, my brother, and Rita, my sister, and I went walking, wading into the ocean south of Lunenburg, Nova Scotia—where our mother had been born—to cast her ashes into the air above the Atlantic. Then there was almost music and we rejoiced because our mother had finally gained her freedom from a life that had become intolerable. But in Dieppe, when I shook my father's ashes out of their envelope, there was no rejoicing. None.

I felt, in fact, as if I had brought the body of an infidel into a holy place and laid it down amongst the true believers. Still, this was what my father had wanted—and how could I refuse him? Neither Cy nor Rita would do it for him. *Gone*, they had said. *Good riddance.*

And so it fell to me.

I was always the least informed. I was always the most inquisitive. During my childhood nobody told me—aside from the single word *Dieppe*—what it was that had happened to my father. And yet, perhaps because I knew the least and because I was the youngest and seemed the most naïve and willing, it was more than often me he focused on.

His tirades would begin in silence—the silence we had been warned of when he first returned. He would sit at the head of the table, eating a piece of fish and drinking from a glass of beer. The beer was always dark in colour. Gold.

Our dining-room had a window facing west. Consequently winter sunsets in particular got in his eyes.

Curtain, he would say at his plate—and jab his fork at me.

If I didn't understand because his mouth was full, my mother would reach my sleeve and pull it with her fingers. *The curtain, Ben*, she would say: *Your father's eyes.*

Yes, ma'am. Down I'd get and pull the curtain.

Then, no sooner would I be reseated than my father—still addressing his plate—would mumble *lights.* And I would rise and turn on the lights. Then, when I was back at last in my chair, he would look at me and say, without apparent rancour, *Why don't you tell me to shove the goddamn curtain up my ass?*

You will understand my silence in response to this if you understand that—before he went away—the worst my father had ever said in our presence had been *damn* and *hell*. The ultimate worst had been *Christ!* when he'd nearly sliced his finger off with a knife. Then, however, he hadn't known that anyone was listening. And so, when he started to talk this way—and perhaps especially at table—it paralysed me.

Cy or Mother would sometimes attempt to intervene, but he always cut them off with something worse than he'd said to me. Then he would turn his attention back in my direction and continue. He urged me to refuse his order, then to upbraid him, finally to openly defy him—call him the worst of the words he could put in my mouth and hit him. Of course I never did any of these things, but the urging, the cajoling, and ultimately the begging never ceased.

One night he came into the bedroom where I slept in the bunk-bed over Cy and he shouted at me *why don't you fight back?* Then he dragged my covers off and threw me onto the floor against the bureau. All this was done in the dark, and after my mother had driven me down in the truck to the Emergency Ward of Wellesley Hospital, the doctors told her that my collar-bone was broken. I heard my mother saying *yes, he fell out of bed.*

Everyone—even I—conspired to protect him. The trouble was, my father had no wish to protect himself. At least it seemed that way until a fellow veteran of Dieppe turned up one day in the shop and my father turned on him with a pair of garden shears and tried to drive him back onto Yonge Street. Far from being afraid of my father, the other man took off his jacket and threw it in my father's face and all the while he stood there, the man was yelling at my father: *Coward! Coward! Yellow Bastard!*

Then he turned around and walked away. The victor.

Thinking for sure the police would come, my mother drew the blind and closed the shop for the rest of the day.

But that was not the end of it. She gathered us together out on the porch and Cy was told to open a can of pork and beans and to make what our mother called a *passel of toast*. He and Rita and I were to eat this meal in the kitchen, after which Cy, who'd been handed a dollar bill my mother had lifted from the till, was to take us down to the Uptown Theatre where an Abbott and Costello film was playing. All these ordinary things we did. Nonetheless, we knew that our father had gone mad.

It was summer then, and when the movie was over, I remember Cy and Rita and I stood on the street and the sidewalks gave off heat and the air around us smelled of peanuts and popcorn and Cy said: 'I don't think it's safe to go home just yet.' For almost an hour, we wandered on Yonge Street, debating what we should do and, at last, we decided we would test the waters by going and looking at the house and listening to see if there was any yelling.

Gibson Avenue only has about twenty houses, most of them semi-detached—and all of them facing south and the park. The porches and the stoops that night were filled with our neighbours drinking beer from coffee cups and fanning themselves with paper plates and folded bits of the *Daily Star*. They were drinking out of cups—you could smell the beer—because the law back then forbade the public consumption, under any circumstance, of alcohol. Whatever you can hide does not exist.

Passing, we watched our neighbours watching us—the Matlocks and the Wheelers and the Conrads and the Bolts—and we knew they were thinking *there go the Max kids and David Max, their father, tried to kill a man today in his store with gardening shears.* . . .

'Hello, Cy.'

'Hello.'

'Ben. Rita.'

'Hi.'

'Good-night . . .'

We went and stood together on the sidewalk out in front of our house.

Inside, everything seemed to be calm and normal. The lights

were turned on in their usual distribution—most of them downstairs. The radio was playing. Someone was singing *Praise the Lord and Pass the Ammunition*.

Cy went up the steps and turned the handle. He was brave—but I'd always known that. Rita and I were told to wait on the porch.

Two minutes passed—or five—or ten—and finally Cy returned. He was very white and his voice was dry, but he wasn't shaking and all he said was: 'You'd best come in. I'm calling the police.'

Our father had tried to kill our mother with a hammer. She was lying on the sofa and her hands were broken because she had used them trying to fend off the blows.

Father had disappeared. The next day he turned himself in because, as he told the doctors, he had come to his senses. He was kept for a year and a half—almost until the war was over—at the Asylum for the Insane on Queen Street. None of us children was allowed to visit him there—but our mother went to see him six months after he had been committed. She told me they sat in a long, grey room with bars on all the windows. My father wore a dressing gown and hadn't shaved. Mother said he couldn't look her in the eyes. She told him that she forgave him for what he had done. But my father never forgave himself. My mother said she never saw his eyes again.

Two weeks after our father had tried to kill our mother, a brick was thrown through the window of Max's Flowers. On the brick, a single word was printed in yellow chalk.

Murderer.

Mother said: 'There's no way around this, now. I'm going to have to explain.'

That was how we discovered what had gone wrong with our father at Dieppe.

Our mother had known this all along, and I still have strong suspicions Cy had found it out and maybe Rita before our mother went through the formal procedure of sitting us down and telling us all together. Maybe they had thought I was just too young to understand. Maybe Cy and maybe Rita hadn't known. Maybe they had only guessed. At any rate I had a very strong sense that I was the only one who received our mother's news in a state of shock.

Father had risen, since his enlistment in 1939, all the way up from an NCO to the rank of captain. Everyone had adored him in the army. He was what they called a natural leader. His men were particularly fond of him and they would, as the saying goes, have followed him anywhere. Then came Dieppe. All but a handful of those who went into battle there were Canadians. This was our Waterloo. Our Gettysburg.

There isn't a single history book you can read—there isn't a single man who was there who won't tell you—there isn't a single scrap of evidence in any archive to suggest that the battle of Dieppe was anything but a total and appalling disaster. Most have called it a slaughter.

Dieppe is a port and market town on the coast of Normandy in northern France. In 1942, the British High Command had chosen it to be the object of a practice raid in preparation for the invasion of Europe. The Allies on every front were faltering, then. A gesture was needed, and even the smallest of victories would do.

And so, on the 19th of August 1942, the raid on Dieppe had taken place—and the consequent carnage had cost the lives of over a thousand Canadians. Over two thousand were wounded or taken prisoner. Five thousand set out; just over one thousand came back.

My father never left his landing craft.

He was to have led his men ashore in the second wave of troops to follow the tanks—but, seeing the tanks immobilized, unable to move because the beaches were made of stone and the stones had jammed the tank tracks—and seeing the evident massacre of the first wave of troops whose attempt at storming the shore had been repulsed by machine-gun fire from the cliffs above the town—my father froze in his place and could not move. His men—it is all too apparent—did not know what to do. They had received no order to advance and yet, if they stayed, they were sitting ducks.

In the end, though a handful escaped by rushing forward into the water, the rest were blown to pieces when their landing craft was shelled. In the meantime, my father had recovered enough of his wits to crawl back over the end of the landing craft, strip off his uniform and swim out to sea where he was taken on board a British destroyer sitting offshore.

The destroyer, H.M.S. *Berkley*, was ultimately hit and everyone on board, including my father—no one knowing who he was—was transferred to another ship before the *Berkley* was scuttled where she sat. My father made it all the way back to England, where his burns and wounds were dressed and where he debated taking advantage of the chaos to disappear, hoping that, in the long run, he would be counted among the dead.

His problem was, his conscience had survived. He stayed and, as a consequence, he was confronted by survivors who knew his story. He was dishonourably discharged and sent home to us. Children don't understand such things. The only cowards they recognize are figures cut from comic books or seen on movie screens.

Fathers cannot be cowards.

It is impossible.

His torment and his grief were to lead my father all the way to the grave. He left our mother, in the long run, though she would not have wished him to do so and he lived out his days in little bars and back-street beer parlours, seeking whatever solace he could find with whores and derelicts whose stories might have matched his own. The phone would ring and we would dread it. Either it was him or news of him—either his drunken harangue or the name of his most recent jail.

He died in the Wellesley Hospital, the place where I was

born—and when he was dying he asked to see his children. Cy and Rita 'could not be reached', but I was found—where he'd always found me—sitting within yelling distance. Perhaps this sounds familiar to other children—of whatever age—whose parents, whether one of them or both of them, have made the mistake of losing faith too soon in their children's need to love.

I would have loved a stone.

If only he had known.

He sensed it, maybe, in the end. He told me he was sorry for everything—and meant it. He told me the names of all his men and he said he had walked with them all through hell, long since their deaths, to do them honour. He hoped they would understand him, now.

I said they might.

He asked if his ashes could be put with theirs.

Why not, I thought. *A stone among stones.*

The beaches of Dieppe can throw you off balance. The angle at which they slope into the water is both steep and dangerous. At high tide you can slide into the waves and lose your footing before you've remembered how to swim. The stones are treacherous. But they are also beautiful.

My father's ashes were contraband. You can't just walk about with someone's remains, in whatever form, in your suitcase. Stepping off the *Sealink* ferry, I carried my father in an envelope addressed to myself in Canada. This was only in case I was challenged. There was hardly more than a handful of him there. I had thrown the rest of him into the English Channel as the coast of Normandy was coming into view. It had been somewhat more than disconcerting to see the interest his ashes caused amongst the gulls and other sea birds. I had hoped to dispose of him in a private way, unnoticed. But a woman with two small children came and stood beside me at the railing and I heard her explain that *this nice gentleman is taking care of our feathered friends.* I hoped that, if my father was watching, he could laugh. I had to look away.

The ferry arrived in the early afternoon and—once I had booked myself into La Présidence Hotel—I went for a walk along the promenade above the sea-wall. It being May, the offshore breeze was warm and filled with the faintest scent of apple trees in bloom.

I didn't want to relive the battle. I hadn't come to conjure ghosts. But the ghosts and the battle are palpable around you there, no matter what your wishes are. The sound of the tide rolling back across the stones is all the cue you need to be reminded of that summer day in 1942. I stood that evening, resting my arms along the wall and thinking *at last, my father has come ashore*.

In the morning, before the town awoke, I got up in the dark and was on the beach when the sun rose inland beyond the cliffs. I wore a thick woollen sweater, walking shorts and a pair of running shoes. The envelope was in my pocket.

The concierge must have thought I was just another crazy North American off on my morning run. He grunted as I passed and I pretended not to know that he was there. Out on the beach, I clambered over retaining walls and petrified driftwood until I felt I was safely beyond the range of prying eyes.

The stones at Dieppe are mostly flint—and their colours range from white through yellow to red. The red stones look as if they have been washed in blood and the sight of them takes your breath away. I hunkered down above them, holding all that remained of my father in my fist. He felt like a powdered stone—pummelled and broken.

I let him down between my fingers, feeling him turn to paste—watching him divide and disappear.

He is dead and he is gone.

Weekends, our parents used to take us walking under the trees on Crescent Road. This was on the Rosedale side of Yonge Street. My brother Cy and I were always dressed in dark blue suits whose rough wool shorts would chafe against our thighs. Our knee socks—also blue—were turned down over thick elastic garters. Everything itched and smelled of Sunday. Cy had cleats on his shoes because he walked in such a way as to wear his heels *to the bone*, as my mother said—and causing much expense. The cleats made a wondrous clicking noise and you could always hear him coming. I wanted cleats, but I was refused because, no matter how I tried, I couldn't walk like that.

The houses sat up neat as pins beyond their lawns—blank-eyed windows, steaming chimneys—havens of wealth and all the mysteries of wealth.

Father often walked behind us. I don't know why. Mother walked in front with Rita. Rita always wore a dress that was either red or blue beneath her princess coat and in the wintertime she wore a sort of woollen cloche that was tied with a knitted string beneath her chin. Her Mary Jane shoes were just like Shirley Temple's shoes—which, for a while, was pleasing to Rita; then it was not. Rita always had an overpowering sense of image.

After the advent of our father's return, she said from the corner of her mouth one Sunday as we walked on Crescent Road that she and Cy and I had been named as if we were manufactured products: *Cy Max Office Equipment; Rita Max Household Appliances* and *Ben Max Watches*. This, she concluded, was why our father had always walked behind us. Proudly, he was measuring our performance. Now, he had ceased to walk behind us and our mother led us forward dressed in black.

Tick. Tick. Tick. That's me. The Ben Max Watch.

I have told our story. But I think it best—and I like it best—to end with all of us moving there beneath the trees in the years before the war. Mister and Mrs David Max out walking with their children any Sunday afternoon in any kind of weather but the rain.

Colonel Matheson, striding down his walk, is caught and forced to grunt acknowledgement that we are there. He cannot ignore us, after all. We have seen him every weekday morning, choosing his boutonnière and buying it from us.

CYNTHIA FLOOD

A Young Girl-Typist Ran to Smolny:[1] Notes for a Film

Street corner in Burnaby.[2] Hot summer day. Time now. Three young women. One's cute, one's punkoid, and one's neither. She looks as though she's trying to be someone.[3] Some of her clothes fit. Punkoid smokes and Cute giggles. All three carry sheaves of a revolutionary newspaper,[4] subscription forms, pencils. Street: small tidy stucco houses, small tidy green lawns; a few larger, scruffier frame dwellings; some humans at work with hedge clippers; gnomes and flamingos stand about; curtains[5] drawn everywhere.

Cute, giggling, 'Isn't the anarchist house around here?'

Experienced Punkoid frowns. 'Yeah somewhere,' indifferently.

Unsure one has millisecond vision of black dwarves massing by the barbecues, TV aerials flaming with black flags.[6]

Dissolve to Punkoid's cross face and sharp voice. 'Kate, you

[1] So says A.J.P. Taylor in his Introduction to John Reed's *Ten Days That Shook The World*, Penguin, 1982, p. xv. NB see if Trotsky or Deutscher refer to her.

[2] Boring bedroom suburb of Vancouver, British Columbia, Canada.

[3] Lots of room here for directional creativity. Wd be interesting to see what F and M directors would do. (In the women's dorm at college in the late 50s the phone-message book included a column showing initially the sex of each caller. Still done?)

[4] NB devise suitable name.

[5] Priscillas.

[6] Consider music for this bit—in fact consider soundtrack throughout. Shd be highly patterned. Maybe silences for all the inner visions though?

take this block, both sides. Meet you back here in an hour. And *don't* get tied up talking, okay?' Cute goes on way, combing her hair, and Punkoid another, not. CU on Kate, whose adam's-apple[7] jigs as she swallows; not attractive.

The stairs of the first house are cartoonly tall, looming. Kate can tell there's someone behind the glass-windowed and curtained door.[8] Her knock sounds explosive. East Indian woman in sari, festooned with small children, opens.

Kate, brightly, 'Good morning! I'm visiting in your neighbourhood to introduce our[9] paper *Da Da Da Da*[10] [EIW remains expressionless—camera on her throughout Kate's remarks], and I'm sure it will be of interest to you. We cover the international scene from a revolutionary perspective,[11] and each monthly issue also contains [here Kate's voice starts running down like an old Victrola; camera is still on EIW's unchanging face] up-to-date analysis of events in the Canadian labour movement, the women's movement, the. . . .' Behind the EIW appears a handsome teenage boy. He takes a paper from the top of Kate's pile, looks at it, hands it back, says 'No.'[12] His glance moves over the little bump Kate's right nipple[13] makes in the close-fitting fabric of her shirt, and he closes the door in her face. Immediately, Punjabi bursts out multiply within.

[7]Obvious question, but let's ask it anyway: What about eve's-apple? If it's supposed to be all her fault, how come she doesn't even get the damn thing named after her? Or did the apple just slide down her evil throat as smooth as milk?

[8]Shot here through letter-slot, about eight inches from bottom of door—the sari and the bundle of kids' legs.

[9]Note that this is never explained.

[10]Making up a name will be hard. Sarcasm and flippancy are easy, but irrelevant here. Can't use any extant. Many of the non-extant have too many connotations, resonances (go easy on that lit crit stuff, okay?).

[11]The extreme disjuncture between the contents of these two sentences is echoes in the changing tones of Kate's voice. Readers/viewers may feel the impulse to laugh; they are invited, since they are so smart, to think up other and better ways to do door-to-door selling of a revolutionary newspaper in late 20th century North America.

[12]He does all this quickly, decisively; no hesitation whatsoever.

[13]The left is concealed by the revolutionary press.

Kate walks farther down the street.[14]

Next house. Flowers planted geometrically. Razor edge between grass and sidewalk.[15] Door, freshly-painted, bears sign in stick-on letters. The Jone's. Kate winces. Then we see her from the back as she positions herself at an angle to the doorway so as not to seem invasive to the opener. She knocks gently. Middle-aged man, prim-faced, appears. We see Kate's lips moving tentatively and then with more determination, and come in on 'women's movement, the anti-imperialist and third-world struggles. We[16] are also active in the NDP across Canada. . . .' Man disappears. Victrola effect. Kate waits, nervous. Man reappears. Kate's eyes are wide open and eager, the man's narrowed and suspicious.

'We take the *Trib*.'[17] He closes his door, precisely and not noisily.

Kate walks further down the street.

Next house. Geometry and razor-edge again. Kate pauses at first step, arranges sheaf of papers, has pencil ready. We watch her from the top of the stairs this time; she comes up sturdily and rings the bell in a confident manner, stands feet apart directly in front of the door. Woman opens main door (screen door remains closed): early forties, tall, glasses, curly grey hair, big build. Stares. We see Kate's lips moving again, and come in on 'across Canada. Right now we're offering a special rate, twelve issues for five dollars and three back issues thrown in free. [The woman stares with a little smile. Kate is unnerved but continued.] Or if

[14]This sequence can repeat exactly whenever needed. Kate has to look extremely alone. Camera behind her, the long street stretching out.

[15]Could have shot of a man using an edger here.

[16]Never explained.

[17]Newspaper of Communist Party in British Columbia. Kate's reference to the New Democratic Party tipped her prospect off that her newspaper is likely Trotskyist. (Though he would say 'Trotskyite'. Why this curious distinction obtains could be the theme of a very interesting little dissertation. Cf. Marxian, Marxist; economism, economist; racist, racialist; socialite, socialist. Consideration in order of distinctions between/among American, Canadian, and British usage.)

you like you can buy a single issue now and see if you like it.[18] [The woman's smile widens.] I'm sure you will, you know. It's really a very good paper. . . .' Victrola effect again, and Kate shifts her feet about miserably.

The woman says, 'I'll take a subscription.' Kate fumbles delightedly among her papers. There is a mixup over who will open the screen door[19] and whether Kate will give the form or the woman will simply take it off the top of the pile. Kate watches while the woman deliberately, too slowly, fills in the form. There is something not quite right about her manner.[20] Kate connects with this fact at the moment when the woman hands back the subscription form. Her accepting hand hesitates, indicating her realization that this is not a 'real' sub.[21] But it *is* a sub. Kate leaves. The woman watches her go down the steps to the sidewalk and turn to continue her journey.

Kate walks farther down the street.

She thinks about that young girl-typist who ran to Smolny, ran with a message of crucial importance that Trotsky had to receive or . . . ? What kind of place was Smolny, anyway? A suburb like Burnaby? Kate visualizes herself running from Georgia and Granville out to Boundary and Hastings. But 1917, in Russia . . . fragmentary images of snow-howling steppes, Lenin addressing the crowd, onion spires, Peter and Paul.[22] Kate shakes her head,

[18]Mistake. At the training session back at the hall Kate was told to suggest a single-issue sale only if *sure* the prospect wouldn't take a sub.

[19]A metal screen door, ugly, noisy, with stiff latch and handle. This model, now ubiquitous, is in every way inferior to the wood-framed screen doors of yore, the sound of whose closing on summer days has been eulogized by innumerable middle-class writers doing an E.B. White 'Once More To The Lake' number.

[20]The woman has a look something like when a person who ordinarily wears glasses goes without them—drugged, lost, out of sync. Her clothing also can suggest mental illness (not the garments themselves but the way they are worn, the movement of the body beneath them).

[21]'Real' would be when the prospect and Kate had engaged in a brisk, vigorous, informed political discussion *as a result of which* the p. was convinced (not persuaded but convinced) to buy the newspaper. Kate does not believe she is able to carry on such a discussion. For the present she is right.

[22]Also possibly the pram-on-the-Odessa-Steps scene from *Potemkin* and the massed pennanted spears from *Alexander Nevsky*.

annoyed at her own ignorance and romanticism, waves her arm to brush the images away. She says, 'I can't see how to see it.' And the young woman herself, what is she like? Kate puts her on a country road, straight and flat, files of elms to either side,[23] and dresses her *seriatim* in professional Ukrainian peasant dance costume, Canadian Girls in Training uniform circa 1914, and 1920s flapper style. In all cases she has long blonde hair coiled in braids about her head, and she runs with long powerful strides.[24] Kate shakes her head again.

Next house. Frame, three-storey, beat-up but handsome still. Children's toys, tricycles, playpen littering front yard. Stacks of beer cartons and old newspapers on front porch. Door with long oval window, *no* curtains. Kate is still abstracted when she rings the bell; she waits, thinking. The runner image again, now in modern Olympics outfit complete with torch. Rings again. Door opens. Young man, plain, intelligent, scruffy.

'Yeah,' he says, 'don't I know you?'

'At the demo last Saturday I think,' she says. Her face is shimmering between friendliness and urgency to begin her spiel. Young man's eyes drop to newspapers she's carrying. Face changes,[25] lengthens, goes tight, works in an ugly way. Mouth opens.

'Kronstadt!' he bellows. '*Kronstadt!* Trotsky murdered

[23] A Dutch landscape, Hobbema or Ruisdael.

[24] Kate is thinking of the Modern Library logo, and then by association of the Everyman Library motto, 'Everyman, I will go with thee and be thy guide/In thy most need to go by thy side.' Everywoman is not mentioned, though many do use books as armour. For example, the woman to whom Kate has just sold a subscription: The day she ended her marriage, she went to the Kingsgate Branch of the Vancouver Public Library and read Dick Francis's *Rat Race* in its entirety. With that padding of 150-odd pages of cheap thriller between herself and the morning's experience, she felt able to go home and tell her children.

There are limits though. In 1975 gifted British Columbia poet Pat Lowther was hammered to death by her unadjectived husband in the bedroom of the East Vancouver home they shared (you could say). In her most need, where were you, Erato?

[25] This must happen *instantly*.

them!'[26] Glare. Spit.[27] Slam.[28] Glass of window in door vibrates.

Kate walks farther down the street, her step uncertain. She turns; she has only done four houses; she turns and the long street stretches out.

'Well. That was the anarchist house.'

She walks.

'I wonder if anyone knows what her name was?'[29]

Now a sequence in which we don't see or hear the details of Kate's experiences. She goes up and down steps, from house to next house. A couple of times the pencil and the subscription form pass back and forth, there is briefly a smile on her face, her step is resilient—but essentially what we watch is the strengthening power of routine exerting its influence upon an individual.[30] Kate is passing through her 'first time on the sub-drive' initiation. She is learning how to do this work of the

[26]The sailors of the Kronstadt naval base on the Baltic were among the most loyally revolutionary supporters of the Bolsheviks throughout the revolution, and Trotsky was a particular hero of theirs. In 1921 this relationship soured; the Kronstadt navy 'mutinied against the Soviet government, and took possession of the fortress and two ironclads. After a bombardment lasting many days, the Soviet troops made a night attack across the ice and the revolt was crushed with much severity.' So says the *Encyclopedia Britannica*, 14th ed., 1929. (Incidentally the excellent entry on V.I. Lenin in this edition is by L.D. Trotsky.) The *Britannica* then austerely concludes its remarks on Kronstadt by noting that the port 'is icebound for 140 to 160 days each year, from about the beginning of December until April', and does not comment on Trotsky's approbation of the Bolshevik decision to crush the sailors' revolt. Whether this action should or should not have been carried out is a question which has since generated savage and unhealable differences among leftists.

[27]He's not had time to work up a good supply of saliva; nonetheless a visible glob lands on Kate's shirt.

[28]This is a really purposeful slam.

[29]If Trotsky knew, he didn't tell; he identifies her as a 'working-girl from the Bolshevik printing-plant' (*History of the Russian Revolution*, Sphere Books, London, 1967, Vol. 3, p. 194). Was she a typesetter, not a typist, in fact? He also says she was accompanied by 'A worker' (male, obviously), and that these two 'ran panting to Smolny'. NB remember to see what Deutscher says if anything.

[30]This is a tricky concept in revolutionary work. Too little routine in an organization leads to sloppiness and inefficiency. Too much generates an inability to respond to anything unfamiliar. An organization afflicted by this particular type of blindness is said to be suffering from routinism.

revolution. It *is* work, she now realizes, combining in itself work's too-common attributes of difficulty and tedium. Occasionally there are brief flickering images of the young girl-typist.

Kate finishes one side of the block and crosses the street, and this new side stretches out and out before her. She is just half-done, is already tiring. She starts down the block. At the third house the camera meets her on the porch, a quick approach, nothing special about the building. She knocks. Brief wait. Then heavy sounds beyond the door; it opens. Tall, big-chested old man[31] with crutch under his right arm, newspaper under his left. His jeans and check shirt are clean and neat but he is not a person who is interested in them. He looks intently at Kate, who speaks without much expression.

'I'm selling *Voice of Revolution*, a monthly newspaper. We cover [the man blinks at the copy Kate extends to him] the international scene from a revolutionary perspective [his eyes widen], and each issue also contains up-to-date analysis of events in the Canadian labour movement, the women's movement [frown of puzzlement], the anti-imperialist and Third World struggles. We are also active in the NDP [his lips frame the initials CCF] across Canada. Right now we're offering a special rate [a smile begins to form on his cheeks and he looks Kate up and down; she becomes self-conscious but is determined to get to the end], twelve issues for five dollars and three back issues thrown in free. Would you like to examine[32] our new issue for a few moments? I'm sure. . . .' No Victrola effect this time; the man's deep warm voice simply obliterates hers.

'The *Voice*! Are you selling the *Voice* then?[33] Come in, yes, do come in, put it down here so I can take a good look. The *Voice*

[31]Camera can explore this last adjective. Conclusion: this human is not as old as he initially appears. Poverty and hunger do a fine job in achieving this older-than-you-are look. So do the heavier emotions. So sometimes do intellectual struggles.

[32]This should be 'look at', but at least she's saying the right thing this time.

[33]This telltale sentence construction is the kind that encourages right-wing Letter-to-the-Editor writers in deploring the too-strong influence of Scottish trade unionists in Our Canadian Labour Movement.

now! I've not seen it in years.'

They go past a small fanatically clean living-room and ditto kitchen and enter a TV room currently metamorphosed to a guest-room. The base is clear but the superstructure comprises open suitcases, books and magazines flung about, a couple of canes, a tobacco tin, some Guinness bottles. A crocheted throw on the hide-a-bed has been tossed back as by one arising from a nap.

'Now I'm Mac, Mac Ferguson, and what's your name, comrade?'

'I'm Kate Steele.' Her face is nervous (inside house of totally strange man, remember that look on the porch), excited (this must be an old member, what luck), shy (what can middle-class Kate possibly have to say to this towering hulk of a worker?).

'Been in long?'

'Just a few months. I joined in the spring, after all the cutbacks demonstrations the teachers had.'

'Ah, an intellectual. That's good, the party always needs some. Think of Trotsky himself.'[34]

Abruptly Mac sits down on a chair and feels for his glasses. Kate sees them lying on top of the TV and hands them over; he does not say Thank you, just puts them on and is at once absorbed. Kate looks amused.[35] Mac reads, muttering. 'This NDP convention now, what's the line?'[36] They'll never go for that, the social democrats . . . That's right, tell the leadership where to get off . . . And this nuclear . . . terrible thing, terrible

[34]Kate does not consider herself an intellectual and is bothered, but does not know what to say.

[35]Such a reaction would be suspect in many left-wing and feminist circles. I like her amusement because it shows she has relaxed a bit and is focused on him, not herself; likely it's a relief after her experience of the last while *not* to be the object of attention.

[36]This term, meaning the official opinion or analysis of a revolutionary organization, has been subject to much abuse in the North American left from (a) people too cowardly to accept the political commitment which *having* a line demands, and (b) people unable to move a political inch without the starch of an organizational viewpoint in their spinal columns.

it is. Well . . . never win a strike that way, never happened that way yet on God's green earth. [Kate sits down on the hide-a-bed.] Latin America. Poor damn buggers. Poor damn buggers. Here there's food anyhow . . . Abortion rights. I don't like that now, no no . . . [Kate's face sinks; is she going to have to argue that one with this old comrade?] The International. The Four Eye . . . Ah, the masthead.' He reads in intense searching silence, then drops the paper and looks at Kate. Fragmentary vision of the young girl-typist, lights of a town ahead of her now along the narrow road, with darkness coming. 'Nobody I know left.'

Kate takes the leap delightedly. 'Were you a member then?'

'Aye, yes, we're comrades, eh? Not really though. I dropped to sympathizer—oh, years ago now.' He reaches for a tobacco tin, wincing; quite often in the rest of this scene he shifts his right leg about, seeking comfort. He starts rolling a cigarette. Kate watches his hands. CU to her face; adam's-apple activity again. Then she says, 'What Happened?'

Silence while Mac finishes rolling his cigarette, lighting it, dousing the match, inhaling, looking at Kate. Quite a long silence, which must establish that there is going to be an answer, that it will be serious and truthful, and that Kate is going to hear things she hasn't heard before.

'Comrade,[37] I honestly don't know if you could understand it without being in the Cold War. I mean, I started with the movement in the Depression, the Left Opposition, I went through the War—how old are you?'

'Twenty-seven,' says poor Kate, feeling it a most puny age.

'The Second War. Oh yes, terrible, but the Cold War . . . that McCarthyism . . . what that did to people on the Left. Oh yes, here in Canada too, don't ever let them fool you on that, it didn't stop at the border. Awful divisions. In the movement. We were responding to the outside pressure, you see, it was hard to know that then. Fighting for our lives, we were. Oh, the factions.

[37]Camera on Kate's face through most of this speech, which comes slowly, with pauses and gaps.

Comrades dropping out and dropping out, just a few of us . . . when you're so very few you're precious, see? You love each other and you hate each other too, somehow. Things go bitterly wrong.'[38]

'Was it for personal reasons that you left then, Mac?'[39]

'Hard to say.[40] And I was a marked man in the union too, see. They got at me every way they could, the right-wingers, and they had plenty. Fight to be allowed to speak at meetings. Hell, fight to be told the meetings were happening! Fight to get work. Fight to keep it. And to watch those "labour statesman" trading up their cars every two years . . . boom, see. Oh it was a bad time. My wife left me[41] [this very quick, en passant]. And then I got this,' touching his right leg. 'At Powell River. The mill. They wouldn't even take on the Compensation board like they should have. I don't get half the compo I should, not half.' Mac is going to develop this theme, but recalls himself with a glance at Kate. Brief image of the girl-typist runner, freeze-frame, as if listening.

'So it was very bad. This was the early sixties by now, I was still trying to get back to work with this leg, took me another five years to realize I'd never work in the mill again. I was still trying. And we were having a big faction fight in the movement. Was right round when the NDP was forming, eh? No more CCF.

[38]Now to Mac's face, looking at Kate. Shows (a) the gratitude of a deeply lonely person talking to someone who at least understands the terms he's using; (b) consciousness of her youth and his age; (c) consciousness of her sex.

[39]Kate thinks these would be separate from and inferior to any political reasons, no matter how misguided the latter. She thinks so in spite of a year's participation in a women's group and a careful reading of Rowbotham's *Beyond The Fragments* and analogous work. She doesn't even know that she thinks so. Consideration of power, depth, and subtlety of bourgeois ideology is in order.

[40]Mac is not interested in answering the question but in saying what he wants to say anyway. This is true of about ninety per cent of all answerers to all questioners.

[41]Throughout Mac's story, speculation is encouraged *re* whether he would have spoken thus, or even considered speaking thus, if the revolutionary sales-person arriving on his doorstep had been male. Interested readers/viewers may care also to imagine versions in which inhabitant of house and sales-person are respectively female and male, or both female. Such time-wasting fantasies can be most instructive.

Again and once again, the question of the NDP.[42] So at this one branch meeting I got up to speak, and the comrade in the chair ruled me out of order. And—what's your name again?'

'Kate.'

'And Kate, you know what I did?' He looks in appeal at her.[43] 'I cried. Couldn't help it. It was like everything was all of a piece, the movement, the union, my wife, the right-wingers everywhere. I cried. [Kate sees the girl-typist, clad now in a fifties-style skirt-and-sweater set, running along narrow city streets lined with old European apartment-buildings. She must be tired but she keeps a steady pace. She does not carry any parcel or envelope, so the crucial message for Trotsky must be in her braided head.[44]] And I walked out then, and I never went back.' [CU on Mac's hands, which are large and thick-fingered; the tops of three fingers on the left hand aren't there. The ropy veins on hands, wrists, arms stand out in high relief. Camera shifts to Kate's face, which shows that she cannot think of a single thing to say.]

'Now you'll be wanting your money,' Mac says suddenly and heaves himself up. 'My daughter, she keeps me short, but I know where her bus-money stash is. No no, none of that, the press has to pay its own way, eh?'

Mac and Kate go into the kitchen's antiseptic neatness and he gets a cocoa tin down from the cupboard and counts out twenty quarters.

[42]Kate has heard this sentence spoken with sarcasm and as invective. Mac says the words with plain sadness.

[43]This expression contrasts with Mac's big masculine head and face in a way commonly thought more moving than if it appears on the face of a woman or a child.

[44]Deutscher tells us that on 23 October Kerensky banned *Rabochyi Put* (title of *Pravda* since the July days) and ordered its editorial offices and printing-press closed. 'A working girl [NB he puts her *first*] and a man from the press rushed to the Military Revolutionary Committee, saying that they were prepared to break the seals on the premises of *Rabochyi Put* and to go on producing the paper if the Committee gave them an effective military escort.' (Isaac Deutscher, *The Prophet Armed: Trotsky 1879-1921*, New York/London: Oxford University Press, 1954, p. 307.) Deutscher further states that this proposition, 'breathlessly made by an unknown working girl, comes to Trotsky like a flash.'

'Och yes she'll fuss, but what can she do, see? Next month I'm off to the one in Williams Lake and she's a lot easier on me—so I'll put her address on your form.' He does, in a clear spiky hand which owes nothing to H.B. McLean.[45]

'Do you live part of the time with one and part with the other, then?'

'That's right. When I'm not in some damn hospital with this [slams leg]. Neither of them wants me, really, but what are daughters for, eh?' He folds the receipt and gets out his wallet. 'I'm useful still, though. Do repairs here, look after the kids there. Her man here, though, he's an awful right-winger. "Trade unions are not political organizations" [this in an assumed whiny tone]. Thinks it's terrible when the young Turks now,[46] they bring resolutions on Nicaragua to the meeting. I tell him he should go down Stateside and help Mr Reagan.' Mac and Kate laugh briefly. Mac takes a photograph from his wallet. 'Here I was.'

A young soldier, smiling. A casual snapshot. There is nothing to say. [The young girl-typist has reached a large building, windows lit from top to bottom, guards' figures black against the grey of the coming night.[47]]

'Will you take tea? Och, I should have asked before. No,

[45]System of handwriting instruction favoured for many years in Canadian public schools, and designed to pulverize any individuality in students' methods of moving pens across paper. Each lesson begins with 'Ready for printing—Desks cleared—printing materials ready (practice paper, pencils, and compendiums on desk). Pupils adopt attitude of attention . . . All pupils should sit in a comfortable, hygienic position.' (H.B. MacLean and Grace Vollet, *The MacLean Method of Writing*, rev. ed., Agincourt, Ont., Gage Ltd, 1966-67, *passim.*)

[46]The OED says that this term identifies the Ottomans who in the early years of this century tried to rejuvenate and Europeanize the Turkish empire. It also defines the expression as applicable to anyone having qualities 'attributed to the Turks', i.e., unmanageability and violence. By quoting a question posed in a 1908 newspaper, 'Will the glorification of the "Young Turk" kill this expression as one of reproach to be used in the nursery?', the OED suggests that the child-classifying expression used in Britain predated the 20th c. political term of reference.

[47]By one of those ironies Clio frequently produces—so sharp that in any 'creative' or 'fictional' work they would be roundly condemned as vulgar—Smolny, which was a building in Moscow, had in its previous incarnation been a finishing school for bourgeois young ladies.

you've to get on, I see that.'

Kate is out on the front porch. She is down the steps and almost at the sidewalk. She looks down at her own arms and legs.

She sees the young woman now mounting the steps of the big building, Smolny, about to step inside tall ornate doors, about to break the seals of history and vanish nameless. The doors swing open and the typist turns to show Kate's face, an old face, worn, heavy, heavy, with the weight of human years. Then she's gone.[48]

'Kate! *Kate!*' Cute and Punkoid are down at the next corner, waiting and waving.

Kate walks farther down the street.

She turns in at the next house. She will complete her assignment.

[48]Trotsky, according to Deutscher, had been waiting for some provocative action from Kerensky, and the seals were precisely that. He sent riflemen and sappers to guard the printing-press, the machinery rolled once more, and the next day the rising started. (Deutscher, op. cit., pp. 307 ff.)

Presumably if this specific provocation had not come to Trotsky's attention some other would have, the revolution would still have taken place, etc. However, it did take place in just this particular way because of the thought and action of one particular young woman. For further discussion, see History, role of individual in. Plekhanov's essay is as good a place to start as any.

MAVIS GALLANT

Lena

In her prime, by which I mean in her beauty, my first wife, Magdalena, had no use for other women. She did not depend upon women for anything that mattered, such as charm and enjoyment and getting her bills paid; and as for exchanging Paris gossip and intimate chitchat, since she never confided anything personal and never complained, a man's ear was good enough. Magdalena saw women as accessories, to be treated kindly— maids, seamstresses, manicurists—or as comic minor figures, the wives and official fiancées of her admirers. It was not in her nature to care what anyone said, and she never could see the shape of a threat even when it rolled over her, but I suspect that she was called some of the senseless things she was called, such as 'Central European whore' and 'Jewish adventuress', by women.

Now that she is nearly eighty and bedridden, she receives visits from women—the residue of an early wave of Hungarian emigration. They have small pink noses, wear knitted caps pulled down to their eyebrows, and can see on dark street corners the terrible ghost of Béla Kun. They have forgotten that Magdalena once seemed, perhaps, disreputable. She is a devout Catholic, and she says cultivated, moral-sounding things, sweet to the ears of half a dozen widows of generals and bereft sisters of bachelor diplomats. They crowd her bedside table with bottles of cough mixture, lemons, embroidered table napkins, jars of honey, and covered bowls of stewed plums, the juice from which always spills. They call Magdalena 'Lena'.

She occupies a bed in the only place that would have her—a hospital on the northern rim of Paris, the colour of jails, daubed with graffiti. The glass-and-marble lobby commemorates the flashy prosperity of the nineteen-sixties. It contains, as well as a vandalized coffee machine and a plaque bearing the name of a forgotten Minister of Health, a monumental example of the art of twenty years ago: a white foot with each toenail painted a different colour. In order to admire this marvel, and to bring Magdalena the small comforts I think she requires, I need to travel a tiring distance by the underground suburban train. On these expeditions I carry a furled umbrella: the flat, shadeless light of this line is said to attract violent crime. In my wallet I have a card attesting to my right to sit down, because of an accident suffered in wartime. I never dare show the card. I prefer to stand. Anything to do with the Second World War, particularly its elderly survivors, arouses derision and ribaldry and even hostility in the young.

Magdalena is on the fourth floor (no elevator) of a wing reserved for elderly patients too frail to be diverted to nursing homes—assuming that a room for her in any such place could be found. The old people have had it drummed into them that they are lucky to have a bed, that the waiting list for their mattress and pillow lengthens by the hour. They must not seem too capricious, or dissatisfied, or quarrelsome, or give the nurses extra trouble. If they persist in doing so, their belongings are packed and their relatives sent for. A law obliges close relatives to take them in. Law isn't love, and Magdalena has seen enough distress and confusion to make her feel thoughtful.

'Families are worse than total war,' she says. I am not sure what her own war amounted to. As far as I can tell, she endured all its rigors in Cannes, taking a daily walk to a black-market restaurant, her legs greatly admired by famous collaborators and German officers along the way. Her memory, when she wants to be bothered with it, is like a brief, blurry, self-centred dream.

'But what were you *doing* during those years?' I have asked her. (My mother chalked Gaullist slogans on walls in Paris. The father of my second wife died deported. I joined the Free French in London.)

'I was holding my breath,' she answers, smiling.

She shares a room with a woman who suffers from a burning rash across her shoulders. Medicine that relieves the burning seems to affect her mind, and she will wander the corridors, wondering where she is, weeping. The hospital then threatens to send her home, and her children, in a panic, beg that the treatment be stopped. After a few days the rash returns, and the woman keeps Magdalena awake describing the pain she feels—it is like being flogged with blazing nettles, she says. Magdalena pilfers tranquillizers and gets her to take them, but once she hit the woman with a pillow. The hospital became nasty, and I had to step in. Fortunately, the supervisor of the aged-and-chronic department had seen me on television, taking part in a literary game ('Which saint might Jean-Paul Sartre have wanted most to meet?'), and that helped our case.

Actually, Magdalena cannot be evicted—not just like that. She has no family, and nowhere to go. Her continued existence is seen by the hospital as a bit of a swindle. They accepted her in the first place only because she was expected to die quite soon, releasing the bed.

'Your broken nose is a mistake,' she said to me the other day. My face was damaged in the same wartime accident that is supposed to give me priority seating rights in public transportation. 'It lends you an air of desperate nerve, as if a Malraux hero had wandered into a modern novel and been tossed out on his face.'

Now, this was hard on a man who had got up earlier than usual and bought a selection of magazines for Magdalena before descending to the suburban line, with its flat, worrying light. A man who had just turned sixty-five. Whose new bridge made him lisp. She talks the way she talked in the old days, in her apartment with the big windows and the sweeping view across the Seine. She used to wear white, and sit on a white sofa. There were patches of red in the room—her long fingernails and her lipstick, and the Legion of Honour on some admirer's lapel. She had two small, funny dogs whose eyes glowed red in the dusk.

'I heard you speaking just the other day,' she went on. 'You were most interesting about the way Gide always made the rounds of the bookstores to see how his work was selling. Actually, I think I told you that story.'

'It couldn't have been just the other day,' I said. 'It sounds like a radio program I had in the nineteen-fifties.'

'It couldn't have been you, come to think of it,' she said. 'The man lisped. I said to myself, "It *might* be Édouard."'

Her foreign way of speaking enchanted me when I was young. Now it sharpens my temper. Fifty years in France and she still cannot pronounce my name, 'Édouard', without putting the stress on the wrong syllable and rolling the 'r'. 'When you come to an "r",' I have told her, 'keep your tongue behind your lower front teeth.'

'It won't stay,' she says. 'It curls up. I am sorry.' As if she cared. She will accept any amount of petulance shown by me, because she things she owes me tolerance: she sees me as youthful, boyish, to be teased and humoured. She believes we have a long, unhampered life before us, and she expects to occupy it as my wife and widow-to-be. To that end, she has managed to outlive my second wife, and she may well survive me, even though I am fourteen years younger than she is and still on my feet.

Magdalena's Catholic legend is that she was converted after hearing Jacques Maritain explain Neo-Thomism at a tea party. Since then, she has never stopped heaping metaphysical rules about virtue on top of atavistic arguments concerning right and wrong. The result is a moral rock pile, ready to slide. Only God himself could stand up to the avalanche, but in her private arrangements he is behind her, egging her on. I had to wait until a law was passed that allowed divorce on the ground of separation before I was free to marry again. I waited a long time. In the meantime, Magdalena was writing letters to the Pope, cheering his stand on marriage and urging him to hold firm. She can choose among three or four different languages, her choice depending on where her dreams may have taken her during the night. She used to travel by train to Budapest and Prague wearing white linen. She had sleek, fair hair, and wore a diamond hair clip behind one ear. Now no one goes to those places, and the slim linen suits are crumpled in trunks. Her mind is clear, but she says absurd things. 'I never saw her,' she said about Juliette, my second wife. 'Was she anything like me?'

'You did see her. We had lunch, the three of us.'

'Show me her picture. It might bring back the occasion.'

'No.'

They met, once, on the first Sunday of September 1954—a hot day of quivering horizons and wasps hitting the windshield. I had a new Renault—a model with a reputation for rolling over and lying with its wheels in the air. I drove, I think, grimly. Magdalena was beside me, in a nimbus of some scent—jasmine, or gardenia—that made me think of the opulent, profiteering side of wars. Juliette sat behind, a road map on her knee, her finger on the western outskirts of Fontainebleau. Her dark hair was pulled back tight and tied at the nape of her neck with a dark-blue grosgrain ribbon. It is safe to say that she smelled of soap and lemons.

We were taking Magdalena out to lunch. It was Juliette's idea. Somewhere between raspberries-and-cream and coffee, I was supposed to ask for a divorce—worse, to coax from Magdalena the promise of collusion in obtaining one. So far, she had resisted any mention of the subject and for ten years had refused to see me. Juliette and I had been living together since the end of the war. She was thirty now, and tired of waiting. We were turning into one of those uneasy, shadowy couples, perpetually waiting for a third person to die or divorce. I was afraid of losing her. That summer, she had travelled without me to America (so much farther from Europe then than it is today), and she had come back with a different coloration to her manner, a glaze of independence, as though she had been exposed to a new kind of sun.

I remember how she stared at Magdalena with gentle astonishment, as if Magdalena were a glossy illustration that could not look back. Magdalena had on a pale dress of some soft, floating stuff, and a pillbox hat tied on with a white veil, and long white gloves. I saw her through Juliette's eyes, and I thought what Juliette must be thinking: Where does Magdalena think we're taking her? To a wedding? Handing her into the front seat, I had shut the door on her skirt. I wondered if she had turned into one of the limp, pliant women whose clothes forever catch.

It was Juliette's custom to furnish social emptiness with some rattling anecdote about her own activities. Guests were often grateful. Without have to cast far, they could bring up a narrative of their own, and the result was close to real conversation. Juliette spoke of her recent trip. She said she was wearing an American dress made of a material called cotton seersucker. It washed like a duster and needed next to no ironing.

For answer, she received a side view of Magdalena's hat and a blue eye shadowed with paler blue. Magdalena was not looking but listening, savouring at close quarters the inflections of the French Protestant gentry. She knew she was privileged. As a rule, they speak only to one another. Clamped to gearshift and wheel, I was absolved of the need to comment. My broken profile had foxed Magdalena at first. She had even taken me for an impostor. But then the remembered face of a younger man slid over the fraud and possessed him.

Juliette had combed through the *Guide Michelin* and selected a restaurant with a wide terrace and white umbrellas, set among trees. At some of the tables there were American officers, in uniform, with their families—this is to show how long ago it was. Juliette adjusted our umbrella so that every inch of Magdalena was in shade. She took it for granted that my wife belonged to a generation sworn to paleness. From where I was sitting, I could see the interior of the restaurant. It looked cool and dim, I thought, and might have been better suited to the soft-footed conversation to come.

I adjusted my reading glasses, which Magdalena had never seen, and stared at a long handwritten menu. Magdalena made no move to examine hers. She had all her life let men decide. Finally, Juliette wondered if our guest might not like to start with asparagus. I was afraid the asparagus would be canned. Well, then, said Juliette, what about melon. On a hot day, something cool followed by cold salmon. She broke off. I started to remove my glasses, but Juliette reminded me about wine.

Magdalena was engaged in a ritual that Juliette may not have seen before and that I had forgotten: pulling off her tight, long gloves finger by finger and turning her rings right side up. Squeezed against a great sparkler of some kind was a wedding ring. Rallying, Juliette gave a little twitch to the collar of the washable seersucker and went on about America. In Philadelphia, a celebrated Pentecostal preacher had persuaded the Holy Spirit to settle upon a member of the congregation, a woman whose hearing had been damaged when she was brained by a flying shoe at a stock-car race. The deaf woman rose and said she could hear sparrows chirping in High German, on which the congregation prayed jubilant thanks.

Juliette did not stoop to explain that she was no Pentecostalist. She mentioned the Holy Spirit as an old acquaintance of her own class and background, a cultivated European with an open mind.

We were no longer young lovers, and I had heard this story several times. I said that the Holy Spirit might find something more useful to attend to than a ruptured eardrum. We were barely ten years out of a disastrous war. All over the world, there were people sick, afraid, despairing. Only a few days before, the President of Brazil had shot himself to death.

Juliette replied that there were needs beyond our understanding. 'God knows what he wants,' she said. I am sure she believed it.

'God wanted Auschwitz?' I said.

I felt a touch on my arm, and I looked down and saw a middle-aged hand and a wedding ring.

With her trained inclination to move back from rising waters, Juliette made the excuse of a telephone call. I knew that her brief departure was meant to be an intermission. When she came back, we would speak about other things. Magdalena and I sat quietly, she with her hand still on my arm, as if she had finally completed a gesture begun a long time before. Juliette, returning, her eyes splashed with cold water, her dark hair freshly combed, saw that I was missing a good chance to bring up the divorce. She sat down, smiled, picked up her melon spoon. She was working hard these days, she said. She was translating an American novel that should never have been written. (Juliette revealed nothing more about this novel.) From there, she slid along to the subject of drastic separations—not so much mine from Magdalena as divorcement in general. Surely, she said, a clean parting was a way of keeping life pleasant and neat? This time, it was Magdalena's hearing that seemed impaired, and the Holy Spirit was nowhere. The two women must have been thinking the same thing at that moment, though for entirely different reasons: that I had forfeited any chance of divine aid by questioning God's intentions.

It was shortly before her removal to the hospital that Magdalena learned about Juliette's death. One of her doddering friends may have seen the notice in a newspaper. She at once resumed her place as my only spouse and widow-to-be. In fact, she had never relinquished it, but now the way back to me shone clear. The divorce, that wall of pagan darkness, had been torn down and dispersed with the concubine's ashes. She saw me delivered from an adulterous and heretical alliance. It takes a convert to think 'heretical' with a straight face. She could have seen Juliette burned at the stake without losing any sleep. It is another fact about converts that they make casual executioners.

She imagined that I would come to her at once, but I went nowhere. Juliette had asked to be cremated, thinking of the purification of the flame, but the rite was accomplished by clanking, hidden, high-powered machinery that kept starting and stopping, on cycle. At its loudest, it covered the voice of the clergyman, who affirmed that Juliette was eyeing us with great good will from above, and it prevailed over Juliette's favourite recordings of Mozart and Bach. Her ashes were placed in a numbered niche that I never saw, for at some point in the funeral service I lost consciousness and had to be carried out. This nightmare was dreamed in the crematorium chapel of Père Lachaise cemetery. I have not been back. It is far from where I live, and I think Juliette is not there, or anywhere. From the moment when her heart stopped, there has been nothing but silence.

Last winter, I had bronchitis and seldom went out. I managed to send Magdalena a clock, a radio, an azalea, and enough stamps and stationery to furnish a nineteenth-century literary correspondence. Nevertheless, the letters that reached my sickbed from hers were scrawled in the margins of newspapers, torn off crookedly. Sometimes she said her roommate had lent her the money for a stamp. The message was always the same: I must not allow my wife to die in a public institution. Her pink-nosed woman friends wrote me, too, signing their alien names, announcing their titles—there was a princess.

It was no good replying that everybody dies in hospital now. The very idea made them sick, of a sickness beyond any wasting last-ditch illusion. Then came from Magdalena 'On Saturday at nine o'clock, I shall be dressed and packed, and waiting for you to come and take me away.'

Away from the hospital bed? It took weeks of wangling and soft-soaping and even some mild bribery to obtain it. Public funds, to which she is not entitled, and a voluntary contribution from me keep her in it. She has not once asked where the money comes from. When she was young, she decided never to worry, and she has kept the habit.

I let several Saturdays go by, until the folly had quit her mind. Late in April I turned up carrying a bottle of Krug I had kept on ice until the last minute and some glasses in a paper bag. The woman who shares her room gave a great groan when she saw me, and showed the whites of her eyes. I took this to mean that Magdalena had died. The other bed was clean and empty. The clock and the radio on the table had the look of objects left behind. I felt shock, guilt, remorse, and relief, and I wondered what to do with the wine. I turned, and there in the doorway stood Magdalena, in dressing gown and slippers, with short white hair. She shuffled past me and lay on the bed with her mouth open, struggling for breath.

'Shouldn't I ring for a nurse?' I said, unwrapping the bottle.

'No one will come. Open the champagne.'

'I'd better fetch a nurse.' Instead, I made room on the table for the glasses. I'd brought three, because of the roommate.

Magdalena gasped, 'Today is my birthday.' She sat up, apparently recovered, and got her spectacles out from under the pillow. Leaning toward me, she said, 'What's that red speck on your lapel? It looks like the Legion of Honour.'

'I imagine that's what it is.'

'Why?' she said. 'Was there a reason?'

'They probably had a lot to give away. Somebody did say something about "cultural enrichment of the media".'

'I am glad about the enrichment,' she said. 'I am also very happy for you. Will you wear it all the time, change it from suit to suit?'

'It's new,' I said. 'there was a ceremony this morning.' I sat down on the shaky chair kept for visitors, and with a steadiness that silenced us both I poured the wine. 'What about your neighbour?' I said, the bottle poised.

'Let her sleep. This is a good birthday surprise.'

I felt as if warm ashes were banked round my heart, like a

residue of good intentions. I remembered that when Magdalena came back to Paris after the war, she found her apartment looted, laid waste. One of the first letters to arrive in the mail was from me, to say that I was in love with a much younger woman. 'If it means anything at all to you,' I said, the coals glowing brighter, 'if it can help you to understand me in any way—well, no one ever fascinated me as much as you.' This after only one glass.

'But, perhaps, you never loved me,' she said.

'Probably not,' I said. 'Although I must have.'

'You mean, in a way?' she said.

'I suppose so.'

The room became so quiet that I could hear the afternoon movie on television in the next room. I recognized the voice of the actor who dubs Robert Redford.

Magdalena said, 'Even a few months ago this would have been my death sentence. Now I am simply thankful I have so little time left to wander between "perhaps" and "probably not" and "in a way". A crazy old woman, wringing my hands.'

I remembered Juliette's face when she learned that her menopause was irreversible. I remember her shock, her fright, her gradual understanding, her storm of grief. She had hoped for children, then finally a child, a son she would have called 'Thomas'. 'Your death sentence,' I said. 'Your death sentence. What about Juliette's life sentence? She never had children. By the time I was able to marry her, it was too late.'

'She could have had fifteen children without being married,' said Magdalena.

I wanted to roar at her, but my voice went high and thin. 'Women like Juliette, people like Juliette, don't do that sort of thing. It was a wonder she consented to live with me for all those years. What about her son, her Thomas? I couldn't even have claimed him—not legally, as long as I was married to you. Imagine him, think of him, applying for a passport, finding out he had no father. Nothing on his birth certificate. Only a mother.'

'You could have adopted Thomas,' said Magdalena. 'That

way, he'd have been called by your name.'

'I couldn't—not without your consent. *You* were my wife. Besides, why should I have to adopt my own son?' I think this was a shout; that is how it comes back to me. 'And the inheritance laws, as they were in those days. Have you ever thought about that? I couldn't even make a will in his favour.'

Cheek on hand, blue eyes shadowed, my poor, mad, true, and only wife said, 'Ah, Édouard, you shouldn't have worried. You know I'd have left him all that I had.'

It wasn't the last time I saw Magdalena, but after that day she sent no more urgent messages, made no more awkward demands. Twice since then, she has died and come round. Each time, just when the doctor said, 'I think that's it,' she has squeezed the nurse's hand. She loves rituals, and she probably wants the last Sacraments, but hospitals hate that. Word that there is a priest in the place gets about, and it frightens the other patients. There are afternoons when she can't speak and lies with her eyes shut, the lids quivering. I hold her hand, and feel the wedding ring. Like the staunch little widows, I call her 'Lena', and she turns her head and opens her eyes.

I glance away then, anywhere—at the clock, out the window. I have put up with everything, but I intend to refuse her last imposition, the encounter with her blue, enduring look of pure love.

KATHERINE GOVIER

The King of Siam

Jane is in Paris when the news comes: her mother is dead in the apple orchard in the Okanagan, where she and Jane's father have retired, supposedly at peace. And Jane remembers her mother dancing. Not with her father, Saturday night in the living-room, after a discussion about how much hip she could use in the rhumba. He would be leading, driving her with both shoulders as one would a wheelbarrow. 'That much, no more,' he ruled. Her slim hip poked out; he put it back in its place, a stern man with a measuring eye.

'Here I go with my best foot backward,' her mother would say, waggishly, because the man always led, and his forward steps made her step out behind.

No, that is not what she remembers, but her mother dancing, alone, weekday mornings, letting loose, elbows pumping, her mouth a soundless smile. She looks like Mary Martin. The words she sings are Mary's: 'I'm gonna wash that man right outa my hair. . . .' The record spins in the dusty-bright air.

The house glares; the cloudless sky and the flat, snow-whitened lawns and streets bounce sunbeams through the picture windows. The beams explode geometrically again and again on motes of dust in the dry inside air, creating a painful brightness in all directions. Alone with the smallest child when the others have gone to school, her mother walks around in the forced-air heat with narrowed eyes, sometimes shading her brows with a forearm. The beige curtains are closed, to filter the light which could take two shades out of the upholstery in one season.

The house is a lightbox, her mother has two dimensions, like a paper doll glued onto sticks. The records are old ones in small jackets, the songs simple, like rhymes.

'Oh what a beautiful morning, oh what a beautiful day, I've got a wonderful feeling, everything's going my way.'

Every morning it is the same. They have things to do. They will just put on a record while they work. They listen a few minutes and pretend to dust or sort tea-towels but inevitably are seduced. First, certain pieces of furniture have to be moved, his stuffed footstool and the glass-topped coffee-table with the three cones for legs. Then the choice—*Brigadoon? Carousel? The King and I?* They take off their shoes.

They are dancing. Not with each other, no, they move off into separate orbits, there in the veiled brilliance of the living room. Socks on the pink-beige carpet give shocks if they touch each other or the velvet chair. Bits of them arc through the hall mirror, and also in the glass of the picture frames. Cheap clichés these move-ments, but wildly sincere. The arched eyebrows, hands on knees, bug eyes for the benefit of the audience beyond the curtains fluttering over the forced-air vent. The faces out of which such words can come:

'I'm gonna wash that man right outa my hair, and send him on his way!'

Or the supple, breathy swaying, mouth slightly open:

'Some enchanted evening, you may see a stranger, you may see a stranger, across a crowded room . . .'

The room where such events can happen is somewhere else. But somewhere else is a place, a place you can get to, if you just keep going, going

until

it is not Jane, but just her mother dancing, Jane watching. Her mother fabulous and strong, her mother tough and funny. And Jane knows a kind of peace, almost holy. Her mother, the light, the music.

We are talking about the fifties, in the West. A growing city with a university, an industry; a small box house on a too wide street;

her father working out of town on the oil rigs. The Oil Capital of
Canada! Gateway to the North! But outside its boundaries,
nowhere. West, but not coast, flattish, but not prairie, that was
farther south. The American term 'Midwest', conjuring visions
of cornfields, did not apply. They call it parkland, but there were
no parks, only a place where they sometimes went to see a herd
of captive buffalo, brought back from near-extinction. During
the gold rush, expeditions embarked from here for the Yukon;
some lost their way; in all one hundred and twenty-eight people
perished.

And there was the river, muscular, army-green, so wide it
would lead Jane, years later, to scorn the Seine as puny. The
North Saskatchewan's deep valley cut an S through the city,
curling below Lolly Bacon, the treacherous toboggan hill, running straight under the High Level Bridge (One of the Seven
Wonders of the World!) and looping the hill where stood the
giant blue-roofed railway hotel. Then it straightened out to pass
the refinery—when lit at night its scaffolds, arms and towers a
fairy castle—and swept east, toward everything else.

In summer the family walked alongside the river, on a narrow
path by the Outdoors Club, watching out for quicksand. In winter
her father and the boys skied, on long light planks with leather
lace-up boots. Jane stood by the back door looking after them
down the walk. On either side the heaps of snow were piled over
her head; she was too small to go out. Later, she went along, but
she was clumsy and fell, and they were impatient.

Winter lasted from October to May. They were farther north
than any other city of size except Moscow. In the depth of winter,
the sun didn't come up until nine, and it was setting by four.
Strange, then, it was not the dark she remembered, but the light.
Winter days were dazzling: a clear sky and diamond sun on the
packed dry snow, snowblindness as common as frostbite. And
her mother dancing.

The rigs went south and so did they. Her mother's eyes went
down, her back began to stoop. Something was wrong. Her

mother seemed the victim of some terrible disease, consumed by things she wanted to be, or do, and couldn't. She never danced alone, only with him, her father, and it was not dancing any more, it was just obedience. He worked in an office by then.

By the time her father comes home, her mother is trussed with an apron, hands sticky with flour and water, facing into the corner where the sink is. It is a fascinating corner; the mouse is said to live in the back of the cupboard. Jane feels kin to that mouse: she was a mouse in her dance recital, and her father calls her Mouse. There are windows above the sink, looking into the backyard, at the flowering crab-apple tree which the waxwings visit in winter. Probably Jane is at the table drawing, invisible behind the door when her father pushes it open.

'Hi, honey.'

He comes up behind and slaps her bottom. Her mother stiffens, turning her face toward him for the kiss, but keeping the chin down.

'My hands,' she says, excusing herself. He opens the cupboard doors, taking a glass down with a hard click, banging the door shut again, opening and shutting the refrigerator noisily. His movements are square, angry. He is already on his way back to the den, where he will sit and read the paper 'in peace'. Halfway down the hall his voice is louder.

'Kids out again?'

Her mother turns, whispers. 'Go see your father. Talk to him.'

She rises, looking down at her colouring book. The only thing that makes this bearable is that they are working together, mother and daughter. She knows she is an offering to forestall a perhaps inevitable wrath.

'Dad?'

'Is that you, Mouse?'

Still standing outside the door, not moving until requested to.

'Come in.'

She pushes open the door. His feet are closest to her, on the footstool in socks; wide, almost square feet, with toes that arch and curl as if by their own inclination. He is behind these feet leaning back in the armchair; the paper is folded in his lap. He has put down the paper. Now she must prove herself worthy of his attention.

She is invited up close, to sit on his lap. He gives her a rough hug; she ducks his face because of the scratchy whiskers. His head is like a bullet, his neck thick and pocked. Everything about him is strange and threatening. She is perched there when another faint tap comes on the door. Her mother, without the apron, with clean hands. There is a discreet change in his voice, and he sits up. 'I have work to do, girls.' They both slip out.

He doesn't want music on, music disturbs him at this hour. As dinner cooks Jane studies the record album. Anna and the King of Siam in sunset colours, before the flock of little round-faced children with blue-black hair.

'Shall we dance, On a bright cloud of music shall we fly? Shall we dance, shall we then say goodnight and mean goodbye?'

Anna was a beautiful, gentle woman who went to a strange land to look after the children. They were the King's children, not hers. The King was bald and mean, with blazing eyes and a very straight back, like Jane's father. He had unpredictable rages, he even put people to death if they displeased him. He was primitive, a brute. But Anna fell in love. Jane cannot understand what Anna sees in the King. And why did Anna go there in the first place? Reading closely, Jane discovers that Anna had another love, her true love, who died. Perhaps this was the case with her mother.

At five-thirty her father calls out his door about dinner—is it almost ready, or does someone want to get him another Scotch? Jane is sent to retrieve his glass. He has seated himself, by this time, at his desk and is working with a pencil and a ruler on large sheets of squared paper which roll up at the corners. She takes the glass to her mother, who pours more Scotch in it. By the time she reaches his door it happens. He cannot find the gum eraser.

'Nona! Nona!' he roars.

Now Jane is in the hall outside his door, and can see them both. In the kitchen her mother's head, ever ready for alarm, rises up like some deer's hearing distant gunfire. She pushes in the drawer where she is counting out table-napkins. Jane hates the panicky, hobbled sound of her mother's heels.

'What is it, dear?' sweetly, anxious.

'Who's been in this drawer? I told you not to let the kids at my things. Now I can't find my eraser.'

'I don't think they have been. I've told them so many times.'

Jane shrinks in the background. Has she taken the eraser? The accusation is so strong she thinks she must have.

His drawer slams.

'Oh, what's the point?' (bitterly, bitterly) 'I can't get anything done around here.'

After eating in silence, he pushes back his chair and announces that he has to go back to the office. Jane and her mother do the dishes together. After, her mother finds the eraser in the drawer, under a pile of envelopes. She reads to Jane, *The House at Pooh Corner*, before bed and she laughs, very hard, about Tigger falling out of the tree.

Jane lies awake in bed. Eventually her father comes home. His voice is still loud, and cross. Her mother murmurs, placating. They go to bed, in the room next to Jane. Jane doesn't want to hear the noises, so she sings to herself.

'Or perchance, when the *last leetle star* has leaved the sky, shall we still be together, with our arms around each other, and shall you be my new romance?'

Later the family found little to recommend these cities, little to remember. They moved to British Columbia, and her mother became more bitter, more crippled. Jane went away without regret. She didn't like ties, didn't want a man, never thought about it. She studied art, as her mother wished her to, and went to Paris. But she didn't paint. As she often said, she had nothing to paint. She worked, when she felt like it, writing features for Canadian newspapers. Her pieces always had some Canadian angle, that was how she sold them.

The day she learns that her mother has killed herself, not just died, passively, but died actively, by her own hand, all in the new blossoms of spring, Jane has lined up an interview with an artist. It is her father who telephones. Her father is sorry, he has been sorry for years, but he does not say so. And Jane, who thought she had forgiven him, is filled with hate. All she can think of is his impatience, the way he beat her mother down, the way her mother shrank. She puts down the telephone. Then, because Jane is alone and has nothing better to do, she goes to the interview.

The artist lives in the sixteenth district. Jane travels by Métro, getting off at the stop he named, turns up narrower streets than those she's passed through, and finds his door with a tiny gold nameplate. He greets Jane sternly, and turns his back. In the sitting room he brings a trolley, serves tea, and madeleines (à la Proust! he points out in a way not convivial but instructive). The artist is prairie Canadian, and very good; Jane wept in the gallery looking at his pictures. He shows her more. They are painted in egg tempera and are of people in empty rooms, of light from two windows hitting a corner, or sunglasses reflecting a flat horizon. She says she is from Edmonton. He was recently there.

'A terrible place full of awful people! And they all look just like you!'

The madeleines are crumbly and taste like dust. She mentions a few names.

'Oh yes! I saw him! He looks like he just came in from bashing baby seals. And the students! So lazy! All they ever asked me about was money. How much they could make as artists. Mind you, they were better than the faculty. These people, they were so lost, so ignorant. A dreadful, dreadful place.'

Something causes her to be polite, eager to please. She doesn't dare make her usual joke, that the North Saskatchewan is wider than the Seine.

'The only nice person in the whole city was a taxi-driver. He drove me along the river valley,' says the artist.

'It's beautiful, isn't it?'

He glares and presses his lips together. 'You don't know Paris if you think that any other city is beautiful.'

Jane trips, stumbles from the staircase onto the sidewalk, turns this way and that in the crowded streets. The Métro stop is not where it was. She discovers another. She stares down at the rails in the tunnel. She reassesses the man's paintings. They are unreasonable, relentless, unforgiving. There is a clinical coldness to them; but they have taught her something. They have made her see in terrible relief. The city is split into layers, levels one on top of each other. Gaps and improbabilities occur.

For instance, there on the dull shine of the train rail, a creature is moving. It has a familiar down-tilted, pear-shaped body and scaly tail. The rat looks her in the eye. It stands up on its hind legs as if to declare itself. Jane has never actually seen a rat before. There is a special program for rat control in Alberta, successful to an extraordinary degree.

Jane screams, clamping her hand on her mouth. She begins to tremble. She is falling apart, and on foreign soil. The train pulls into the station and the doors sigh open, with pressure. She enters the car with others. Parisians are so rude, they take the outside seat as if to dare you to climb over their knees to get to the other chair. She does. There is a boy sitting across from her. He has dirty, long hair and a huge Adam's apple. He leans forward in his chair, sensing weakness.

'You speak English?'

She stares straight ahead.

'Mademoiselle, you speak English.'

She does not answer.

'Français?'

She keeps staring, hoping to be taken for a deaf mute.

'Mademoiselle, you are American.'

That trips her into shaking her head.

'Not American; German, perhaps?'

The other passengers find this amusing. The young man slurs and leans, perhaps he is on drugs, he doesn't seem to be drunk. He puts his hand on her knee. He keeps asking her where she is from, he lists half the countries in Europe, but he really thinks she is English-speaking, and returns compulsively to 'America, America'. She shrinks in her seat. She is afraid to push him away, to push his hand off her knee; she thinks then he might leap on her.

The man who would not move over is watching. He cocks an eye as if to say, 'Why are you putting up with this? Why don't you fight back?' Women smirk. No one in the crowd will help her. They are waiting for her to speak. She cannot speak. Why should she expect them to defend her, if she can't defend herself? The only thing she can do is run away. The next time the train stops she springs over the man in the seat and out the door. People are laughing behind her. The hollow station magnifies her shame.

Jane walks, runs, sweating, through streets that are completely strange, not the Paris she knows. The faces around her are black; words from shopfront conversations fall around her ears like pebbles. The boy on the train has laid a curse on her: she understands no known language, she comes from nowhere. She carries on like this for a while, crying, while passersby look at her incuriously or not at all. When the tears are reduced to hiccups and shudders, she realizes that she is hungry and gathers her courage to enter a little restaurant. There at last, coffee before her, she become calm. She sits for a long time.

The man at a table by the window looks like the philosopher-king whose picture Jane has seen in the newspaper. He is very dark, with a beard, and a long, bony nose, long, narrow eyes. She looks past him at the street and recognizes a certain hare-lip

newspaper vendor: there is the passage she calls Avenue des
Crottes; around the corner from that must be Square Saint-Sulpice.
She has made her way back somehow to 'her' Paris. She smiles
at her empty cup. She lifts her eyes. He is gazing at her.

They leave the café together. He corrects her French as they
climb five floors to his room. As if he cares, as if he has been
asking, she tells him she is from Canada. He is disappointed. He
is crazy about things American, 'bask*ets*', which turn out to be
track shoes, and Broadway music. *West Side Story. South
Pacific*. He has all the records. And a bottle of wine.

The sun is going down pale peach beyond the gummy grey
windows. She realizes that the light is wrong, there is a film on
everything, the dirty air, the dusty desk top. There must be light.
He plays records one after another. *Camelot, My Fair Lady.*
Then, *The King and I*. She begins to sing the words. He knows
them too, but not what they mean, he tests them in his mouth like
unfamiliar candies. He rubs her nipples, hard, and they undress.
His body is long and narrow and dark, with a rectangle of hair
like a flag on his chest. When they make love, he is making love
to America, but she doesn't care.

After, she gets up to dance, putting on his shirt. The philo-
sopher—she doesn't even know his name, but somehow he is
making all this possible—focuses a reading light on her. Tears
slide over her cheeks, down her throat. By then she is stoned
enough to forget about the rat and the terrible boy on the Métro,
and the upbeat story she will have to write about the frightening
artist—but not about her wasted, horribly dead mother, who has
now turned into an ache running from the base of her rib on the
left side right into her neck.

But Jane does not stop, she keeps on and she has all the moves,
the snap wrists, the jammed-out hip, open mouth and fake
innocent eyes; she is all those saucy heroines of the musicals.
She is Nona, in the fifties, Nona in her lip-sync revolt.

'Oh, Mother, Mother, Mother,' she cries. It is all right to do
it; the French understand these things. Didn't de Beauvoir write

that Sartre himself cried out for his mother in sleep? She cries and she lets loose and she keeps going

until

it visits her again, that feeling of having no edges, nothing to defend, nothing to fear, that only-one-word-for-it peace from when she was four, or five, in the living-room, watching her mother dance. And this peace is the gift, not the emptiness, not the ticket to leave. There was love, before the end. And Jane too may find it. She may even find it with the King of Siam.

JANICE KULYK KEEFER

A Really Good Hotel

'Taxi, mum?'

Mrs Paxton pursed her lips. Ordinarily, she would have swept past this sort of person—bearded, stooped, an emerald turban clenching an unfathomable mass of hair. Ordinarily, there would have been a car waiting for her and a uniformed chauffeur: youngish, deferential, inoffensive. But this was intolerable— there hadn't even been a porter to help her with her luggage. Never mind that she was travelling unusually light this time. There were certain attentions she had come to expect, attentions due to elderly travellers who hadn't the vigour, the indis- criminate good humour of the young.

'You want a taxi, mum?'

Mrs Paxton frowned. Why hadn't the hotel sent a car round? The doctor had assured her all details had been taken care of. As soon as she was shown to her room she'd sit down and fire off a letter of complaint to the manager. Outrageous, unheard of.... Little blots of light dribbled across her eyes, like rain on the windshield of a moving car. Nothing serious, the doctor had assured her, nothing to worry about. All the same, she would have to sit down somewhere, calm herself, set things back to rights.

'I take your bag, mum.' He held the door open, gesturing with his hand to the waiting seat. The powder-blue upholstery was covered with indescribably dingy vinyl. Heaven knew how many bodies had slid in and out of this cab. She shouldn't get in, she knew she shouldn't—the fumes of patchouli would choke her long before she reached the hotel. This was an airport, not a bazaar—what were men with turbans doing driving taxi cabs? What sort of man would condescend to wear a turban? He had shifty eyes, Mrs Paxton decided—he looked like a thief. She shuddered a small, violent shudder, then slid into the sweetened darkness of the cab.

Before the driver could turn the key in the ignition, Mrs Paxton was leaning forward, clutching her collar tighter round her throat. 'I want the Shady Nook Hotel. They were supposed to have sent a car. Can you tell me what the fare will be?'

The man nodded, then made a curious gesture with his hand, turning it palm downward and moving it from side to side as if to indicate that there would be no charge, or at least the regular fares did not apply. Perhaps, then this was the driver sent by the hotel? Unthinkable. Yet before she could protest, the car had started up and they were rolling out of the airport into a sunstruck afternoon, curiously like summer, though it was still the bleakest part of March. Trees on either side of the highway were in flagrant leaf—a perverse sort of evergreen, decided Mrs Paxton, who'd always excelled at botany, though there were some who swore she couldn't tell parsley from poison ivy.

Trees in heavy, slumberous leaf almost blocking out the sky. Several times the car arched over bridges—there seemed to be a remarkable quantity of rivers in this part of the country, Mrs Paxton observed. She patted at her hair, tucking stray wisps under the hairnet which was her only adornment. She scorned any make-up other than fine floury powder, and had the lowest opinion of women who painted their toe- and fingernails. In her prime, Mrs Paxton hadn't needed to resort to trick and feints. She'd been, in her husband's words, a 'demmed fine gel' and it was generally acknowledged that she'd aged impressively.

The driver showed no signs of spying on her through his rear-view mirror. His eyes were given over to the highway down which the cab was bearing with utmost gravity, if little speed. There was no sign of a meter, and he still hadn't given her any idea of the fare. Well, if it were excessive, she would simply refuse to pay. She'd no luggage in the trunk—she would just step out of the cab and into the hotel and have done with the whole unpleasant business. Mrs Paxton licked lips that seemed to be dissolving, like rice paper, under her tongue. She could do, she decided, she could very well do with that glass of fortified wine which the doctor had prescribed to keep up her appetite.

Abruptly, the car turned a corner and began, if possible, to slow. At first, Mrs Paxton thought the driver had realized he'd taken a wrong turning. Then, as the trees seemed to be thickening on either side of the car—white trunks on the right, black on the left, and everywhere that suffocating foliage—Mrs Paxton's gloved hands went up to her mouth. Shutting her eyes, she recalled with distressing accuracy all those items on the front pages of the papers she disdained to read at the supermarket checkout counter—women raped down lonely country roads, bludgeoned in library stacks, assaulted in elevators. Women of advanced age producing miracle babies—often twins and some-times quintuplets. Had she even checked the cab? Was it from a reliable company? She racked her brains for the name painted on the doors and on the triangular light perched over the car roof, but could only dredge up a handful of letters. S—was it an S? And somewhere an I and D—or was it a V? Whatever it was, the car had come to a complete halt. She was reaching for her shoe—not alas, a very high-heeled shoe—as the car door burst open—

'—the last time I taken one a them goddam intercontinental buses. Jeez, we came in fifty minutes late. *And* the service stinks. But the restrooms—let me tell ya—I swear there was snakes come creepin' outta the toilet. Holy Smokes—excuse my Greek—but a girl could get bit but *good.*'

The person sliding in beside Mrs Paxton had the voice of Betty Boop and the carriage of the late Queen Mary. In fact, she was wearing a mourning veil and a severe black suit which reminded Mrs Paxton of those photographs of the Dowager Queen which had so cowed her in childhood. Yet on a chain round her neck the woman wore the most ridiculous mess of ornaments: a Coptic Cross, a Star of David, a tiny replica of the Koran, Nefertiti's profile and a miniature cornucopia. 'Ivy da Silva', the creature pronounced, offering Mrs Paxton a lace-gloved hand. Mrs Paxton refused the hand but managed a vestigial nod.

Behind her veil, Mrs da Silva seemed to grin. 'I guess you flew in. Me, I got this thing about airplanes. Bill, he went down with that 747 back in—oh, back a helluva long time ago. Almost as bad as the Titanic. Remember the Titanic?'

This time Mrs Paxton didn't bother with civilities. She leaned away from the pungent cloud of her travelling companion's breath—gin? whiskey? Evening in Paris?—and spoke commandingly to the driver. 'This is quite ludicrously far to go. I never agreed to sharing a cab, and I won't be held accountable—'

'Hotel round the next bend, mum. Sign on the left—you see?'

And indeed there was a sign. Under a painting of an old stone house with shuttered windows and a lake lapping at its walls she found the words, 'The Shady Nook'. 'Sure to be damp,' sniffed Mrs Paxton, rather more relieved than she cared to show.

'Ca-rumba, I'll be glad to get outta these clothes and inta a hot tub,' screeched the da Silva woman. Mrs Paxton couldn't help but silently agree, for the reek of gin and patchouli had impregnated the glazed linen of her suit, even the kid of her gloves. She would insist that her room be as many floors away as possible from this interloper's. Doubtlessly they would run into one another in the dining room or on the grounds, but then a nod would suffice—there'd be scarcely any call for them to speak. At her time of life, Mrs Paxton prized her privacy. Hell, she'd heard it said, was other people. She was not inclined to disagree.

As the taxi pulled up in front of the hotel, Mrs Paxton drew to the extreme edge of the back seat, so decisively that the door handle cut into her side. But it didn't stop Ivy da Silva from leaning across and squeezing her companion's arm.

'Whatta ya say, Judy? Just what the doctor ordered, eh? Did ya know there's a lake out back? You betcha—I even brought my bikini.'

To begin with, the bellhop was an albino. Mrs Paxton had nothing against that particular deformity, but she thought it tactless of the management to present their guests with so visible a proof of what they'd come to the hotel to forget—namely, that all in all, life had rather less order and decorum than a rubbish tip. People were known to have been with heads swollen to the size of beachballs, and without a trace of brain; in the course of one's daily business one could, with no warning at all, lose legs or eyes or life, as if legs and eyes and life were of no more account than a handbag or a pair of gloves. Gifted children perished in infancy; drooling idiots survived into the monstrosity of advanced old age, at which point they couldn't be distinguished from those who'd been the brightest and most beautiful of their peers. That was the reason Mrs Paxton had never consented to have children. If it had been possible to pick out one's offspring from a display case or nursery, the way one did with bedding plants, then it might have been a different story. Incalculable, were children, and she'd never been one for gambling.

The bellhop was an albino, and the manager had not been at the desk, nor had his wife, who was presumably attending to some crisis in the kitchen, from what the chambermaid—a flittery, bat-like creature—had been able to tell her. Nevertheless, the room was satisfactory, that had to be admitted at once. The furniture was white, quasi-French provincial, but not in any Sears catalogue way. The vase of lilies on the desk turned out to be acrylic, to Mrs Paxton's relief—she was allergic to pollen in all its forms. Later she would discover that the lacquered wood of bed and chair and desk was in fact a cunning form of plastic, and that even the luxurious wool carpet underfoot was nothing more than a *trompe-pied*. Ingenious things could be done with polyester these days, reflected Mrs Paxton, folding her devastated linen suit into the bag marked *Laundry Services*, and entering the tub.

Judy, she had called her. No one had dared to address her as Judy since grade school; even Gilbert, on their wedding night, had permitted himself no greater liberty than, 'Judith, my dear...'. But how ever did the creature know her? How could a gin soak have been a former schoolfellow of Judith Paxton, née Dreedle? Preposterous. It only showed what good hotels were coming to these days. Mrs Paxton began soaping herself energetically with the loofah she had brought from home. Would Wilson remember to water the geraniums? Should she have trusted her with forwarding the mail? Now that Gilbert was dead and the business closed down, now that she finally had a house of her own, why had she ever agreed to leave it? It was all her doctor's doing—he was responsible for sending her here, he was responsible for everything, and she would write to tell him so.

Climbing out of the tub, Mrs. Paxton wrapped her dressing gown tight as a shroud around her and walked to the window. It was the old-fashioned kind, two panes that opened into the room so as not to disturb the vine burdening the ledge outside. Mrs Paxton leaned over the sill, breathing in great gulps of curiously cool and scented air—jasmine and nicotiana and mint, creasing the stillness. Overhead, in that shockingly blue sky, clouds like stray lambs browsed upon a light so clear it stung her eyes. Mrs Paxton looked quickly down at the water licking the walls of the hotel. No sign, thank heavens, of that dreadful da Silva woman drifting by on an air mattress, martini in hand. No, the only thing to trouble the surface of the lake was a lighted window, rising like some great golden carp from the blackness of the water.

Mrs Paxton took her morning coffee in the library. At least she assumed it was morning—she seemed to have mislaid her watch, though she entertained suspicions *vis à vis* the chambermaid. Certainly, Mrs Paxton had lain down to sleep after her bath, having decided she'd dispense with dinner. And equally certainly, she'd risen from the bed after a most tiresome dream in which she'd been trekking across endless plains composed of either sand or snow. Wakened by the barking of a pack of dogs—another item to be added to the list of her complaints—she'd opened the window onto the same azure sky and hurried to put on her coolest dress, only to find all the lamps lit in the lobby, the dining room curtains drawn. She was about to tug them open when a bearded man at a corner table called out,' You mustn't. It's bad for them. They're imported, you see.' He was pointing to a huge vase of purplish flowers. 'Rubbish,' replied Mrs Paxton, but all the same she left the curtains be and made her way into the library.

It was a splendidly cavernous room, without any windows to let light leak in and scald the bindings. Mrs Paxton was a tireless reader, not of novels but of educational works: histories of civilization, surveys of philosophy, comparative studies of the world's great religions. Greedily, she homed in to one of the towering shelves. Really, they ought to have a stepladder handy. How did they expect people to reach the more interesting volumes, the ones with gold-embossed and dust-embedded spines promising revelations far beyond the facts disgorged by mere encyclopedias? Right now she fancied something weighty, something to settle the butterflies which capered in her stomach and beat blurry wings behind her eyes. She felt distinctly queasy. This was to be expected, of course, this derangement of one's whole being that travelling entailed: different time zones, parasites in the water, disruption of one's personal schedule and physiological clock. A history of the early church would be the very thing. On the topmost shelf were stacked some ecclesiastical-looking volumes—she would just reach up and see....

'Kee-roust, I can't believe this one. All I want is a magazine—you'd think that wouldn't be too hard to get a hold of. They call this a hotel? I'd like to see the manager, I'd just like to see him. You'd think he was Harry Houdini or something. A hotel without a magazine rack—I don't care how old a magazine, anything would do, even a bunch of pictures—'

A startlingly high-heeled, abrasively crimson shoe, pumping from the depths of a wing-chair at right angles to Mrs Paxton. A whiff of some syrupy but not altogether offensive scent. It was to be hoped that Ivy da Silva was talking to herself, that Mrs Paxton in her grey piqué, her sensible shoes, would blend in with the books, but this was not to be. Ivy had heaved herself out of the wing-chair and stomped across to her before Mrs Paxton could grab her coffee and flee the room. Only this wasn't Ivy, or at least it wasn't the woman who had shared her taxi the night before and who'd accosted her with such gross familiarity as 'Judy'. This woman was a good twenty years younger. Her hair was platinum blonde, whirled like cotton candy round her head, and she was wearing the most inappropriate of morning dresses: a red satin, sequin-studded bustière, even more outlandish than the skyscraper heels. Yet the sloppy diction, the petulant intonation could only belong to that aged creature with the lilac hair who had so precipitately clutched Mrs Paxton's arm in the cab and spoken of bikinis.

'Hey, let me help you with that. These got to be good for something besides slipping my discs. You want this one? What about a couple more?'

Mrs Paxton gave the kind of grimace which can often be mistaken for a smile. 'Thank you. I wouldn't dream of troubling you any further.'

'Aw, don't mention it. Listen sister, we've got to stick together—I mean, we're not going to let them sell us a bill of goods, right? And a hotel without a magazine—. Aw, cripes, I'm going to go and find the manager. Right *now*.'

Mrs Paxton blinked as the red satin skin over the alarming breasts and buttocks bounced in the direction of the lobby. Her coffee was by now stone-cold—the cream had formed cataracts inside the cup. There must be a bell somewhere to summon an attendant, though they seemed in singularly short supply here.

Apart from the bellhop and chambermaid she'd seen on her first night, there seemed to be no staff at all. According to the brochure, the manager's wife did all the cooking—she grew her own fruit and vegetables in the gardens that were supposed to be at the back of the hotel, though Mrs Paxton hadn't caught so much as a glimpse of them from any of the windows. 'How irritating,' she thought. Even though she deplored the vulgarity of the da Silva woman, she had to admit that it was an excellent idea to speak to the manager, an idea *she* ought to have acted upon instead of leaving it to that tarty piece of goods. If one didn't make one's presence known, the staff would simply ride rough-shod over one. Mrs Paxton had stayed in innumerable hotels in the course of her seventy-odd years. She had been an equal partner in her husband's import-export business, and they had travelled wherever new markets presented themselves. What would Gilbert have made of this hotel? As if for an answer, Mrs Paxton opened the tome which Ivy da Silva had got down from the shelf and which looked indisputably like a work by one of the Nicaean Fathers.

'*A Treasury of Golden Hours for the Little Ones*, by Mrs Isabella St John Sims.'

This simply would not do. Mrs Paxton went back to the shelves, pulling out volumes at random, but all she could find were more children's books. Not even the classics, just dreary texts preached by writers named Lapwing and Ewer and Stodgson, sermons against dirtying one's pinafore, maiming one's cat, drowning one's brother. She would have to see the manager—no, better, she would ring for a servant and have the manager fetched before her. After all, if she were spending good money in this place for four, possibly six weeks (depending on what her doctor decided) then something would have to be done about the deplorable absence of reading matter. Were there no bookshops? Were there no lending libraries?

But before Mrs Paxton could make her displeasure known, she was overcome by the clanging of what sounded unpleasantly like a churchbell. She rose to her feet, smoothed her collar and strode out of the library into what ought to have been the lobby, but which turned out to be something different altogether.

'C'mon, sit by me, Jude. I'm an old hand at this. I'll show you what to do.'

Ivy addressed her from behind a long plank which reminded Mrs Paxton of the desks in country schoolrooms, in which four children sat to a row and memorized multiplication tables. This time she had not doubt it was Ivy speaking, though her head was shaved, all save a zigzag of stiff orange strips across her scalp. She was wearing a black leather jacket big enough for three, and a pair of satin trousers into which a child of ten could have barely squeezed. She had no shoes on and her toenails, painted vermilion, were pierced through with little feathered rings.

'C'mon, or you'll miss the beginning—that's the most important part. He's such an asshole,' continued Ivy. 'He reminds me of Frankie, but then Frankie—'

'I presume you found the manager? interrupted Mrs Paxton, who'd decided, not long after first youth, that reminiscence was a sign of weakness. Forget everything and you will have no regrets, that was her credo. 'The manager,' she repeated, in a carrying voice. For answer, Ivy held up a finger to her lips, then tore a few sheets of paper off a writing pad embossed with the name of the hotel. 'Jude, Jude—you mean you didn't even bring a pen?' Ivy's voice was surprisingly low and gentle. She didn't wait for Mrs Paxton's reply, but broke her own pencil in half, dug a pocket knife out of the black leather jacket and whittled the stub to a serviceable point. 'Here,' she whispered. 'Now just keep your eyes peeled, and do like me—it's the only way.'

'Only way to what?' demanded Mrs Paxton, but Ivy's eyes were fixed on the exact centre of the rotunda, to which a man with a top hat and black silk cape was striding. In one white-gloved hand he held a long carved baton. He was no albino—his face was a deep smouldering blue, like the flowers on the dining room table. 'That's the manager,' Ivy ventured, chewing on a bit of fingernail. Not someone, thought Mrs Paxton, to whom one would voice trifling complaints about the dishonesty of chambermaids or the dearth of anything but children's books in the recesses of the library.

The manager lifted his hands wearily, as though oppressed by the weight of rings he wore on every finger—gold and rubies, sapphires and silver, diamonds, emeralds, platinum. Lights exploded from the jewels, reminding Mrs Paxton of those little comets which no longer burned out over her eyes—perhaps there *was* something salubrious in the air of this country, perhaps her doctor had been right after all. Though it was the most curious hotel—how, for example, could so large and unusually shaped a room fit into the confines of the Shady Nook? Why hadn't she remarked on the existence of a rotunda when she'd got out of the cab the night before? But then, she'd been exhausted, distressed. Sometimes the mind would simply not accept the evidence of the senses. Even now.... This room reminded her of a Roman basilica; indeed, the domed ceiling was paved entirely with golden tiles, except for the centre at which an enormous, unlidded blue eye stared down at them all. Where the pupil should have been painted there seemed to be nothing but a hole. No, that would be impossible. How would one keep out the rain and the snow? Though, it was, perhaps, a very little hole....

'Ladies and Gentlemen. We are ready to begin.'

At first Mrs Paxton thought they'd all been summoned to a gigantic bingo game. Indignantly, she started to her feet when suddenly she felt Ivy's hand upon her arm. It was the transparency of Ivy's hand, the waxy thinness of her face which arrested Mrs Paxton, so that she fell back into her seat, grasping the pencil Ivy had given her. She wished that it were a candy, even a stick of chewing gum. She would have offered it to Ivy, who looked as though she hadn't eaten anything for the longest time, at least not since her arrival at The Shady Nook. Mrs Paxton could understand her reluctance, of course. Breakfast had been appalling. Nothing but that muesli business, burnt toast and something which may or may not have been scrambled eggs. She had contented herself with a spoonful of jelly—it was sour, mostly seeds, and a dismal shade of red.

'Try to remember,' Ivy whispered, as the manager pulled a gigantic stopwatch out of his pocket. Slowly, deliberately, he scanned the circular rows of benches. People were hunched over papers, pencils raised expectantly in a silence Mrs Paxton could only liken to the yellow roaring in one's ears before one is about to faint.

'Ready, Steady—Go!'

Suddenly the geometrical frieze along the rim of the dome pulsed and cracked. Jagged bits streamed up inside where they became circles or sticks, remarkably, as Mrs Paxton observed, like the letters of an alphabet. They were, in fact, an alphabet in a strangely familiar foreign tongue, swarming higgledy-piggledly over the golden tiles. But no sooner did the letters combine into something that looked like a word, an ordinary pronounceable word, than they would break apart and recombine into some quite other arrangement. 'If only one could pin them down,' wailed Mrs Paxton, but Ivy wasn't listening. Like everyone else she was scribbling fractions of indecipherable words over her sheets of paper, one word across another and another on top of that, till the page looked like a verbal whirlwind.

Mrs Paxton sat helplessly before her blank sheet, staring at the manager, who stood, stopwatch in hand, tapping the floor with his baton. She'd accustomed herself to the irregularity of his complexion—most likely a birth defect, a variation on a port wine stain. She tried to catch his attention, but he looked right through her as though she were merely another member of that scribbling mob. And so, Mrs Paxton fixed her eyes on the dome, which looked like nothing so much as a gigantic pool of honey, heaving with flies. All these people madly writing, writing—. Why on earth had they come here on holiday, only to go back to school? What was the point in trying to fit the letters into some readable combination—what sort of message could they possible convey. And to whom?

'What on earth—' began Mrs Paxton, but before anyone could answer her a buzzer sounded. People dropped their pencils in panic, or else gripped them so tightly she thought the knuckle bones would pop straight through the skin. Ivy had let her pencil roll to the floor—she closed her black-lidded eyes and slumped in her seat, as if she had fainted. 'Ivy,' Mrs Paxton shouted, groping with her hand in the direction of her neighbour. 'Ivy, this is no time—'

'What? I can't hear you, speak louder.' Ivy had jumped out of her seat, quite wide-awake—even a little insolent. 'Oh, it's no use, you'll only get us into trouble. Look, I'm going for a swim—why don't you join me?'

'I can't, you know that's quite out of the question.' Mrs Paxton had a fearful headache after the session in the rotunda. She muttered something about going to lie down in her room. Would Ivy be so good as to stop in after her swim? She had something rather important to ask her.

Ivy took Mrs Paxton's arm and guided her to the elevator, an affair of swirling metal bars within a spiral shaft. Mrs. Paxton was loath to step inside, but Ivy insisted, pushing her in and locking the gate. Mrs. Paxton stretched out her arms through the bars, calling Ivy's name.

'Don't do that—it's dangerous. You should know better than that by now,' Ivy scolded. She pushed the button at the side of the shaft. Mrs. Paxton clung to the bars as the cage ascended. Except—she had the strangest feeling that instead of going up, the elevator was taking her slantwise down, around and around like a corkscrew into a stoppered bottle.

Her room was stuffy—of course the chambermaid had forgotten to air it out while making up the bed. Mrs Paxton went directly to the window and fiddled with the latch. But it would not give. The wood must have swelled somehow—the window would not open. Maddening. She so wanted to put her head outside and find Ivy rippling through the moat like some comic-strip Ophelia. For if she were to fill her eyes with Ivy, she wouldn't have to think of Gilbert, and it was necessary not to think of Gilbert because she thought—she couldn't be sure, everything was so confusing here—she thought she'd caught a glimpse of Gilbert in the crowd pushing its way out of the rotunda. She couldn't be sure—she hadn't seen anything so direct and deliberate as a face. It had been nothing more than the particular configuration of a bald patch, a certain hunch of the shoulders—the way his shoulders always hunched when she'd sent him away from her, when she'd refused him things for which he had no call to ask.

But no matter how closely she pressed her face to the glass, all she could see was a blue blaze overhead, an impenetrable gloom of leaves below, and in the moat encircling her the multiplied reflections of a lighted window, an endless row of drowning lamps.

If only she could decide whether it were sand or snow through which she were trudging, Mrs Paxton could have settled on an appropriate image of rescue. An oasis, or a log cabin with a friendly plume of smoke beckoning from the chimney. But she simply could not tell. It was most extraordinary, but for the first time in her life she could not seem to distinguish between what should have been black and white, chalk and cheese. Why was everything blurred and shifting, here? Why in this hotel was nothing straight or sharply edged—why was the décor all arabesques and circles? Even the glass in the windows bulged out and in, even the stems of the artificial lilies spiralled in the crescents of their vases.

Would Wilson remember to water the geraniums. Why had she trusted Wilson? And how had she consented to this holiday, this forcible removal from the one place that was at last her own, after all those years in hotel suites and furnished rooms and houses taken only for the summer. Of course she had agreed to go on the urging of her doctor, an obstreperous, an obtuse man for all the diplomas and certificates on his office walls. Making her undress for the examination, as if that were necessary at her age. Strip to the skin, though draughts came pouring through the windows, a polar wind whirling her veins. And yet how hot had been the lights over the examining table, probing her limbs and heart and the gorge of her womb.... A most impertinent man. She would write a letter of complaint to the College of Physicians and Surgeons. She would do that straight away, instead of wasting her time in that awful rotunda place with all the others.

Where was Ivy? She'd promised she would come to her. She would ask Ivy to explain what was going on—Ivy would know. Yet they'd been at the hotel for exactly the same amount of time—why should Ivy have got so far ahead of her, making herself so free? Dressing up, going for swims, stomping off to see that most distressing-looking Manager. Where *was* Ivy? Mrs Paxton sat up in her bed, waited for a few moments more, then pulled on her dressing gown. She hadn't any idea what time it could be. Since she had dreamed, she must have slept, but there was no way of knowing for how long. She should have reported the loss—the theft—of her watch that very morning. But had there been anyone to whom to report? Stealthily, Mrs. Paxton unbolted the door and ventured out along the corridor. Everywhere lights were burning—not lights, but torches, smouldering in the dark.

'Too much, this is simply too, too much,' rasped Mrs Paxton. 'Why, I might be burnt to a crisp in my bed. Torches indeed. I'll pack my things tonight. I won't even wait for Ivy, I'll call a cab right now and drive to the airport and taken the first flight home.'

When Mrs Paxton returned to her room a breeze, half mist, half wind, was teasing the curtains. There on the window sill, swinging her legs, sat Ivy in a cloud of a dress, her hair floating white and filmy all about her. She looked no older than a child; indeed, she was holding something in her arms that looked like a doll. Except that it wasn't a doll—it was a baby and the baby was sucking at Ivy's small, pale breasts. 'Oh Judith,' she called, 'Judith, where have you been? I've waited as long as I could.'

'Nonsense,' declared Mrs Paxton, shutting the door behind her, refusing to be flustered by this apparition in the window. Apparition indeed, for all round the cloudy hair and dress, even round the milk spurting from Ivy's breasts, hung a golden mist that made Mrs Paxton think of pollen, of the mosaic tiles on the rotunda dome, the unbearable heat of the lamps on the doctor's examining table. Mists and contagion. She didn't like this, she didn't like it one little bit.

'Ivy!' commanded Mrs Paxton. 'Explain yourself! What exactly is going on here?'

'Exactly? Ivy echoed. 'Why, I don't know—exactly.' She smiled, unlatching the baby from her breasts. 'Oh Judith—just let go. You'll see. Everything will run on wheels.'

'Run?' repeated Mrs Paxton, folding her arms and digging her heels into the carpet. 'Run where? My dear girl, do you realize I've been in this wretched hotel for—heaven knows how long— and I've never once been let outside? So how can you talk about wheels? Tell me, do—where will they run?'

Ivy smiled, dangling the baby in her arms. 'Where? Why backwards, of course.'

Mrs Paxton took a long measured step towards the window.

'Ivy, Ivy, this is most unfair of you. I ask a simple question and you—'

'Backwards and over and away you go. Child's play, you see?'

Mrs Paxton retreated a pace and stared. Ivy's voice sounded amazingly pure, as high and lilting as a child's. Indeed it seemed as if it were no longer Ivy speaking, but the baby itself.

'Ivy!' Mrs Paxton called again, but the name came out as no more than a whisper. 'You have to tell me what to do. Ivy? Wherever are you going?'

Inside the line of golden fog the girl appeared to be trembling and fading, like an image on a distant screen. Heaven knew where the words came from, but Mrs Paxton heard them quite distinctly.

'You forgot the driver, so I paid for both of us. Remember, Judith—just let go. *Addio*.'

Mrs Paxton still hasn't been able to decide what happened next. One moment a woman transparent as gauze was sitting on a window sill holding an increasingly distinct and vigorous baby. The next moment both had vanished, exactly as if they'd done a backwards somersault. But there hadn't even been a splash from the water below. Mrs Paxton had run to the window and leaned out as far as she dared. All she could see was a fine white ring that stung her eyes, exactly like a paper cut. And then it vanished into the water.

Mrs Paxton hung down her head into the cool, tangled scents of mint, jasmine and nicotiana. The sun beat upon her hair till she felt her whole head must be on fire. And she kept on calling out, impetuous, imploring,

'Sand or snow, Ivy? Tell me, sand or snow?'

NORMAN LEVINE

Something Happened Here

I felt at home soon as I got out of the Paris train and waited for a taxi outside the railway station. I could hear the gulls but I couldn't see them because of the mist. But I could smell the sea. The driver brought me to a hotel along the front. It was a residential hotel beside other residential hotels with the menu in a glass case by the sidewalk. It had four storeys. Its front tall windows, with wooden shutters and small iron balconies, faced the sea. On the ground level was the hotel's dining-room. The front wall was all glass. And there was a man sitting alone by a table.

It looked a comfortable family hotel. The large wooden staircase belonged to an earlier time when it had been a family house. The woman who now owned and ran it liked porcelain. She had cups and saucers on large sideboards, on every landing, as well as grandfather clocks and old clocks without hands. They struck the hour at different times. There were fresh and not so fresh flowers in porcelain vases. There were large mirrors, in wooden frames, tilted against the wall, like paintings. There were china plates, china cups, and china teapots on top of anything that could hold them.

My room on the third floor didn't face the sea but a courtyard. I watched a short man in a chef's hat cutting vegetables into a pot. The room was spacious enough but it seemed over-furnished. It had a large double-bed with a carving of two birds on the headboard. A tall wooden closet, a heavy wooden sideboard, a solid table, several chairs, a colour television, and a small fridge fully stocked with wine, brandy, champagne, mineral water, and fruit juices. On the fridge was a pad and pencil to mark what one drank.

After I partly unpacked and washed I went down to the dining-room and was shown to a table by the glass wall next to the man sitting alone. He was smoking a cigarette and drinking coffee. He had on a fawn shirt with an open collar and a carefully tied black-and-white cravat at the neck. He also had fawn-coloured trousers. He looked like Erich von Stroheim.

The proprietress came to take my order. She wobbled, coquettishly, on high heels. Medium height, a little plump, in her late forties or early fifties perhaps. She had a sense of style. She wore a different tailored dress every day I was there. A striking person. She had a white complexion and black hair. And looked in fine health. Her teeth were very good. There was a liveliness in her dark eyes. Every time I walked by the desk and the lounge she never seemed far away: doing accounts, dealing with the staff, talking to guests.

I gave her my order in English. I ordered a salad, an omelette, and a glass of *vin rosé*.

When she had gone the man at the next table said in a loud voice.

'Are you English or American?'

'Canadian.'

He began to talk in French.

Although I understood some of what he said I replied. 'I can't speak French well. I'm *English* Canadian.'

'I speak English,' he said. 'I had lessons in Paris at the Berlitz school. My English teacher, she was a pretty woman, said I was very good because I could use the word barbed-wire in a sentence. My name is Georges.'

I told him mine. But for some reason he called me Roman.

'Roman, what do you do?'

'I am a writer.'

'Come, join me,' he said. 'I like very much the work of Somerset Muffin and Heavelin Woof. Are you staying in the hotel?'

'Yes. I arrived a half-hour ago.'

'I live in the country. Since my wife is dead I come here once a week to eat. What do you write?'

'Short stories,' I said, 'novels.'

'I read many books—but not novels. I read books of ideas. The conclusion I have come to is that you can divide the people of the world. There are the sedentary. There are the nomads. The sedentary—they are registered. We know about them. The nomads—they leave no record.'

A young waiter, in a white double-breasted jacket, poured more coffee.

'Do you know Dieppe?'

'No, this is my first time here.'

'I will show you.'

And he did. When I finished eating he took me along the promenade. A brisk breeze was blowing but the sea remained hidden by mist. He brought me to narrow sidestreets, main streets, and squares. He walked with a sense of urgency. A short, stocky man, very compact and dapper, with lively brown eyes and a determined-looking head. He had a bit of a belly and his trousers were hitched high-up. He carried his valuables in a brown shoulder-bag.

In a street for pedestrians only we were caught up in a crowd. It was market day. There were shops on both sides and stalls in the middle.

'Look, Roman, at the *wonderful* colours,' Georges said loudly of the gladioli, the asters, lilies, roses, geraniums. Then he admired the peaches, apricots, butter, tomatoes, carrots, the heaped strands of garlic and onions. He led me to a stand that had assorted cheeses and large brown eggs, melons, leeks, and plums. And to another that had different sausages and salamis. On one side he showed me live brown-and-white rabbits in hutches. And laughed when, directly opposite, brown-and-white rabbit skins were for sale. The street fascinated him. He stopped often and talked loudly to anyone whose face happened to interest him.

We had a Pernod at a table outside a café that had a mustard and orange façade. He lit a French cigarette. I a Canadian cigarillo. The pleasure of the first puffs made us both silent. Nearly all the tables were occupied, shoppers were passing, and music came loudly from a record store.

I asked Georges, 'What do you think of Madame who runs the hotel?'

'*Très intelligente*,' he said and moved his hands slowly to indicate a large bosom. '*Et distinguée.*' He moved his hands to his backside to indicate large buttocks. And smiled.

He had a way of talking English which was a lot better, and more amusing, than my French.

He brought me inside an old church. He was relaxed until he faced the altar. He stiffened to attention, slid his left leg forward as if he was a fencer, and solemnly made the sign of the cross. He remained in that position for several seconds looking like the figurehead at the prow of a ship. When he moved away he relaxed again. And pointed to a small statue of the Virgin with her arms open.

'Roman, the Virgin has opened her legs in welcome.'

I was feeling tired when we came out of the church. The train journey, the sightseeing, the conversation . . . but Georges walked on. He was heading for the docks. I said I would go back to the hotel as I had some letters to write.

'Of course,' he said, 'forgive me. You must be exhausted. Tomorrow, would you like to see where I live in the country? I will come for you after breakfast.'

And he was there, as I came out of the hotel, at 8:30, sitting in a light blue Citroën, dressed in the same clothes.

'Did you sleep Roman?'

'For eight hours.'

I could not see the sun because of the mist. But the surf, breaking on the pebbles, glistened. As he drove inland it began to brighten up. He drove fast and well. And he talked continually. Perhaps because he needed someone he could talk English to.

He said he had been an officer in the French navy. That in the last war he had been a naval architect in charge of submarines at their trials.

'I was at Brest, Cherbourg, Toulon, Marseille. My daughter was born when I was stuck in submarine in the mud. My wife told me the nurse came to say, "The baby she is lovely. But the father—it is dead."' And he laughed.

'On a low hill, ahead, a large institution-like building with many windows and fire-escapes.

'Lunatic asylum,' Georges said, 'full of patriots.'

The government, he said, had a publicity campaign for the French to drink more of their wine and appealed to their patriotism. After this, whenever he mentioned anyone who liked to drink, Georges called him 'a patriot'. And if anyone looked more than that. '*Very* patriotic'.

The asylum was beside us. A cross on top. And all the top windows barred.

'When I was a boy . . . this place made big impression. Before a storm . . . the wind is blowing . . . and the people in lunatic asylum scream. I will never forget.'

He drove through empty villages, small towns. He stopped, walked me around, and did some shopping. I noticed that the elaborate war memorials, by the churches, were for the 1914-1918 war. The only acknowledgement of the Second World War was the occasional stone, suddenly appearing in the countryside, at the side of the road, that said three or four members of the Resistance had been shot at this spot.

'I have been to America,' Georges said. 'I like the Americans. But sometimes they are infantile. Nixon—dustbin. Carter—dustbin.'

He drove up a turning road by a small, broken stone bridge that had rocks and uprooted trees on either side. 'There is a plateau,' he said, 'high up. It has many meadows. The water gathers there for many rivers. Once in a hundred years the water very quickly goes down from the plateau to the valley and turns over houses, bridges, trees. Last September a priest on the plateau telephone the Mayor and say the water looks dangerous. But the Mayor, a young man, say it is only an old man talking. Half-hour later the water come down and drown thirty people and took away many houses. It was Sunday so many people were away from the houses otherwise more drown. All happen last September. In a half-hour. But it will not happen for another hundred years. And no one will be here who knows it. The young won't listen. They will, after some years, build houses in the same place. And it will happen all over again.'

In one of the large towns he stopped and showed me the cemetery where his family is buried. It was a vault, all stone, no grass around. Nor did any of the others have grass anywhere. On the stone was a vertical tablet with two rows of de Rostaings. The first was born in 1799. 'He was town architect.' A few names down. 'He had lace factory.... He build roads.... See how the names become larger as we come nearer today.'

'Will you be buried here?'

'No. My wife is Parisian. She is buried in Paris. I will lie with her.'

He continued on the main road, then turned off and drove on a dirt road. Then went slowly up a rough slope until he stopped, on the level, by the side of a converted farmhouse.

'We are here,' he said.

We were on a height. Below were trees and small fields—different shades of green, yellow, and brown. Instead of fences or hedgerows, the fields had their borders in trees. And from this height the trees gave the landscape a 3-D look.

Georges introduced me to Marie-Jo, a fifteen-year-old school-girl from the next farm who did the cooking and cleaning during the summer. Short blonde hair, blue eyes, an easy smile. She was shy and tall for her age and walked with a slightly rounded back. While Marie-Jo barbecued salmon steaks at the far end of the porch, under an overhanging chimney, Georges walked me around. In front of the house, under a large elm, was a white table and white chairs. It was very quiet. A light wind on the small leaves of the two near poplars. 'They say it will rain,' he said. And beside them a border of roses, geraniums, and lobelia.

We ate outside on a white tablecloth. I could hear people talking from the farm below. Further away someone was burning wood. The white smoke rose and thinned as it drifted slowly up. On top of the house was a small stone cross. A larger metal cross was imbedded in the concrete of the front fence.

'I am Catholic,' Georges said. 'There are Protestants here too. My sister married a Jew. A Pole. From Bialystok.'

Marie-Jo brought a round wooden board with cows' and goats' cheeses on it. And Georges filled my glass with more red wine.

'When I was a young boy of seven we had great distilleries in my country. We hear the Russians are coming. We wait in the street. It is beginning to snow. But I do not want to go home. Many people wait for the Russians.

'Then they come. They look giants with fur hats and big boots and long overcoats. *Very* impressive.

'After a while—what happens? First the women. They say to Russian soldiers—you want drink? They give them drink. A little later, in the street, you see the women wearing the Russian furs for—'

Georges indicated with his hands.

'Muffs,' I said.

'Yes, muffs, muffs. The women all have muffs.

'Then the French men give drink. Later, the French men you see in the street—they are wearing the Russian boots.

'The peasants—they *drowned* the Russians.'

Marie-Jo brought ripe peaches, large peaches, lovely colours, dark and light, red to crimson. They were juicy and delicious.

'How did your sister meet her husband?'

'At the Sorbonne. My sister always joking. He serious. I did not think they would stay together. When she go to Poland to meet his family we are worried. We Catholic. They Jew. They have two children. Then the war. The Nazis. He is taken away. My mother, a tough woman, get priest and doctor to make fake certificate—say the two boys baptized. But my mother did not think that was enough. She tell me to take the boys to a farmer she know in the Auvergne. I take them. When I meet the farmer I begin to tell story. But the farmer just shake my hand. Say nothing. The children stay with him for the war.'

'What happened to the Polish Jew?'

'He died.'

We went to have coffee in the barn. The main room of the house. High ceiling with large windows and the original beams. To get to it from the inside you would go up some stairs. But you could walk to it from the garden by going up a grass slope. 'All farmers have this for the cattle to go up and down,' Georges said.

It was also his studio. On the walls were oil paintings by his uncle who was dead. Impressionist paintings of the landscape around here. 'They sell for 40,000 francs,' Georges said. 'I have about thirty good ones. Some in the flat in Paris, some in the flat in Cannes. A few here.' He also had his own paintings—on the wall, and one on an easel—like his uncle's but not as good.

Marie-Jo appeared with a jug full of coffee.

'I am working on book,' he said. 'I have contract with Paris publisher. Eleven years—I am not finished. It will be traveller's dictionary of every place in world that someone has written.'

We had coffee. He lit a cigarette and went over to his record player.

'Roman—have you heard the Japanese Noh?'

I answered 'No' with a movement of my face.

'Very strange. Sounds like a cat . . . and a chain with bucket . . . and a man flogging his wife. I was twenty, a midshipman on cruiser. We visit Japan. Suddenly I was put there, for six hours, listening to this.'

He put a record on. 'This is the cat . . .' a single note vibrated . . . 'looking for another cat . . .' Georges was standing, talking with gestures. 'Now, the long chain with a bucket going down well . . . it needs oil.... This is a man flogging his wife....'

He stopped the record.

'The Japanese they are different from the French. They believe the dead are with us all the time.'

He showed me a photograph of his wife, Colette.

She looked a determined woman, in her late forties. A strong jaw, thin lips, blonde hair pulled back on her head, light eyes.

'She had beautiful voice,' Georges said. 'One of the things I like in people is the voice. If they have bad voice it is difficult for me to stay long with them.'

'How long is it since she died?'

'Three years.'

He must have thought of something else for he said abruptly, 'If you do not come into the world—then you cannot go.'

He took me for a walk through the countryside. There were all kinds of wild flowers I didn't know and butterflies and some, like the small black and white, I had not seen before either. But it was the trees that dominated. And I like trees. Probably because I have lived so long in Cornwall facing stone streets and stone terraces.

I wondered why Georges was not curious about my past. He appeared not interested in my personal life. Though I did give him bits of information.

'How long will you be in Dieppe?'

'Two, maybe three days more,' I said. 'I want to go to England, to a flat I have in Cornwall, and do some work.'

It was after nine, but still light, when we got back to Dieppe. 'I know a small place but good,' Georges said. And brought me to a restaurant opposite the docks called *L'Espérance*.

We were both tired and for a while didn't talk. I ordered marinated mackerel, a salad, and some chicken. And Georges ordered a half-melon, veal, and cheese. Also coffee and a bottle of red wine.

Two tables away a man and a woman, both plump, in their late fifties or early sixties, were eating with relish. The woman had a large whole tongue on her plate to start with, the man a tureen of soup. He tucked his napkin into his open-neck shirt. Then they both had fish, then meat with potatoes, then cheese, then a large dessert with whipped cream on top.... And all the time they were eating they didn't speak.

Beside them, going away towards the centre of the restaurant, were two young men. They were deaf and dumb. They were talking with their hands. They also mimed. When they saw us looking they included us in their conversation. One of the men looked Moroccan, with a black moustache on the top lip and down the side of his face. He was lean. And he mimed very quickly and well. He pointed at Georges's cigarette and at my cigarillo. And shook his head. He touched his chest and pretended he was coughing. And shook his head. He then showed himself swimming, the breast stroke. He was smiling. He showed us that he was also a long distance walker, getting up and staying in one place, he moved heel and toe, heel and toe, and that curious rotation of the hips.

'Roman,' Georges said loudly. 'The woman you see is fat. Her husband is fat. Look how they eat. Beside them two men, slim, young. They have to talk with their hands. They look happy—all the time the food comes—they are talking. But the two beside them—they do not talk at all—they concentrate on next bite. If I had movie camera—that is all you need. No words. No explanation. If I was young man, Roman, I would make films.'

As he drove me to the hotel, Georges could not forget the scene in the restaurant. On the hotel's front door there was a sign saying it was full.

'Tomorrow,' Georges said, 'I no see you.'

As tomorrow was Sunday I asked him if he was going to church.

'No, I do not like the clergy. The elm tree need spray. They get disease. I know a young man. He will do it. But I have to get him. And I go to see an old friend. He was officer with me. He now alone in Rouen. We eat lunch on Sunday when I am here.

Two old men. I see you the day after.'

And we shook hands.

Next morning I opened the large window of the room. The sun was out. It was warm. A blue sky. After breakfast I decided to go for a walk. I crossed the harbour by an iron bridge. And went up a steep narrow street of close-packed terraced houses. It looked working-class. The houses were small, drab, unpainted. And the sidewalks were narrow and in need of repair. They had red and pink geranium petals that had fallen from the window boxes on the small balconies.

I passed an upright concrete church with a rounded top. It stood by itself, stark, against the skyline. I went through tall undergrowth and, when clear of it, I saw I was on top of cliffs. They were an impressive sight: white-grey, sheer, and at the bottom pebbles with the sea coming in.

I walked along for about an hour, on top of the cliffs, when I noticed the path becoming wider as it started to slope down. The cliffs here went back from the sea and left a small pebbled beach. People were on it.

I was looking at the dirt path, as I walked down, because it was uneven and steep when I saw a shrew, about two inches long, over another shrew lying on its side. The one on its side was flattened as if a roller had gone over it. I watched the head of the live shrew over the belly of the dead one—there didn't seem to be any movement. Then, for no reason, I whistled. The live shrew darted in to the grass. And I saw the open half-eaten belly of the one on its side, a brilliant crimson. The colour was brighter than any meat I had seen at the butcher's.

The small beach wasn't crowded. The surf gentle . . . the water sparkled . . . a family was playing boules. Someone was wind-surfing across the length of the beach . . . going one way then turning the sail to go the other, and often falling in. A man in a T-shirt brought a dog, a terrier, on a leash. Then he let him go into the shallows. Under an umbrella a young woman was breast-feeding a baby. Nearer to the water a tall woman with white skin and red hair was lying on her back, topless. People were changing, using large coloured towels . . . with the continual sound of the low surf as it came in, breaking over the pebbles and sliding back.

I had brought a picnic: bread, a hard-boiled egg, cheese, tomatoes, a pear. And a can of cider to wash it down. After I had eaten I took off my shirt, shoes, socks, and lay down on the stones.

A loud noise woke me. It was two boys running over the stones between my head and the cliffs. I sat up. I didn't know how long I had been asleep. The surface of the water sparkled. The click of the boules was still going. From somewhere a dog was barking. The cliffs, a few yards behind me and on both sides, had light green streaks in the massive white grey. And high up, on the very top, a thin layer of grass.

The tide was coming in. I put on shirt, socks, and shoes, and walked over the pebbles to a paved slope that led from the beach to the road. I could now see a narrow opening between the cliffs. And as I walked up the slope the opening fanned out to show a suburb of houses with gardens, green lawns, and trees. As I came to the top of the paved slope I saw, across the road, on a stone, in French and English:

> *On this beach*
> *Officers and Men of the*
> *Royal Regiment of Canada*
> *Died at Dawn 19 August 1942*
> *Striving to Reach the Heights Beyond*
>
> *You who are alive on this beach*
> *remember that these men died far from home*
> *that others here and everywhere might freely*
> *enjoy life in God's mercy.*

When I got back to the hotel the 'full' sign had been taken down. Madame greeted me with a smile.

'You have caught the sun. I have surprise for you.'

She soon reappeared with a thin blonde girl of about twelve or thirteen.

'This is Jean. She is from Canada,' Madame said proudly. 'From Alberta.'

'Where from in Alberta?' I asked.

'Edmonton,' the girl replied in a quiet voice.

'How long will you be in Dieppe?'

'I live here. I go to school.'

'When were you in Edmonton?'

'Three weeks ago.'

'Is your father there?'

'No, he is somewhere else. He travels. I'm with my mother.'

'Can you speak French as well as you can English?'

'I can speak it better,' she said.

And she was glad to go off with Madame's only daughter, who was older and not as pretty, to roller skate on the promenade.

'She is charming,' Madame said as we watched both girls run to get out.

'I went for a walk today, Madame,' I said, 'and came to the beach where in the war the Canadians—'

'*Ah.*' She interrupted and shook her head, then raised an arm, in distress or disbelief. She tried to find words—but couldn't.

'I have read many books about it,' she said quickly. 'Do you want to see the cemetery?'

'No,' I said.

That evening, while in the dining-room, I decided to leave tomorrow. For over three weeks I had been travelling in France. All inland, until Dieppe. It had been a fine holiday. I had not been to France before. But now I wanted to get back to the familiar. I was also impatient to get back to work. I had brought with me a large notebook but I had written nothing in it.

I said to Madame at the desk. 'I will be leaving tomorrow. Could you have my bill ready?'

'Of course,' she said, 'you will have it when you come down for breakfast.'

'It is a very comfortable hotel. Are you open all year?'

'In December we close.'

'Has it been a good season?'

'I think I go bankrupt,' she said loudly. 'Oil—up three times in two months. It is impossible to go on—' She held up a sheaf of bills.

'I will tell my friends,' I said.

'Is kind of you,' she said quietly. And gave me several brochures that said the hotel would be running a weekly cookery course in January and February of next year.

Late next morning, with my two cases in the lounge, I was having a coffee and smoking a cigarillo, when Georges appeared. He saw the cases.

'Yes,' I said. 'I'm going today.'

'What time is your boat?'

'It goes in an hour.'

'I will take you.'

He insisted on carrying the cases to his car. Madame came hurrying away from people at the desk to shake my hand vigorously and hoped she would see me again.

While Georges was driving he gave me a card with his address in the country, in Cannes, and in Paris. And the dates he would be there. Then he gave me a large brown envelope. I took out what was in it—a small watercolour of Dieppe that he had painted. It showed the mustard-and-orange café, with people sitting at the outside tables and others walking by. On the back he had written: 'For Roman, my new friend, Georges.'

'When I get to England,' I said, 'I will send you one of my books.'

'Thank you. I should like to improve my English. Perhaps I find in it something for my traveller's dictionary.'

At the ferry I persuaded Georges not to wait.

'Roman, I do not kiss the men.'
We shook hands.

I sat in a seat on deck, at the stern, facing Dieppe. They ferry turned slowly and I saw Dieppe turn as well. The vertical church with the rounded top, the cathedral, the square, the houses with the tall windows, and wooden shutters, and small iron balconies.

Then the ferry straightened out and we were in the open sea. After a while it altered course. And there were the cliffs where I had walked yesterday and the narrow opening. I kept watching the cliffs and the opening. And thought how scared they must have been coming in from the sea and seeing this.

The sun was warm, the sea calm. And when I next looked at the cliffs the opening had disappeared. All that was there was the white-grey stone sticking up. I thought of gravestones . . . close together on a slope.... You could see nothing else. Just gravestones. And they were gravestones with nothing on them. They were all blank.

On the loudspeaker the captain's voice said that coming up on the left was one of the world's largest tankers. People hurried to the rails with their cameras.

I went down to a lower deck and stood in the queue for the duty-free.

DANIEL DAVID MOSES

King of the Raft

There was a raft in the river that year, put there, anchored with an anvil, just below a bend, by the one of the fathers who worked away in Buffalo, who could spend only every other weekend, if that, at home. The one of the mothers whose husband worked the land and came in from the fields for every meal muttered as she set the table that that raft was the only way the father who worked in the city was able to pretend he cared about his sons. Her husband, also one of the fathers, who had once when young gone across the border to work and then, unhappy there, returned, could not answer, soaking the dust of soil from his hands.

Most of the sons used the raft that was there just that one summer in the usually slow-moving water during the long evenings after supper, after the days of the fieldwork of haying and then combining were done. A few of them, the ones whose fathers and mothers practised Christianity, also used it in the afternoons on sunny Sundays after the sitting through church and family luncheons. And the one of the sons who had only a father who came and went following the work—that son appeared whenever his rare duties or lonely freedom became too much for him.

The sons would come to the raft in Indian file along a footpath the half-mile from the road and change their overalls or jeans for swimsuits among the goldenrod and milkweed on the bank, quickly, to preserve modesty and their blood from the mosquitoes, the only females around. Then one of the sons would run down the clay slope and stumble in with splashing and a cry of shock or joy for the water's current temperature. The other sons would follow, and, by the time they all climbed out onto the raft out in the stream, through laughter would become boys again.

The boys used that raft in the murky green water to catch the sun or their breaths on or to dive from where they tried to touch the mud bottom. One of the younger ones also used to stand looking across the current to the other side, trying to see through that field of corn there, the last bit of land that belonged to the reserve. Beyond it the highway ran, a border patrolled by a few cars flashing chrome in the sun or headlights through the evening blue like messages from the city. Every one of the boys used the raft several times that summer to get across the river and back, the accomplishment proof of their new masculinity. And once the younger one, who spent time looking at that other land, crossed and climbed up the bank there and explored the shadows between the rows of corn, the leaves like dry tongues along his naked arms as he came to the field's far edge where the asphalt of that highway stood empty.

Toward the cool end of the evenings, any boy left out on the raft in the lapping black water would be too far from shore to hear the conversations. They went on against a background noise of the fire the boys always built against the river's mist and mosquito lust, that they sometimes built for roasting corn, hot dogs, marshmallows. The conversations went on along with or over games of chess. Years later, one of the older boys, watching his own son play the game with a friend in silence, wondered if perhaps that was why their conversations that year of the raft about cars, guitars, and girls—especially each other's sisters— about school and beer, always ended up in stalemate or check. Most of the boys ended up winning only their own solitariness from the conversations by the river. But the one who had only a father never even learned the rules of play.

One sunny Sunday after church, late in the summer, the one who had only a father already sat on the raft in the river as the rest of the boys undressed. He smiled at the boy who had gone across through the corn, who made it into the water first. Then he stood up and the raft made waves as gentle as those in his blue-black hair—I'm the king of the raft, he yelled, challenging the boy who had seen the highway to win that wet, wooden square. And a battle was joined, and the day was wet and fair, until the king of the raft, to show his strength to the rest of the boys still on shore, took a hank of the highway boy's straight hair in hand and held the highway boy underwater till the highway boy saw blue fire and almost drowned. The story went around among the mothers and the fathers, and soon that son who had only a father found himself unwelcome. Other stories came around, rumour about his getting into fights or failing grades or how his father's latest girlfriend had dyed her Indian hair blonde. And the boy who almost had drowned found he both feared the king of the raft and missed the waves in his blue-black hair.

One muggy evening when pale thunderheads growled in from the west, the boy who had almost drowned, who had the farthest to go to get home, left the raft and the rest by the river early. On the dark road he met the king, who had something to say. They hid together with a case of beer in a cool culvert under the road. The king of the raft was going away with his father to live in Buffalo in the United States and thought the boy who had almost drowned could use what was left of this beer the king's father would never miss. The boy who had almost drowned sipped from his bottle of sour beer and heard the rain beginning to hiss at the end of the culvert. He crawled and looked out in time to see the blue fire of lightning hit a tree. In the flash he was again the waves in the king's blue-black hair, the grin that offered another beer. The boy who had almost drowned felt he was going down again, and, muttering some excuse, ran out into the rain. The king yelled after him that old insult boys use about your mother wanting you home.

The boy who had almost drowned found he could cross through the rain, anchored by his old running shoes to the ground, though the water came down like another river, cold and clear and wide as the horizon. He made it home and stood on the porch, waiting for the other side of the storm, hearing hail hitting the roof and water through the eaves filling up the cistern. Later, out of the storm, he could still hear far-off a gurgling in the gully and a quiet roar as the distant river tore between its banks. The storm still growled somewhere beyond the eastern horizon.

The raft was gone the next evening when the boys came to the bank, and the current was still too cold and quick to swim in. No one crossed the river for the rest of the summer. The king of the raft never appeared again anywhere. In the fall, a rumour came around about his going to work in the city and in the winter another one claimed he had died. The boy who had crossed through the rain thought about going down even quicker in winter river water. Then a newspaper confirmed the death. In a traffic accident, the rain boy read. None of the boys had even met that impaired driver, that one of the fathers, surviving and charged without a licence. One of the mothers muttered as she set another mother's hair about people not able to care even about their kids. The rain boy let the king of the raft sink into the river, washing him away in his mind and decided he would someday cross over and follow the highway through that land and find the city.

ALICE MUNRO

Meneseteung

I

Columbine, bloodroot,
And wild bergamot,
Gathering armfuls,
Giddily we go.

Offerings the book is called. Gold lettering on a dull-blue cover.
The author's full name underneath: Almeda Joynt Roth. The
local paper, the *Vidette*, referred to her as 'our poetess'. There
seems to be a mixture of respect and contempt, both for her
calling and for her sex—or for their predictable conjuncture. In
the front of the book is a photograph, with the photographer's
name in one corner, and the date: 1865. The book was published
later, in 1873.

The poetess has a long face; a rather long nose; full, sombre
dark eyes, which seem ready to roll down her cheeks like giant
tears; a lot of dark hair gathered around her face in droopy rolls
and curtains. A streak of grey hair plain to see, although she is,
in this picture, only twenty-five. Not a pretty girl but the sort
of woman who may age well, who probably won't get fat. She
wears a tucked and braid-trimmed dark dress or jacket, with a
lacy, floppy arrangement of white material—frills or a bow—
filling the deep V at the neck. She also wears a hat, which might
be made of velvet, in a dark colour to match the dress. It's the
untrimmed, shapeless hat, something like a soft beret, that
makes me see artistic intentions, or at least a shy and stubborn

eccentricity, in this young woman, whose long neck and forward-inclining head indicate as well that she is tall and slender and somewhat awkward. From the waist up, she looks like a young nobleman of another century. But perhaps it was the fashion.

'In 1854,' she writes in the preface to her book, 'my father brought us—my mother, my sister Catherine, my brother William, and me—to the wilds of Canada West (as it then was). My father was a harness-maker by trade, but a cultivated man who could quote by heart from the Bible, Shakespeare, and the writings of Edmund Burke. He prospered in this newly opened land and was able to set up a harness and leather-goods store, and after a year to build the comfortable house in which I live (alone) today. I was fourteen years old, the eldest of the children, when we came into this country from Kingston, a town whose handsome streets I have not seen again but often remember. My sister was eleven and my brother nine. The third summer that we lived here, my brother and sister were taken ill of a prevalent fever and died within a few days of each other. My dear mother did not regain her spirits after this blow to our family. Her health declined, and after another three years she died. I then became housekeeper to my father and was happy to make his home for twelve years, until he died suddenly one morning at his shop.

'From my earliest years I have delighted in verse and I have occupied myself—and sometimes allayed my griefs, which have been no more, I know, than any sojourner on earth must encounter—with many floundering efforts at its composition. My fingers, indeed, were always so clumsy for crochetwork, and those dazzling productions of embroidery which one sees often today—the overflowing fruit and flower baskets, the little Dutch boys, the bonneted maidens with their watering cans—have likewise proved to be beyond my skill. So I offer instead, as the product of my leisure hours, these rude posies, these ballads, couplets, reflections.'

Titles of some of the poems: 'Children at Their Games', 'The

Gypsy Fair', 'A Visit to My Family', 'Angels in the Snow', 'Champlain at the Mouth of the Meneseteung', 'The Passing of the Old Forest', and 'A Garden Medley'. There are other, shorter poems, about birds and wildflowers and snowstorms. There is some comically intentioned doggerel about what people are thinking about as they listen to the sermon in church.

'Children at Their Games': The writer, a child, is playing with her brother and sister—one of those games in which children on different sides try to entice and catch each other. She plays on in the deepening twilight, until she realizes that she is alone, and much older. Still she hears the (ghostly) voices of her brother and sister calling. *Come over, come over, let Meda come over.* (Perhaps Almeda was called Meda in the family, or perhaps she shortened her name to fit the poem.)

'The Gypsy Fair': The Gypsies have an encampment near the town, a 'fair', where they sell cloth and trinkets, and the writer as a child is afraid that she may be stolen by them, taken away from her family. Instead, her family has been taken away from her, stolen by Gypsies she can't locate or bargain with.

'A Visit to My Family': A visit to the cemetery, a one-sided conversation.

'Angels in the Snow': The writer once taught her brother and sister to make 'angels' by lying down in the snow and moving their arms to create wing shapes. Her brother always jumped up carelessly, leaving an angel with a crippled wing. Will this be made perfect in Heaven, or will he be flying with his own makeshift, in circles?

'Champlain at the Mouth of the Meneseteung': This poem celebrates the popular, untrue belief that the explorer sailed down the eastern shore of Lake Huron and landed at the mouth of the major river.

'The Passing of the Old Forest': A list of all the trees—their names, appearances, and uses—that were cut down in the original forest, with a general description of the bears, wolves, eagles, deer, waterfowl.

'A Garden Medley': Perhaps planned as a companion to the forest poem. Catalogue of plants brought from European countries, with bits of history and legend attached, and final Canadianness resulting from this mixture.

The poems are written in quatrains or couplets. There are a couple of attempts at sonnets, but mostly the rhyme scheme is simple—*a b a b* or *a b c b*. The rhyme used is what was once called 'masculine' ('shore'/'before'), though once in a while it is 'feminine' ('quiver'/'river'). Are those terms familiar anymore? No poem is unrhymed.

II

> *White roses cold as snow*
> *Bloom where those 'angels' lie.*
> *Do they but rest below*
> *Or, in God's wonder, fly?*

In 1879, Almeda Roth was still living in the house at the corner of Pearl and Dufferin Streets, the house her father had built for his family. The house is there today; the manager of the liquor store lives in it. It's covered with aluminum siding; a closed-in porch has replaced the veranda. The woodshed, the fence, the gates, the privy, the barn—all these are gone. A photograph taken in the eighteen-eighties shows them all in place. The house and fence look a little shabby, in need of paint, but perhaps that is just because of the bleached-out look of the brownish photograph. The lace-curtained windows look like white eyes. No big shade tree is in sight, and, in fact, the tall elms that overshadowed the town until the nineteen-fifties, as well as the maples that shade it now, are skinny young trees with rough fences around them to protect them from the cows. Without the shelter of those trees, there is a great exposure—back yards, clotheslines, woodpiles, patchy sheds and barns and privies—all bare, exposed, provisional-looking. Few houses have anything like a lawn, just a patch of plantains and anthills and raked dirt.

Perhaps petunias growing on top of a stump, in a round box. Only the main street is gravelled; the other streets are dirt roads, muddy or dusty according to season. Yards must be fenced to keep animals out. Cows are tethered in vacant lots or pastured in back yards, but sometimes they get loose. Pigs get loose, too, and dogs roam free or nap in a lordly way on the boardwalks. The town has taken root, it's not going to vanish, yet it still has some of the look of an encampment. And, like an encampment, it's busy all the time—full of people, who, within the town, usually walk wherever they're going; full of animals, which leave horse buns, cow pats, dog turds that ladies have to hitch up their skirts for; full of the noise of building and of drivers shouting at their horses and of the trains that come in several times a day.

I read about that life in the *Vidette*.

The population is younger than it is now, than it will ever be again. People past fifty usually don't come to a raw, new place. There are quite a few people in the cemetery already, but most of them died young, in accidents or childbirth or epidemics. It's youth that's in evidence in town. Children—boys—rove through the streets in gangs. School is compulsory for only four months a year, and there are lots of occasional jobs that even a child of eight or nine can do—pulling flax, holding horses, delivering groceries, sweeping the boardwalk in front of stores. A good deal of time they spend looking for adventures. One day they follow an old woman, a drunk nicknamed Queen Aggie. They get her into a wheelbarrow and trundle her all over town, then dump her into a ditch to sober her up. They also spend a lot of time around the railway station. They jump on shunting cars and dart between them and dare each other to take chances, which once in a while result in their getting maimed or killed. And they keep an eye out for any strangers coming into town. They follow them, offer to carry their bags, and direct them (for a five-cent piece) to a hotel. Strangers who don't look so prosperous are taunted and tormented. Speculation surrounds all of them—it's like a cloud of flies. Are they coming to town to start up a new business, to persuade people to invest in some scheme, to sell cures or gimmicks, to preach on the street corners? All these things are possible any day of the week. Be on your guard, the *Vidette* tells people. These are times of opportunity and danger. Tramps, confidence men, hucksters, shysters, plain thieves are travelling the roads, and particularly the railroads. Thefts are announced: money invested and never seen again, a pair of trousers taken from the clothesline, wood from the woodpile, eggs from the henhouse. Such incidents increase in the hot weather.

Hot weather brings accidents, too. More horses run wild then, upsetting buggies. Hands caught in the wringer while doing the washing, a man lopped in town at the sawmill, a leaping boy killed in a fall of lumber at the lumberyard. Nobody sleeps well. Babies wither with summer complaint, and fat people can't catch their breath. Bodies must be buried in a hurry. One day a man goes through the streets ringing a cowbell and calling, 'Repent! Repent!' It's not a stranger this time, it's a young man who works at the butcher shop. Take him home, wrap him in cold wet cloths, give him some nerve medicine, keep him in bed, pray for his wits. If he doesn't recover, he must go to the asylum.

Almeda Roth's house faces on Dufferin Street, which is a street of considerable respectability. On this street, merchants, a mill owner, an operator of salt wells have their houses. But Pearl Street, which her back windows overlook and her back gate opens onto, is another story. Workmen's houses are adjacent to hers. Small but decent row houses—that is all right. Things deteriorate toward the end of the block, and the next, last one becomes dismal. Nobody but the poorest people, the unrespectable and undeserving poor, would live there at the edge of a boghole (drained since then), called the Pearl Street Swamp. Bushy and luxuriant weeds grow there, makeshift shacks have been put up, there are piles of refuse and debris and crowds of runty children, slops are flung from doorways. The town tries to compel these people to build privies, but they would just as soon go in the bushes. If a gang of boys goes down there in search of adventure, it's likely they'll get more than they bargained for. It is said that even the town constable won't go down Pearl Street on a Saturday night. Almeda Roth has never walked past the row housing. In one of those houses lives the young girl Annie, who helps her with her housecleaning. That young girl, herself, being a decent girl, has never walked down to the last block or the swamp. No decent woman ever would.

But that same swamp, lying to the east of Almeda Roth's house, presents a fine sight at dawn. Almeda sleeps at the back of the house. She keeps to the same bedroom she once shared with her sister Catherine—she would not think of moving to the large front bedroom, where her mother used to lie in bed all day, and which was later the solitary domain of her father. From her window she can see the sun rising, the swamp mist filling with light, the bulky, nearest trees floating against that mist, and the trees behind turning transparent. Swamp oaks, soft maples, tamarack, butternut.

III

Here where the river meets the
*   inland sea,*
Spreading her blue skirts from the
*   solemn wood,*
I think of birds and beasts and
*   vanished men,*
Whose pointed dwellings on these
*   pale sands stood.*

One of the strangers who arrived at the railway station a few years ago was Jarvis Poulter, who now occupies the next house to Almeda Roth's—separated from hers by a vacant lot, which he has bought, on Dufferin Street. The house is plainer than the Roth house and has no fruit trees or flowers planted around it. It is understood that this is a natural result of Jarvis Poulter's being a widower and living alone. A man may keep his house decent, but he will never—if he is a proper man—do much to decorate it. Marriage forces him to live with more ornament as well as sentiment, and it protects him, also, from the extremities of his own nature—from a frigid parsimony or a luxuriant sloth, from squalor, and from excessive sleeping or reading, drinking, smoking, or freethinking.

In the interests of economy, it is believed, a certain estimable gentleman of our town persists in fetching water from the public tap and supplementing his fuel supply by picking up the loose coal along the railway track. Does he think to repay the town or the railway company with a supply of free salt?

This is the *Vidette*, full of shy jokes, innuendo, plain accusation that no newspaper would get away with today. It's Jarvis Poulter they're talking about—though in other passages he is spoken of with great respect, as a civil magistrate, an employer, a churchman. He is close, that's all. An eccentric, to a degree. All of which may be a result of his single condition, his widower's life. Even carrying his water from the town tap and filling his coal pail along the railway track. This is a decent citizen, prosperous: a tall—slightly paunchy?—man in a dark suit with polished boots. A beard? Black hair streaked with grey. A severe and self-possessed air, and a large pale wart among the bushy hairs of one eyebrow? People talk about a young, pretty, beloved wife, dead in childbirth or some horrible accident, like a house fire or a railway disaster. There is no ground for this, but it adds interest. All he has told them is that his wife is dead.

He came to this part of the country looking for oil. The first oil well in the world was sunk in Lambton County, south of here, in the eighteen-fifties. Drilling for oil, Jarvis Poulter discovered salt. He set to work to make the most of that. When he walks home from church with Almeda Roth, he tells her about his salt wells. They are twelve hundred feet deep. Heated water is pumped down into them, and that dissolves the salt. Then the brine is pumped to the surface. It is poured into great evaporator pans over slow, steady fires, so that the water is steamed off and the pure, excellent salt remains. A commodity for which the demand will never fail.

'The salt of the earth,' Almeda says.

'Yes,' he says, frowning. He may think this disrespectful. She did not intend it so. He speaks of competitors in other towns who are following his lead and trying to hog the market. Fortunately, their wells are not drilled so deep, or this evaporating is not done so efficiently. There is salt everywhere under this land, but it is not so easy to come by as some people think.

Does this not mean, Almeda says, that there was once a great sea?

Very likely, Jarvis Poulter says. Very likely. He goes on to tell her about other enterprises of his—a brickyard, a limekiln. And he explains to her how this operates, and where the good clay is found. He also owns two farms, whose woodlots supply the fuel for his operations.

Among the couples strolling home from church on a recent, sunny Sabbath morning we noted a certain salty gentleman and literary lady, not perhaps in their first youth but by no means blighted by the frosts of age. May we surmise?

This kind of thing pops up in the *Vidette* all the time.

May they surmise, and is this courting? Almeda Roth has a bit of money, which her father left her, and she has her house. She is not too old to have a couple of children. She is a good enough housekeeper, with the tendency toward fancy iced cakes and decorated tarts that is seen fairly often in old maids. (Honourable mention at the Fall Fair.) There is nothing wrong with her looks, and naturally she is in better shape than most married women of her age, not having been loaded down with work and children. But why was she passed over in her earlier, more marriageable years, in a place that needs women to be partnered and fruitful? She was a rather gloomy girl—that may have been the trouble. The deaths of her brother and sister, and then of her mother, who lost her reason, in fact, a year before she died, and lay in her bed talking nonsense—those weighed on her, so she was not lively company. And all that reading and poetry—it seemed more of a drawback, a barrier, an obsession, in the young girl than in the middle-aged woman, who needed something, after all, to fill her time. Anyway, it's five years since her book was published, so perhaps she has got over that. Perhaps it was the proud, bookish father encouraging her?

Everyone takes it for granted that Almeda Roth is thinking of Jarvis Poulter as a husband and would say yes if he asked her. And she is thinking of him. She doesn't want to get her hopes up too much, she doesn't want to make a fool of herself. She would like a signal. If he attended church on Sunday evenings, there would be a chance, during some months of the year, to walk home after dark. He would carry a lantern. (There is as yet no street lighting in town.) He would swing the lantern to light the way in front of the lady's feet and observe their narrow and delicate shape. He might catch her arm as they step off the boardwalk. But he does not go to church at night.

Nor does he call for her, and walk with her *to* church on Sunday mornings. That would be a declaration. He walks her home, past his gate as far as hers; he lifts his hat then and leaves her. She does not invite him to come in—a woman living alone could never do such a thing. As soon as a man and woman of almost any age are alone together within four walls, it is assumed that anything may happen. Spontaneous combustion, instant fornication, an attack of passion. Brute instinct, triumph of the senses. What possibilities men and women must see in each other to infer such dangers. Or, believing in the dangers, how often they must think about the possibilities.

When they walk side by side, she can smell his shaving soap, the barber's oil, his pipe tobacco, the wool and linen and leather smell of his manly clothes. The correct, orderly, heavy clothes are like those she used to brush and starch and iron for her father. She misses that job—her father's appreciation, his dark, kind authority. Jarvis Poulter's garments, his smell, his movements all cause the skin on the side of her body next to him to tingle hopefully, and a meek shiver raises the hairs on her arms. Is this to be taken as a sign of love? She thinks of him coming into her—*their*—bedroom in his long underwear and his hat. She knows this outfit is ridiculous, but in her mind he does not look so; he has the solemn effrontery of a figure in a dream. He comes into the room and lies down on the bed beside her, preparing to take her in his arms. Surely he removes his hat? She doesn't know, for at this point a fit of welcome and submission overtakes her, a buried gasp. He would be her husband.

One thing she has noticed about married women, and that is how many of them have to go about creating their husbands. They have to start ascribing preferences, opinions, dictatorial ways. Oh, yes, they say, my husband is very particular. He won't touch turnips. He won't eat fried meat. (Or he will only eat fried meat.) He likes me to wear blue (brown) all the time. He can't stand organ music. He hates to see a woman go out bareheaded. He would kill me if I took one puff of tobacco. This way, bewildered, sidelong-looking men are made over, made into husbands, heads of households. Almeda Roth cannot imagine herself doing that. She wants a man who doesn't have to be made, who is firm already and determined and mysterious to her. She does not look for companionship. Men—except for her father— seem to her deprived in some way, incurious. No doubt that is necessary, so that they will do what they have to do. Would she herself, knowing that there was salt in the earth, discover how to get it out and sell it? Not likely. She would be thinking about the ancient sea. That kind of speculation is what Jarvis Poulter has, quite properly, no time for.

Instead of calling for her and walking her to church, Jarvis Poulter might make another, more venturesome declaration. He could hire a horse and take her for a drive out to the country. If he did this, she would be both glad and sorry. Glad to be beside him, driven by him, receiving this attention from him in front of the world. And sorry to have the countryside removed for her—filmed over, in a way, by his talk and preoccupations. The countryside that she has written about in her poems actually takes diligence and determination to see. Some things must be disregarded. Manure piles, of course, and boggy fields full of high, charred stumps, and great heaps of brush waiting for a good day for burning. The meandering creeks have been straightened, turned into ditches with high, muddy banks. Some of the crop fields and pasture fields are fenced with big, clumsy uprooted stumps; others are held in a crude stitchery of rail fences. The trees have all been cleared back to the woodlots. And the woodlots are all second growth. No trees along the roads or lanes or around the farmhouses, except a few that are newly planted, young and weedy-looking. Clusters of log barns—the grand barns that are to dominate the countryside for the next hundred years are just beginning to be built—and mean-looking log houses, and every four or five miles a ragged little settlement with a church and school and store and a blacksmith shop. A raw countryside just wrenched from the forest, but swarming with people. Every hundred acres is a farm, every farm has a family, most families have ten or twelve children. (This is the country that will send out wave after wave of settlers—it's already starting to send them—to northern Ontario and the West.) It's true that you can gather wildflowers in spring in the woodlots, but you'd have to walk through herds of horned cows to get to them.

IV

The Gypsies have departed,
Their camping-ground is bare.
Oh, boldly would I bargain now
At the Gypsy Fair.

Almeda suffers a good deal from sleeplessness, and the doctor has given her bromides and nerve medicine. She takes the bromides, but the drops gave her dreams that were too vivid and disturbing, so she has put the bottle by for an emergency. She told the doctor her eyeballs felt dry, like hot glass, and her joints ached. Don't read so much, he said, don't study; get yourself good and tired out with housework, take exercise. He believes that her troubles would clear up if she got married. He believes this in spite of the fact that most of his nerve medicine is prescribed for married women.

So Almeda cleans house and helps clean the church, she lends a hand to friends who are wallpapering or getting ready for a wedding, she bakes one of her famous cakes for the Sunday-school picnic. On a hot Saturday in August, she decides to make some grape jelly. Little jars of grape jelly will make fine Christmas presents, or offerings to the sick. But she started late in the day and the jelly is not made by nightfall. In fact, the hot pulp has just been dumped into the cheesecloth bag to strain out the juice. Almeda drinks some tea and eats a slice of cake with butter (a childish indulgence of hers), and that's all she wants for supper. She washes her hair at the sink and sponges off her body to be clean for Sunday. She doesn't light a lamp. She lies down on the bed with the window wide open and a sheet just up to her waist, and she does feel wonderfully tired. She can even feel a little breeze.

When she wakes up, the night seems fiery hot and full of threats. She lies sweating on her bed, and she has the impression that the noises she hears are knives and saws and axes—all angry implements chopping and jabbing and boring within her head. But it isn't true. As she comes further awake, she recognizes the sounds that she has heard sometimes before—the fracas of a summer Saturday night on Pearl Street. Usually the noise centres on a fight. People are drunk, there is a lot of protest and encouragement concerning the fight, somebody will scream, 'Murder!' Once, there was a murder. But it didn't happen in a fight. An old man was stabbed to death in his shack, perhaps for a few dollars he kept in the mattress.

She gets out of bed and goes to the window. The night sky is clear, with no moon and with bright stars. Pegasus hangs straight ahead, over the swamp. Her father taught her that constellation—automatically, she counts its stars. Now she can make out distinct voices, individual contributions to the row. Some people, like herself, have evidently been wakened from sleep. 'Shut up!' they are yelling. 'Shut up that caterwauling or I'm going to come down and tan the arse off yez!'

But nobody shuts up. It's as if there were a ball of fire rolling up Pearl Street, shooting off sparks—only the fire is noise; it's yells and laughter and shrieks and curses, and the sparks are voices that shoot off alone. Two voices gradually distinguish themselves—a rising and falling howling cry and a steady, throbbing, low-pitched stream of abuse that contains all those words which Almeda associates with danger and depravity and foul smells and disgusting sights. Someone—the person crying out, 'Kill me! Kill me now!'—is being beaten. A woman is being beaten. She keeps crying, 'Kill me! Kill me!' and sometimes her mouth seems choked with blood. Yet there is something taunting and triumphant about her cry. There is something theatrical about it. And the people around are calling out, 'Stop it! Stop that!' or 'Kill her! Kill her!' in a frenzy, as if at the theatre or a sporting match or a prizefight. Yes, thinks Almeda, she has noticed that before—it is always partly a charade with these people; there is a clumsy sort of parody, an exaggeration, a missed connection. As if anything they did—even a murder—might be something they didn't quite believe but were powerless to stop.

Now there is the sound of something thrown—a chair, a plank?—and of a woodpile or part of a fence giving way. A lot of newly surprised cries, the sound of running, people getting out of the way, and the commotion has come much closer. Almeda can see a figure in a light dress, bent over and running. That will be the woman. She has got hold of something like a stick of wood or a shingle, and she turns and flings it at the darker figure running after her.

'Ah, go get her!' the voices cry. 'Go baste her one!'

Many fall back now; just the two figures come on and grapple, and break loose again, and finally fall down against Almeda's fence. The sound they make becomes very confused—gagging, vomiting, grunting, pounding. Then a long, vibrating, choking sound of pain and self-abasement, self-abandonment, which could come from either or both of them.

Almeda has backed away from the window and sat down on the bed. Is that the sound of murder she has heard? What is to be done, what is she to do? She must light a lantern, she must go downstairs and light a lantern—she must go out into the yard, she must go downstairs. Into the yard. The lantern. She falls over on her bed and pulls the pillow to her face. In a minute. The stairs, the lantern. She sees herself already down there, in the back hall, drawing the bolt of the back door. She falls asleep.

She wakes, startled, in the early light. She thinks there is a big crow sitting on her windowsill, talking in a disapproving but unsurprised way about the events of the night before. 'Wake up and move the wheelbarrow!' it says to her, scolding, and she understands that it means something else by 'wheelbarrow'— something foul and sorrowful. Then she is awake and sees that there is no such bird. She gets up at once and looks out the window.

Down against her fence there is a pale lump pressed—a body. *Wheelbarrow.*

She puts a wrapper over her nightdress and goes downstairs. The front rooms are still shadowy, the blinds down in the kitchen. Something goes *plop, plup*, in a leisurely, censorious way, reminding her of the conversation of the crow. It's just the grape juice, straining overnight. She pulls the bolt and goes out the back door. Spiders have draped their webs over the doorway in the night, and the hollyhocks are drooping, heavy with dew. By the fence, she parts the sticky hollyhocks and looks down and she can see.

A woman's body heaped up there, turned on her side with her face squashed down into the earth. Almeda can't see her face. But there is a bare breast let loose, brown nipple pulled long like a cow's teat, and a bare haunch and leg, the haunch showing a bruise as big as a sunflower. The unbruised skin is greyish, like a plucked, raw drumstick. Some kind of nightgown or all-purpose dress she has on. Smelling of vomit. Urine, drink, vomit.

Barefoot, in her nightgown and flimsy wrapper, Almeda runs away. She runs around the side of her house between the apple trees and the veranda; she opens the front gate and flees down Dufferin Street to Jarvis Poulter's house, which is the nearest to hers. She slaps the flat of her hand many times against the door.

'There is the body of a woman,' she says when Jarvis Poulter appears at last. He is in his dark trousers, held up with braces, and his shirt is half unbuttoned, his face unshaven, his hair standing up on his head. 'Mr Poulter, excuse me. A body of a woman. At my back gate.'

He looks at her fiercely. 'Is she dead?'

His breath is dank, his face creased, his eyes bloodshot.

'Yes. I think murdered,' says Almeda. She can see a little of his cheerless front hall. His hat on a chair. 'In the night I woke up. I heard a racket down on Pearl Street,' she says, struggling to keep her voice low and sensible. 'I could hear this—pair. I could hear a man and a woman fighting.'

He picks up his hat and puts it on his head. He closes and locks the front door, and puts the key in his pocket. They walk along the boardwalk and she sees that she is in her bare feet. She holds back what she feels a need to say next—that she is responsible, she could have run out with a lantern, she could have screamed (but who needed more screams?), she could have beat the man off. She could have run for help then, not now.

They turn down Pearl Street, instead of entering the Roth yard. Of course the body is still there. Hunched up, half bare, the same as before.

Jarvis Poulter doesn't hurry or halt. He walks straight over to the body and looks down at it, nudges the leg with the toe of his boot, just as you'd nudge a dog or a sow.

'You,' he says, not too loudly but firmly, and nudges again.

Almeda tastes bile at the back of her throat.

'Alive,' says Jarvis Poulter, and the woman confirms this. She stirs, she grunts weakly.

Almeda says, 'I will get the doctor.' If she had touched the woman, if she had forced herself to touch her, she would not have made such a mistake.

'Wait,' says Jarvis Poulter. 'Wait. Let's see if she can get up.'

'Get up, now,' he says to the woman. 'Come on. Up, now. Up.'

Now a startling thing happens. The body heaves itself onto all fours, the head is lifted—the hair all matted with blood and vomit—and the woman begins to bang this head, hard and rhythmically, against Almeda Roth's picket fence. As she bangs her head, she finds her voice and lets out an openmouthed yowl, full of strength and what sounds like an anguished pleasure.

'Far from dead,' says Jarvis Poulter. 'And I wouldn't bother the doctor.'

'There's blood,' says Almeda as the woman turns her smeared face.

'From her nose,' he says. 'Not fresh.' He bends down and catches the horrid hair close to the scalp to stop the head-banging.

'You stop that, now,' he says. 'Stop it. Gwan home, now. Gwan home, where you belong.' The sound coming out of the woman's mouth has stopped. He shakes her head slightly, warning her, before he lets go of her hair. 'Gwan home!'

Released, the woman lunges forward, pulls herself to her feet. She can walk. She weaves and stumbles down the street, making intermittent, cautious noises of protest. Jarvis Poulter watches her for a moment to make sure that she's on her way. Then he finds a large burdock leaf, on which he wipes his hand. He says, 'There goes your dead body!'

The back gate being locked, they walk around to the front. The front gate stands open. Almeda still feels sick. Her abdomen is bloated; she is hot and dizzy.

'The front door is locked,' she says faintly. 'I came out by the kitchen.' If only he would leave her, she could go straight to the privy. But he follows. He follows her as far as the back door and into the back hall. He speaks to her in a tone of harsh joviality that she has never before heard from him. 'No need for alarm,' he says. 'It's only the consequences of drink. A lady oughtn't to be living alone so close to a bad neighbourhood.' He takes hold of her arm just above the elbow. She can't open her mouth to speak to him, to say thank you. If she opened her mouth, she would retch.

What Jarvis Poulter feels for Almeda Roth at this moment is just what he has not felt during all those circumspect walks and all his own solitary calculations of her probable worth, undoubted respectability, adequate comeliness. He has not been able to imagine her as a wife. Now that is possible. He is sufficiently stirred by her loosened hair—prematurely grey but thick and soft—her flushed face, her light clothing, which nobody but a husband should see. And by her indiscretion, her agitation, her foolishness, her need?

'I will call on you later,' he says to her. 'I will walk with you to church.'

At the corner of Pearl and Dufferin Streets last Sunday morning there was discovered, by a lady resident there, the body of a certain woman of Pearl Street, thought to be dead but only, as it turned out, dead drunk. She was roused from her heavenly—or otherwise—stupor by the firm persuasion of Mr Poulter, a neighbour and a Civil Magistrate, who had been summoned by the lady resident. Incidents of this sort, unseemly, troublesome, and disgraceful to our town, have of late become all too common.

V

I sit at the bottom of sleep,
As on the floor of the sea.
And fanciful Citizens of the Deep
Are graciously greeting me.

As soon as Jarvis Poulter has gone and she has heard her front gate close, Almeda rushes to the privy. Her relief is not complete, however, and she realizes that the pain and fullness in her lower body come from an accumulation of menstrual blood that has not yet started to flow. She closes and locks the back door. Then, remembering Jarvis Poulter's words about church, she writes on a piece of paper, 'I am not well, and wish to rest today.' She sticks this firmly into the outside frame of the little window in the front door. She locks that door, too. She is trembling, as if from a great shock or danger. But she builds a fire, so that she can make tea. She boils water, measures the tea leaves, makes a large pot of tea, whose steam and smell sicken her further. She pours out a cup while the tea is still quite weak and adds to it several dark drops of nerve medicine. She sits to drink it without raising the kitchen blind. There, in the middle of the floor, is the cheesecloth bag hanging on its broom handle between the two chairbacks. The grape pulp and juice has stained the swollen cloth a dark purple. *Plop, plup*, into the basin beneath. She can't sit and look at such a thing. She takes her cup, the teapot, and the bottle of medicine into the dining room.

She is still sitting there when the horses start to go by on the way to church, stirring up clouds of dust. The roads will be getting hot as ashes. She is there when the gate is opened and a man's confident steps sound on her veranda. Her hearing is so sharp she seems to hear the paper taken out of the frame and unfolded—she can almost hear him reading it, hear the words in his mind. Then the footsteps go the other way, down the steps. The gate closes. An image comes to her of tombstones—it makes her laugh. Tombstones are marching down the street on their little booted feet, their long bodies inclined forward, their expressions preoccupied and severe. The church bells are ringing.

Then the clock in the hall strikes twelve and an hour has passed.

The house is getting hot. She drinks more tea and adds more medicine. She knows that the medicine is affecting her. It is responsible for her extraordinary languor, her perfect immobility, her unresisting surrender to her surroundings. That is all right. It seems necessary.

Her surroundings—some of her surroundings—in the dining room are these: walls covered with dark-green garlanded wallpaper, lace curtains and mulberry velvet curtains on the windows, a table with a crocheted cloth and a bowl of wax fruit, a pinkish-grey carpet with nosegays of blue and pink roses, a sideboard spread with embroidered runners and holding various patterned plates and jugs and the silver tea things. A lot of things to watch. For every one of these patterns, decorations seems charged with life, ready to move and flow and alter. Or possibly to explode. Almeda Roth's occupation throughout the day is to keep an eye on them. Not to prevent their alteration so much as to catch them at it—to understand it, to be a part of it. So much is going on in this room that there is no need to leave it. There is not even the thought of leaving it.

Of course, Almeda in her observations cannot escape words. She may think she can, but she can't. Soon this glowing and swelling begins to suggest words—not specific words but a flow of words somewhere, just about ready to make themselves known to her. Poems, even. Yes, again, poems. Or one poem. Isn't that the idea—one very great poem that will contain everything and, oh, that will make all the other poems, the poems she has written, inconsequential, mere trial and error, mere rags? Stars and flowers and birds and trees and angels in the snow and dead children at twilight—that is not the half of it. You have to get in the obscene racket on Pearl Street and the polished toe of Jarvis Poulter's boot and the plucked-chicken haunch with its blue-black flower. Almeda is a long way now from human sympathies or fears or cosy household considerations. She doesn't think about what could be done for that woman or about keeping Jarvis Poulter's dinner warm and hanging his long underwear on the line. The basin of grape juice has overflowed and is running over her kitchen floor, staining the boards of the floor, and the stain will never come out.

She has to think of so many things at once—Champlain and the naked Indians and the salt deep in the earth, but as well as the salt the money, the money-making intent brewing forever in heads like Jarvis Poulter's. Also the brutal storms of winter and the clumsy and benighted deeds on Pearl Street. The changes of climate are often violent, and if you think about it there is no peace even in the stars. All this can be borne only if it is channelled into a poem, and the word 'channelled' is appropriate, because the name of the poem will be—it *is*—'The Meneseteung'. The name of the poem is the name of the river. No, in fact it is the river, the Meneseteung, that is the poem—with its deep holes and rapids and blissful pools under the summer trees and its grinding blocks of ice thrown up at the end of winter and its desolating spring floods. Almeda looks deep, deep into the river of her mind and into the tablecloth, and she sees the crocheted roses floating. They look bunchy and foolish, her mother's crocheted roses—they don't look much like real flowers. But their effort, their floating independence, their pleasure in their silly selves do seem to her so admirable. A hopeful sign. *Meneseteung*.

She doesn't leave the room until dusk, when she goes out to the privy again and discovers that she is bleeding, her flow has started. She will have to get a towel, strap it on, bandage herself up. Never before, in health, has she passed a whole day in her nightdress. She doesn't feel any particular anxiety about this. On her way through the kitchen, she walks through the pool of grape juice. She knows that she will have to mop it up, but not yet, and she walks upstairs leaving purple footprints and smelling her escaping blood and the sweat of her body that has sat all day in the closed hot room.

No need for alarm.

For she hasn't thought that crocheted roses could float away or that tombstones could hurry down the street. She doesn't mistake that for reality, and neither does she mistake anything else for reality, and that is how she knows that she is sane.

VI

I dream of you by night,
I visit you by day.
Father, Mother,
Sister, Brother,
Have you no word to say?

April 22, 1903. At her residence, on Tuesday last, between three and four o'clock in the afternoon, there passed away a lady of talent and refinement whose pen, in days gone by, enriched our local literature with a volume of sensitive, eloquent verse. It is a sad misfortune that in later years the mind of this fine person had become somewhat clouded and her behaviour, in consequence, somewhat rash and unusual. Her attention to decorum and to the care and adornment of her person had suffered, to the degree that she had become, in the eyes of those unmindful of her former pride and daintiness, a familiar eccentric, or even, sadly, a figure of fun. But now all such lapses pass from memory and what is recalled is her excellent published verse, her labours in former days in the Sunday school, her dutiful care of her parents, her noble womanly nature, charitable concerns, and unfailing religious faith. Her last illness was of mercifully short duration. She caught cold, after having become thoroughly wet from a ramble in the Pearl Street bog. (It has been said that some urchins chased her into the water, and such is the boldness and cruelty of some of our youth, and their observed persecution of this lady, that the tale cannot be entirely discounted.) The cold developed into pneumonia, and she died, attended at the last by a former neighbour, Mrs Bert (Annie) Friels, who witnessed her calm and faithful end.

January, 1904. One of the founders of our community, an early maker and shaker of this town, was abruptly removed from our midst on Monday morning last, whilst attending to his correspondence in the office of his company. Mr Jarvis Poulter possessed a keen and lively commercial spirit, which was instrumental in the creation of not one but several local enterprises, bringing the benefits of industry, productivity, and employment to our town.

So the *Vidette* runs on, copious and assured. Hardly a death goes undescribed, or a life unevaluated.

I looked for Almeda Roth in the graveyard. I found the family stone. There was just one name on it—Roth. Then I noticed two flat stones in the ground, a distance of a few feet—six feet?—from the upright stone. One of these said 'Papa', the other 'Mama'. Farther out from these I found two other flat stones, with the names William and Catherine on them. I had to clear away some overgrowing grass and dirt to see the full name of Catherine. No birth or death dates for anybody, nothing about being dearly beloved. It was a private sort of memorializing, not for the world. There were no roses, either—no sign of a rosebush. But perhaps it was taken out. The grounds keeper doesn't like such things; they are a nuisance to the lawnmower, and if there is nobody left to object he will pull them out.

I thought that Almeda must have been buried somewhere else. When this plot was bought—at the time of the two children's deaths—she would still have been expected to marry, and lie finally beside her husband. They might not have left room for her here. Then I saw that the stones in the ground fanned out from the upright stone. First the two for the parents, then the two for the children, but these were placed in such a way that there was room for a third, to complete the fan. I paced out from 'Catherine' the same number of steps that it took to get from 'Catherine' to 'William', and at this spot I began pulling grass and scrabbling in the dirt with my bare hands. Soon I felt the stone and knew that I was right. I worked away and got the whole stone clear and I read the name 'Meda'. There it was with the others, staring at the sky.

I made sure I had got to the edge of the stone. That was all the name there was—Meda. So it was true that she was called by that name in the family. Not just in the poem. Or perhaps she chose her name from the poem, to be written on her stone.

I thought that there wasn't anybody alive in the world but me who would know this, who would make the connection. And I would be the last person to do so. But perhaps this isn't so. People are curious. A few people are. They will be driven to find things out, even trivial things. They will put things together. You see them going around with notebooks, scraping the dirt off gravestones, reading microfilm, just in the hope of seeing this trickle in time, making a connection, rescuing one thing from the rubbish.

And they may get it wrong, after all. I may have got it wrong. I don't know if she ever took laudanum. Many ladies did. I don't know if she ever made grape jelly.

DIANE SCHOEMPERLEN

Red Plaid Shirt

RED PLAID SHIRT that your mother bought you one summer in Banff. It is 100% Pure Virgin Wool, itchy but flattering against your pale skin, your black hair. You got it in a store called Western Outfitters, of the sort indigenous to the region, which stocked only *real* (as opposed to designer) blue jeans, Stetson hats, and $300 hand-tooled cowboy boots with very pointy toes. There was a saddle and a stuffed deer-head in the window.

Outside, the majestic mountains were sitting all around, magnanimously letting their pictures be taken by ten thousand tourists wielding Japanese cameras and eating ice-cream cones. You had tricked your mother into leaving her camera in the car so she wouldn't embarrass you, who lived there and were supposed to be taking the scenery for granted by now.

You liked the red plaid shirt so much that she bought you two more just like it, one plain green, the other chocolate brown. But these two stayed shirts, never acquiring any particular significance, eventually getting left unceremoniously behind in a Salvation Army drop-box in a grocery store parking lot somewhere along the way.

The red plaid shirt reminded you of your mother's gardening shirt, which was also plaid and which you rescued one winter when she was going to throw it away because the elbows were out. You picture her kneeling in the side garden where she grew only flowers, bleeding hearts, roses, peonies, poppies, and a small patch of strawberries. You picture her hair in a bright babushka, her hands in the black earth with her shirt-sleeves rolled up past the elbow. The honeysuckle hedge bloomed fragrantly behind her and the sweet peas curled interminably up the white trellis. You are sorry now for the way you always sulked and whined when she asked you to help, for the way you hated the dirt under your nails and the sweat running into your eyes, the sweat dripping down her shirt-front between her small breasts. You kept her old shirt in a bag in your closet for years, with a leather patch half-sewn onto the left sleeve, but now you can't find it.

You were wearing the red plaid shirt the night you met Daniel in the tavern where he was drinking beer with his buddies from the highway construction crew. You ended up living with him for the next five years. He was always calling it your 'magic shirt', teasing you, saying how it was the shirt that made him fall in love with you in the first place. You would tease him back, saying how you'd better hang onto it then, in case you had to use it on somebody else. You've even worn it in that spirit a few times since, but the magic seems to have seeped out of it and you are hardly surprised.

You've gained a little weight since then or the shirt has shrunk, so you can't wear it any more, but you can't throw or give it away either.

RED: *crimson carmine cochineal cinnabar sanguine scarlet red ruby rouge my birthstone red and blood-red brick-red beet-red bleeding hearts Queen of fire god of war Mars the colour of magic my magic the colour of iron flowers and fruit the colour of meat dripping lobster cracking claws lips nipples blisters blood my blood and all power.*

BLUE COTTON SWEATSHIRT that says 'Why Be Normal?' in a circle on the front. This is your comfort shirt, fleecy on the inside, soft from many washings, and three sizes too big so you can tuck your hands up inside the sleeves when they're shaking or cold. You like to sit on the couch with the curtains closed, wearing your comfort shirt, eating comfort food: vanilla ice-cream, macaroni and cheese, white rice with butter and salt, white toast with CheezWhiz and peanut-butter. Sometimes you even sleep in it.

This is the shirt you wore when you had the abortion three days before Christmas. They told you to be there at nine in the morning and then you didn't get into the operating room until nearly twelve-thirty. So you wore it in the waiting room with the other women also waiting, and the weight you had already gained was hidden beneath it while you pretended to read *Better Homes and Gardens* and they wouldn't let you smoke. After you came to, you put the shirt back on and waited in another waiting room for your friend, Alice, to come and pick you up because they said you weren't capable yet of going home alone. One of the other women was waiting there too, for her boyfriend who was always late, and when he finally got there, first she yelled at him briefly and then they decided to go to McDonald's for a hamburger. At home, Alice pours you tea from the porcelain pot into white china cups like precious opaque stones.

None of this has diminished, as you feared it might, the comfort this shirt can give you when you need it. Alice always puts her arms around you whenever she sees you wearing it now. She has one just like it, only pink.

> BLUE: *azure aqua turquoise delft and navy-blue royal-blue cool cerulean peacock-blue ultramarine cobalt-blue Prussian-blue cyan the sky and electric a space the colour of the firmament and sapphire sleeping silence the sea the blues my lover plays the saxophone cool blue he plays the blues.*

PALE GREY TURTLENECK that you bought when you were seeing Dwight, who said one night for no apparent reason that grey is a mystical colour. You took this judgement to heart because Dwight was more likely to talk about hockey or carburetors and you were pleasantly surprised to discover that he might also think about other things. You spotted the turtleneck the very next day on sale at Maggie's for $9.99.

You took to wearing it on Sundays because that was the day Dwight was most likely to wander in, unannounced, on his way to or from somewhere else. You wore it while you just happened to put a bottle of good white wine into the fridge to chill and a chicken, a roast, or a pan of spinach lasagna into the oven to cook slowly just in case he showed up hungry. You suppose now that this was pathetic, but at the time you were thinking of yourself as patient and him as worth waiting for.

Three Sundays in a row you ended up passed out on the couch, the wine bottle empty on the coffee table, the supper dried out, and a black-and-white movie with violin music flickering on the TV. In the coloured morning, the pattern of the upholstery was imprinted on your cheek and your whole head was hurting. When Dwight finally did show up, it was a Wednesday and you were wearing your orange flannelette nightie with all the buttons gone and a rip down the front, because it was three in the morning, he was drunk, and you had been in bed for hours. He just laughed and took you in his arms when you told him to get lost. Until you said you were seeing someone else, which was a lie, but one that you both wanted to believe because it was an easy answer that let both of you gingerly off the hook.

You keep meaning to wear that turtleneck again sometime because you know it's juvenile to think it's a jinx, but then you keep forgetting to iron it.

Finally you get tough and wear it, wrinkled, grocery-shopping one Saturday afternoon. You careen through the aisles like a crazed hamster, dodging toddlers, old ladies, and other carts, scooping up vegetables with both hands, eating an apple you haven't paid for, leaving the core in the dairy section. But nothing happens and no one notices your turtleneck: the colour or the wrinkles.

Sure enough, Dwight calls the next day, Sunday, at five o'clock. You say you can't talk now, you're just cooking supper: prime rib, wild rice, broccoli with Hollandaise. You have no trouble at all hanging quietly up on him while pouring the wine into the crystal goblet before setting the table for one with the Royal Albert china your mother left you in her will.

GREY: *oyster pewter slate dull lead dove-grey pearl-grey brain my brains silver or simple gone into the mystic a cool grey day overcast with clouds ashes concrete the aftermath of airplanes gun-metal-grey granite and gos-samer whales elephants cats in the country the colour of questions the best camouflage the opaque elegance an oyster.*

WHITE EMBROIDERED BLOUSE that you bought for $80 to wear with your red-flowered skirt to a Christmas party with Peter, who was working as a pizza cook until he could afford to play his sax full-time. You also bought a silken red belt with gold beads and tassels, a pair of red earrings with dragons on them, and ribbed red stockings which are too small but you wanted them anyway. This striking outfit involves you and Alice in a whole day of trudging around downtown in a snowstorm, holding accessories up in front of mirrors like talismans.

You spend an hour in the bathroom getting ready, drinking white wine, plucking your eyebrows, dancing like a dervish, and smiling seductively at yourself. Peter calls to say he has to work late but he'll meet you there at midnight.

By the time he arrives, you are having a complex anatomical conversation with an intern named Fernando who has spilled a glass of red wine down the front of your blouse. He is going to be a plastic surgeon. Your blouse is soaking in the bathtub and you are wearing only your white lace camisole. Fernando is feeding you green grapes and little squares of cheese, com-plimenting your cheekbones, and falling in love with your smooth forehead. You are having the time of your life and it's funny how you notice for the first time that Peter has an inferior bone structure.

> WHITE: *ivory alabaster magnolia milk the moon is full and chalk-white pure-white snow-white moonstone limestone rime and clay marble many seashells and my bones are china bones precious porcelain lace white magic white feather the immaculate conception of white lies wax white wine as a virtue.*

YELLOW EVENING GOWN that you bought for your New Year's Eve date with Fernando. It has a plunging neckline and a dropped sash which flatteringly accentuates your hips. You wear it with black hoop earrings, black lace stockings with seams, and black high-heels that Alice forced you to buy even though they hurt your toes and you are so unco-ordinated that you expect you will have to spend the entire evening sitting down with your legs crossed, calves nicely flexed.

You spend an hour in the bathroom getting ready, drinking pink champagne, applying blusher with a fat brush according to a diagram in a women's magazine that shows you how to make the most of your face. You practise holding your chin up so it doesn't sag and look double. Alice french-braids your hair and teaches you how to waltz like a lady. Fernando calls to say he has to work late but he'll meet you there before midnight.

You go to the club with Alice instead. They seat you at a tiny table for two so that when you sit down, your knees touch hers. You are in the middle of a room full of candles, fresh flowers, lounge music, and well-groomed couples staring feverishly into each other's eyes. The meal is sumptuous: green salad, a whole lobster, home-made pasta, fresh asparagus, and warm buns wrapped in white linen in a wicker basket. You eat everything and then you get the hell out of there, leaving a message for Fernando.

You go down the street to a bar you know where they will let you in without a ticket even though it's New Year's Eve. In the lobby you meet Fernando in a tuxedo with his arm around a short homely woman in black who, when you ask, 'Who the hell are you?', says, 'His wife.' In your black high-heels you are taller than both of them and you know your gown is gorgeous. When the wife says, 'And who the hell are *you*?', you point a long finger at Fernando's nose and say, 'Ask him.' You stomp away with your chin up and your dropped sash swinging.

Out of sight, you take off your high-heels and walk home through the park and the snow with them in your hands, dangling. Alice follows in a cab. By the time you get there, your black lace stockings are in shreds and your feet are cut and you are laughing and crying, mostly laughing.

> YELLOW: *jonquil jasmine daffodil lemon and honey-coloured corn-coloured cornsilk canary crocus the egg yolk in the morning the colour of mustard bananas brass cadmium yellow is the colour of craving craven chicken cats' eyes I am faint-hearted weak-kneed lily-livered or the sun lucid luminous means caution or yield.*

BLACK LEATHER JACKET that you bought when you were seeing Ivan, who rode a red Harley Davidson low-rider with a suicide shift, his black beard blowing in the wind. The jacket has rows of diagonal pleats at the yoke and a red leather collar and cuffs.

Ivan used to take you on weekend runs with his buddies and their old ladies to little bars in other towns where they were afraid of you: especially of Ivan's best friend, Spy, who had been hurt in a bike accident two years before and now his hands hung off his wrists at odd angles and he could not speak, could only make guttural growls, write obscene notes to the waitress on a serviette, and laugh at her like a madman, his eyes rolling back in his head, and you could see what was left of his tongue.

You would come riding up in a noisy pack with bugs in your teeth, dropping your black helmets like bowling balls on the floor, eating greasy burgers and pickled eggs, drinking draft beer by the jug, the foam running down your chin. Your legs, after the long ride, felt like a wishbone waiting to be sprung. If no one would rent you a room, you slept on picnic tables in the campground, the bikes pulled in around you like wagons, a case of beer and one sleeping bag between ten of you. In the early morning, there was dew on your jacket and your legs were numb with the weight of Ivan's head on them.

You never did get around to telling your mother you were dating a biker (she thought you said 'baker') which was just as well since Ivan eventually got tired, sold his bike, and moved back to Manitoba to live with his mother who was dying. He got a job in a hardware store and soon married his high school sweetheart, Betty, who was a dental hygienist. Spy was killed on the highway, drove his bike into the back of a tanker truck in broad daylight: there was nothing left of him.

You wear your leather jacket now when you need to feel tough. You wear it with your tight blue jeans and your cowboy boots. You strut slowly with your hands in your pockets. Your boots click on the concrete and you are a different person. You can handle anything and no one had better get in your way. You will take on the world if you have to. You will die young and in flames if you have to.

> BLACK: *ebon sable charcoal jet lamp-black blue-black bruises in a night sky ink-black soot-black the colour of my hair and burning rubber dirt the colour of infinite space speeding blackball blacklist black sheep blackberries ravens eat crow black as the ace of spades and black is black I want my baby back before midnight yes of course midnight that old black dog behind me.*

BROWN CASHMERE SWEATER that you were wearing the night you told Daniel you were leaving him. It was that week between Christmas and New Year's which is always a wasteland. Everyone was digging up recipes called Turkey-Grape Salad, Turkey Soufflé, and Turkey-Almond-Noodle Bake. You kept vacuuming up tinsel and pine needles, putting away presents one at a time from under the tree. You and Daniel sat at the kitchen table all afternoon, drinking hot rum toddies, munching on crackers and garlic sausage, playing Trivial Pursuit, asking each other questions like:

What's the most mountainous country in Europe?

Which is more tender, the left or right leg of a chicken?

What race of warriors burned off their right breasts in Greek legend?

Daniel was a poor loser and he thought that Europe was a country, maybe somewhere near Spain.

This night you have just come from a party at his friend Harold's house. You are sitting on the new couch, a loveseat, blue with white flowers, which was Daniel's Christmas present to you, and you can't help thinking of the year your father got your mother a coffee percolator when all she wanted was something personal: earrings, a necklace, a scarf for God's sake. She spent most of the day locked in their bedroom, crying noisily, coming out every hour or so to baste the turkey, white-lipped, tucking more Kleenex up her sleeve. You were on her side this time and wondered how your father, who you had always secretly loved the most, could be so insensitive. It was the changing of the guard, your allegiance shifting like sand from one to the other.

You are sitting on the new couch eating cold pizza and trying to figure out why you didn't have a good time at the party. Daniel is accusing you alternately of looking down on his friends or sleeping with them. He is wearing the black leather vest you bought him for Christmas and he says you are a cheapskate.

When you tell him you are leaving (which is a decision you made months ago but it took you this long to figure out how you were going to manage it and it has nothing to do with the party, the couch, or the season), Daniel grips you by the shoulders and bangs your head against the wall until the picture hung there falls off. It is a photograph of the mountains on a pink spring morning, the ridges like ribs, the runoff like incisions or veins. There is glass flying everywhere in slices into your face, into your hands pressed over your eyes, and the front of your sweater is spotted and matted with blood.

On the way to the hospital, he says he will kill you if you tell them what he did to you. You promise him anything, you promise him that you will love him forever and that you will never leave.

The nurse takes you into the examining room. Daniel waits in the waiting room, reads magazines, buys a chocolate bar from the vending machine, then a Coke and a bag of ripple chips. You tell the nurse what happened and the police take him away in handcuffs with their guns drawn. In the car on the way to the station, he tells them he only did it because he loves you. The officer who takes down your report tells you this and he just keeps shaking his head and patting your arm. The police photographer takes pictures of your face, your broken fingers, your left breast which has purple bruises all over it where he grabbed it and twisted and twisted.

By the time you get to the women's shelter, it is morning and the blood on your sweater has dried, doesn't show. There is no way of knowing. There, the other women hold you, brush your hair, bring you coffee and cream of mushroom soup. The woman with the broken cheekbone has two canaries in a gold cage that she carries with her everywhere like a lamp. She shows you how the doors are steel, six inches thick, and the windows are bulletproof. She shows you where you will sleep, in a room on the third floor with six other women, some of them lying now fully-dressed on their little iron cots with their hands behind their heads, staring at the ceiling as if it were full of stars or clouds the drift slowly westward in the shape of camels, horses, or bears. She shows you how the canaries will sit on your finger if you hold very still and pretend you are a tree or a roof or another bird.

BROWN: *ochre cinnamon coffee copper caramel the colour of my Christmas cake chocolate mocha walnut chestnuts raw sienna my suntan burnt umber burning toast fried fricasseed sautéd grilled I baste the turkey the colour of stupid cows smart horses brown bears brown shirt brown sugar apple brown betty brunette the colour of thought and sepia the colour of old photographs the old earth and wood.*

GREEN SATIN QUILTED JACKET in the Oriental style with mandarin collar and four red frogs down the front. This jacket is older than you are. It belonged to your mother, who bought it when she was the same age you are now. In the black-and-white photos from that time, the jacket is grey but shiny and your mother is pale but smooth-skinned, smiling with her hand on her hip or your father's thigh.

You were always pestering her to let you wear it to play dress-up, with her red high-heels and that white hat with the feathers and the little veil that covered your whole face. You wanted to wear it to a Hallowe'en party at school where all the other girls would be witches, ghosts, or princesses and you would be the only mandarin, with your eyes, you imagined, painted up slanty and two sticks through a bun in your hair. But she would never let you. She would just keep on cooking supper, bringing carrots, potatoes, cabbages up from the root cellar, taking peas, beans, broccoli out of the freezer in labelled dated parcels, humming, looking out through the slats of the Venetian blind at the black garden and the leafless rose bushes. Each year, at least one of them would be winter-killed no matter how hard she had tried to protect them. And she would dig it up in the spring by the dead roots and the thorns would get tangled in her hair, leave long bloody scratches all down her arms. And the green jacket stayed where it was, in the cedar chest with the hand-made lace doilies, her grey linen wedding suit, and the picture of your father as a small boy with blond ringlets.

After the funeral, you go through her clothes while your father is outside shovelling snow. You lay them out in piles on the bed: one for the Salvation Army, one for the second-hand store, one for yourself because your father wants you to take something home with you. You will take the green satin jacket, also a white mohair cardigan with multi-coloured squares on the front, a black-and-white striped shirt you sent her for her birthday last year that she never wore, an imitation pearl necklace for Alice, and a dozen unopened packages of pantyhose. There is a fourth pile for your father's friend Jack's new wife, Frances, whom your mother never liked, but your father says Jack and Frances have fallen on hard times on the farm since Jack got the emphysema, and Frances will be glad of some new clothes.

Jack and Frances drop by the next day with your Aunt Jeanne. You serve tea and the shortbread cookies Aunt Jeanne has brought. She makes them just the way your mother did, whipped, with a sliver of maraschino cherry on top. Jack, looking weather-beaten or embarrassed, sits on the edge of the couch with his baseball cap in his lap and marvels at how grown-up you've got to be. Frances is genuinely grateful for the two green garbage bags of clothes, which you carry out to the truck for her.

After they leave, you reminisce fondly with your father and Aunt Jeanne about taking the toboggan out to Jack's farm when you were small, tying it to the back of the car, your father driving slowly down the country lane, towing you on your stomach, clutching the front of the toboggan which curled like a wooden wave. You tell him for the first time how frightened you were of the black tires spinning the snow into your face, and he says he had no idea, he thought you were having fun. This was when Jack's first wife, Winnifred, was still alive. Your Aunt Jeanne, who knows everything, tells you that when Winnifred was killed in that car accident, it was Jack, driving drunk, who caused it. And now when he gets drunk, he beats Frances up, locks her out of the house in her bare feet, and she has to sleep in the barn, in the hay with the horses.

You are leaving in the morning. Aunt Jeanne helps you pack.

You are anxious to get home but worried about leaving your father alone. Aunt Jeanne says she'll watch out for him.

The green satin jacket hangs in your front hall closet now, between your black leather jacket and your raincoat. You can still smell the cedar from the chest and the satin is always cool on your cheek like clean sheets or glass.

One day you think you will wear it downtown, where you are meeting a new man for lunch. You study yourself in the full-length mirror on the back of the bathroom door and you decide it makes you look like a different person: someone unconventional, unusual, and unconcerned. This new man, who you met recently at an outdoor jazz festival, is a free spirit who eats health food, plays the dulcimer, paints well, writes well, sings well, and has just completed an independent study of eastern religions. He doesn't smoke, drink, or do drugs. He is pure and peaceful, perfect. He is teaching you how to garden, how to turn the black soil, how to plant the seeds, how to water them, weed them, watch them turn into lettuce, carrots, peas, beans, radishes, and pumpkins, how to get the kinks out of your back by stretching your brown arms right up to the sun. You haven't even told Alice about him yet because he is too good to be true. He is bound to love this green jacket, and you in it too.

You get in your car, drive around the block, go back inside because you forgot your cigarettes, and you leave the green jacket on the back of a kitchen chair because who are you trying to kid? More than anything, you want to be transparent. More than anything, you want to hold his hands across the table and then you will tell him you love him and it will all come true.

GREEN: *viridian verdigris chlorophyll grass leafy jade mossy verdant apple-green pea-green lime-green sage-green sea-green bottle-green emeralds avocadoes olives all leaves the colour of Venus hope and jealousy the colour of mould mildew envy poison and pain and snakes the colour of everything that grows in my garden fertile nourishing sturdy sane and strong.*

CAROL SHIELDS

Milk Bread Beer Ice

'What's the difference between a gully and a gulch?' Barbara
Cormin asks her husband, Peter Cormin, as they speed south on
the Interstate. These are the first words to pass between them in
over an hour, this laconic, idle, unhopefully offered, trivia-con-
toured question.

Peter Cormin, driving a cautious sixty miles an hour through
a drizzle of rain, makes no reply, and Barbara, from long experience, expects none. Her question concerning the difference
between gullies and gulches floats out of her mouth like a
smoker's lazy exhalation and is instantly subsumed by the hum
of the engine. Two minutes pass. Five minutes. Barbara's
thoughts skip to different geological features, the curious wind-
lashed forms she sees through the car window, and those others
whose names she vaguely remembers from a compulsory geol-
ogy course taken years earlier—arroyos, cirques, terminal
moraines. She has no idea now what these exotic relics might
look like, but imagines them to be so brutal and arresting as to
be instantly recognizable should they materialize on the
landscape. Please let them materialize, she prays to the grooved
door of the glove compartment. Let something, *anything*,
materialize.

This is their fifth day on the road. Four motels, interchange-
able, with tawny, fire-retardant carpeting, are all that have inter-
vened. This morning, Day Five, they drive through a strong
brown and yellow landscape, ferociously eroded, and it cheers
Barbara a little to gaze out at this scene of novelty after seventeen

hundred miles of green hills and ponds and calm, staring cattle. 'I really should keep a dictionary in the car,' she says to Peter, another languid exhalation.

The car, with its new-car smell, seems to hold both complaint and accord this morning. And silence. Barbara sits looking out at the rain, wondering about the origin of the word drizzle—a likeable enough word, she thinks, when you aren't actually being drizzled upon. Probably onomatopoetic. Drizzling clouds. Drizzled syrup on pancakes. She thrashes around in her head for the French equivalent: *bruine*, she thinks, or is that word for fog? 'I hate not knowing things,' she says aloud to Peter. Musing. And arranging her body for the next five minutes.

At age fifty-three she is a restless traveller, forever shifting from haunch to haunch, tugging her blue cotton skirt smooth, examining its weave, sighing and stretching and fiddling in a disapproving way with the car radio. All she gets is country music. Or shouting call-in shows, heavy with sarcasm and whining indignation. Or nasal evangelists. Yesterday she and Peter listened briefly to someone preaching about the seven Fs of Christian love, the first F being, to her amazement, the fear of God, the *feah of Gawd*. Today, because of the rain, there's nothing on the radio but ratchety static. She and Peter have brought along a box of tapes, Bach and Handel and Vivaldi, that she methodically plays and replays, always expecting diversion and always forgetting she is someone who doesn't know what to do with music. She listens but doesn't hear. What she likes are words. *Drizzle*, she repeats to herself, *bruiner*. But how to conjugate it?

In the back seat are her maps and travel guides, a bundle of slippery brochures, a book called *Place Names of Texas* and another called *Texas Wildlife*. Her reference shelf. Her sanity cupboard. She can't remember how she acquired the habit of looking up facts; out of some nursery certitude, probably, connecting virtue with an active, inquiring mind. *People must never stop learning*; once Barbara had believed fervently in this embarrassing cliché, was the first in line for night-school classes, tuned in regularly with perhaps a dozen others to solemn radio talks on existentialism, Monday nights, seven to eight. And she has, too, her weekly French conversation group, now in its fourteenth year but soon to disband.

Her brain is always heating up; inappropriately, whimsically. She rather despises herself for it, and wishes, when she goes on vacation, that she could submerge herself in scenery or fantasy as other people seemed to do, her husband Peter in particular, or so she suspects. She would never risk saying to him, 'A penny for your thoughts', nor would he ever say such a thing to her. He believes such 'openers' are ill-bred intrusions. He told her as much, soon after they were married, lying above her on the living-room floor in their first apartment with the oval braided rug beneath them pushing up its rounded cushiony ribs. 'What are you thinking?' she had asked, and watched his eyes go cold.

The rain increases, little checks against the car window, and Barbara curls her legs up under her, something she seldom does—since it makes her feel like a woman trying too hard to be whimsical—and busies herself looking up Waco, Texas, in her guidebook. There it is: population figures, rainfall statistics, a naive but jaunty potted history. Why at her age does she feel compelled to know such things? What is all this shrewdness working itself up for? Waco, she learns, is pronounced with a long A sound, which is disappointing. She prefers—who wouldn't?—the comic splat of wham, pow, whacko. Waco, Texas. The city rises and collapses in the rainy distance.

Leaning forward, she changes the tape. Its absolute, neat plastic corners remind her of the nature of real things, and snapping it into place gives her more satisfaction than listening to the music. A click, a short silence, and then the violins stirring themselves like iced-tea spoons, like ferns on a breezy hillside. Side two. She stares out the window, watchful for the least variation. A water tower holds her eye for a full sixty seconds, a silver thimble on stilts. *Château d'eau*, she murmurs to herself. Tower of Water. Tower of Babel.

Almost all her conversations are with herself.

Imprisoned now for five long days in the passenger seat of a brand new Oldsmobile Cutlass, Barbara thinks of herself as a castaway. Her real life has been left behind in Toronto. She and Peter are en route to Houston to attend an estate auction of a late client of Peter's, a man who ended his life not long ago with a pistol shot. For the sake of the passage, admittedly only two weeks, she has surrendered those routines that make her feel busy and purposeful. (With another woman she runs an establishment on Queen Street called the Ungift Shop; she also reads to the blind and keeps up her French.) Given the confining nature of her life, she has surprising freedoms at her disposal.

We should have flown is the phrase she is constantly on the point of uttering. Driving had been Peter's idea; she can't now remember his reasons; two reasons he gave, but what were they?

He has a craning look when he drives, immensely responsible. And a way of signalling when he passes, letting his thumb wing out sideways on the lever, a deft and lovely motion. She is struck by the beauty of it, also its absurdity, a little dwarfish, unconscious salute, and silent.

There is too much sorrowful sharing in marriage, Barbara thinks. When added up, it kills words. Games have to be invented; theatre. Out loud she says, like an imitation of a gawking person, 'I wonder what those little red flowers are.' (Turning, reaching for her wildlife book.) 'We don't have those in Ontario. Or do we?'

The mention of the red flowers comes after another long silence.

Then Peter says, not unkindly, not even impatiently, 'A gully's deeper, I think.'

'Deeper?' says Barbara in her dream voice. She is straining her eyes to read a billboard poised high on a yellow bluff. IF YOU SMOKE PLEASE TRY CARLETONS. The word *please*, it's shocking. So!—the tobacco industry has decided to get polite. Backed into a corner, attacked on all sides, they're hitting hard with wheedling courtesies, *please*. Last week Barbara watched a TV documentary on lung cancer and saw a set of succulent pink lungs turning into what looked like slices of burnt toast.

'Deeper than a gulch.'

'Oh,' says Barbara.

'Unless I've got it the wrong way around.'

'Its slang anyway, I think.'

'What?'

'Gully. Gulch. They're not real words, are they? They sound, you know, regional. Cowboy lingo.'

Peter takes a long banked curve. On and on it goes, ninety degrees or more, but finely graded. His hands on the wheel are scarcely required to move. Clean, thick hands, they might be carved out of twin bars of soap. Ivory soap, carbolic. He smiles faintly, but in a way that shuts Barbara out. On and on. Rain falls all around them—*il pleut*—on the windshield and on the twisted landforms and collecting along the roadway in ditches. 'Could be,' Peter says.

'Does that look brighter up ahead to you?' Barbara says wildly, anxious now to keep the conversation going. She puts away the tape, sits up straight, pats her hair, and readies herself for the little fates and accidents a conversation can provide.

Conversation?

Inside her head a quizzing eyebrow shoots up. These idle questions and observations? This dilatory response? This disobliging exchange between herself and her husband of thirty-three years, which is as random and broken as the geological rubble she dully observes from the car window, and about which Peter can scarcely trouble himself to comment? This sludge of gummed phrases? Conversation?

It could be worse, thinks Barbara, always anxious to be fair, and calling to mind real and imaginary couples sitting silent in coffee shops, whole meals consumed and paid for with not a single word exchanged. Or stunned-looking husbands and wives at home in their vacuumed living rooms, neatly dressed and conquered utterly by the background hum of furnaces and air-conditioning units. And after that, what?—a desperate slide into hippo grunts and night coughing, slack, sponge-soft lips and toothless dread—that word *mute* multiplied to the thousandth power. Death.

An opportunity to break in the new car was what Peter had said—now she remembered.

Barbara met Peter in 1955 at a silver auction in Quebec City. He was an apprentice then, learning the business. He struck her first as being very quiet. He stared and stared at an antique coffee service, either assessing its value or awestruck by its beauty—she didn't know which. Later he grew talkative. Then silent. Then eloquent. Secretive. Verbose. Introspective. Gregarious. A whole colony of choices appeared to rest in his larynx. She never knew what to expect. One minute they were on trustworthy ground, feeding each other intimacies, and the next minute they were capsized, adrift and dumb.

'Some things can't be put into words,' a leaner, nervous, younger Peter Cormin once said.

'Marriage can be defined as a lifelong conversation,' said an elderly, sentimental, slightly literary aunt of Barbara's, meaning to be kind.

Barbara at twenty had felt the chill press of rhetorical echo: *a religious vocation is one of continuous prayer, a human life is one unbroken thought.* Frightening. She knew better, though, than to trust what was cogently expressed. Even as a young woman she was forever tripping over abandoned proverbs. She counted on nothing, but hoped for everything.

Breaking in the new car. But did people still break in cars? She hadn't heard the term used for years. Donkey's years. Whatever that meant.

A younger, thinner, more devious Barbara put planning into her conversations. There was breakfast talk and dinner talk and lively hurried telephone chatter in between. She often cast herself in the role of *ingénue*, allowing her husband Peter space for commentary and suggestions. It was Barbara who put her head to one side, posed questions and prettily waited. It was part of their early shared mythology that he was sometimes arrogant to the point of unkindness, and that she was sensitive and put upon, an injured consciousness flayed by husbandly imperative. But neither of them had the ability to sustain their roles for long.

She learned certain tricks of subversions, how with one word or phrase she could bring about disorder and then reassurance. It excited her. It was like flying in a flimsy aircraft and looking at the suddenly vertical horizon, then bringing everything level once more.

'You've changed,' one of her conversations began.

'Everyone changes.'

'For better or worse?'

'Better, I think.'

'You think?'

'I know.'

'You say things differently. You intellectualize.'

'Maybe that's my nature.'

'It didn't use to be.'

'I've changed, people do change.'

'That's just what I said.'

'I wish you wouldn't—'

'What?'

'Point things out. Do you always have to point things out?'

'I can't help it.'

'You could stop yourself.'

'That wouldn't be me.'

Once they went to a restaurant to celebrate the birth of their second son. The restaurant was inexpensive and the food only moderately good. After coffee, after glasses of recklessly ordered brandy, Peter slipped away to the telephone. A business call, he said to Barbara. He would only be a minute or two. From where she sat she could see him behind the glass door of the phone booth, his uplifted arm, his patient explanation, and his glance at his watch—then his face reshaped itself into furrows of explosive laughter.

She had been filled with a comradely envy for his momentary connection, and surprised by her lack of curiosity, how little she cared who was on the other end of the line, a client or a lover, it didn't matter. A conversation was in progress. Words were being mainlined straight into Peter's ear, and the overflow of his conversation travelled across the dull white tablecloths and reached her too, filling her emptiness, or part of it.

Between the two of them they have accumulated a minor treasury of anecdotes beginning with 'Remember when we—' and this literature of remembrance sometimes traps them into smugness. And, occasionally, when primed by a solid period of calm, they are propelled into the blue-tinged pre-history of that epoch before they met.

'When I was in Denver that time—'

'I never knew you were in Denver.'

'My mother took me there once . . .'

'You never told me your mother took you to . . .'

But Barbara is tenderly protective of her beginnings. She is also, oddly, protective of Peter's. Eruptions from this particular and most cherished layer of time are precious and dangerous; retrieval betrays it, smudges it.

'There's something wrong,' Barbara said to Peter some years ago, 'and I don't know how to tell you.'

They were standing in a public garden near their house, walking between beds of tulips.

'You don't love me,' he guessed, amazing her, and himself.

'I love you but not enough.'

'What is enough?' he cried and reached out for the cotton sleeve of her dress.

A marriage counsellor booked them for twelve sessions. Each session lasted two hours, twenty-four hours in all. During those twenty-four hours they released into the mild air of the marriage counsellor's office millions of words. Their longest conversation. The polished floor, the walls, the perforated ceiling tile drank in the unstoppable flow. Barbara Cormin wept and shouted. Peter Cormin moaned, retreated, put his head on his arms. The histories they separately recounted were as detailed as the thick soft novels people carry with them to the beach in the summer. Every story elicited a counter-story, until the accumulated weight of blame and blemish had squeezed them dry. 'What are we doing?' Peter Cormin said, moving the back of his hand across and across his mouth. Barbara thought back to the day she had stood by the sunlit tulip bed and said, 'Something's wrong,' and wondered now what had possessed her. A hunger for words, was that all? She asked the marriage counsellor for a glass of cold water. She feared what lay ahead. A long fall into silence. An expensive drowning.

But they were surprisingly happy for quite some time after, speaking to each other kindly, with a highly specific strategy, little pieces moved on a chess board. What had been tricky territory before was strewn with shame. Barbara was prepared now to admit that marriage was, at best, a flawed and gappy narrative. Occasionally some confidence would wobble forward and one of them, Barbara or Peter, might look up cunningly, ready to measure the moment and retreat or advance. They worked around the reserves of each other's inattention the way a pen-and-ink artist learns to use the reserve of white space.

'Why?' Barbara asked Peter.

'Why what?'

'Why did he do it? Shoot himself.'

'No one knows for sure.'

'There's always a note. Wasn't there a note?'

'Yes. But very short.'

'Saying?'

'He was lonely.'

'That's what he said, that he was lonely?'

'More or less.'

'What exactly did he say?'

'That there was no one he could talk to.'

'He had a family, didn't he? And business associates. He had you, he's known you for years. He could have picked up the phone.'

'Talking isn't just words.'

'What?'

Barbara sees herself as someone always waiting for the next conversation, the way a drunk is forever thinking ahead to the next drink.

But she discounts the conversation of Eros which seems to her to be learned not from life, but from films or trashy novels whose authors have in turn learned it from other secondary and substandard sources. Where bodies collide most gloriously, language melts—who said that? Someone or other. Barbara imagines that listening at the bedroom keyholes of even the most richly articulate would be to hear only the murmurous inanities of *True Romance*. ('I adore your golden breasts,' he whispered gruffly. 'You give me intense pleasure,' she deeply sighed.) But these conversations actually take place. She knows they do. The words are pronounced. The sighing and whispering happen. *Just the two of us, this paradise.*

'We can break in the car,' Peter said to her back in Toronto, 'and have a few days together, just the two of us.'

Very late on Day Five they leave the Interstate and strike off on a narrow asphalt road in search of a motel. The cessation of highway noise is stunningly sudden, like swimming away in a dream from the noises of one's own body. Peter holds his head to one side, judging the car's performance, the motor's renewed, slower throb and the faint adhesive tick of the tires rolling on the hot road.

The towns they pass through are poor, but have seen better days. Sidewalks leading up to lovely old houses have crumbled along their edges, and the houses themselves have begun to deteriorate; many are for sale; dark shaggy cottonwoods bend down their branches to meet the graceful pitch of the roofs.

Everywhere in these little towns there are boarded-up railway stations, high schools, laundries, cafés, plumbing supply stores, filling stations. And almost everywhere, it seems, the commercial centre has shrunk to a single, blinking, all-purpose, twenty-four-hour outlet at the end of town—pathetically, but precisely named: the Mini-Mart, the Superette, the Quik-Stop. These new buildings are of single-storey slab construction in pale brick or cement block, and are minimally landscaped. One or two gas pumps sit out in front, and above them is a sign, most often homemade, saying MILK ICE BREAD BEER.

'Milk ice bread beer', murmurs the exhausted Barbara, giving the phrase a heaving tune. She is diverted by the thought of these four purposeful commodities traded to a diminished and deprived public. 'The four elements.'

In the very next town, up and down over a series of dark hills, they find a subtly altered version: BEER ICE BREAD MILK. 'Priorities,' says Peter, reading the sign aloud, making an ironic chant of it.

Further along the road they come upon BREAD BEER MILK ICE. Later still, the rescrambled BEER MILK ICE BREAD.

Before they arrive, finally, at a motel with air-conditioning, a restaurant, and decent beds—no easy matter in a depressed agricultural region—they have seen many such signs and in all possible variations. Cryptic messages, they seem designed to comfort and confuse Peter and Barbara Cormin with loops of flawed recognition and to deliver them to a congenial late-evening punchiness. As the signs pop up along the highway, they take it in turn, with a rhythmic spell and counter-spell, to read the words aloud. Milk bread beer ice. Ice bread milk beer.

This marks the real death of words, thinks Barbara, these homely products reduced to husks, their true sense drained purely away. Ice beer bread milk. Rumblings in the throats, syllables strung on an old clothesline, electronic buzzing.

But, surprisingly, the short unadorned sounds, for a few minutes, with daylight fading and dying in the wide sky, take on expanded meaning. Another, lesser world is brought forward, distorted and freshly provisioned. She loves it—its weather and depth, its exact chambers, its lost circuits, its covered pleasures, its submerged pattern of communication.

AUDREY THOMAS

Blue Spanish Eyes

Over and over the same question: relatives, friends, husbands
and wives at breakfast tables on both sides of the Atlantic. Why?
Examining the blurry photos again. A sensible woman, a grandmother, staring straight at the camera with an open, friendly
smile. Then, further down, the Indentikit drawing—HAVE YOU
SEEN THIS MAN?

Her daughter wept, her sons. Why? When? (remembering all
the warnings about strangers). Why? And where was she now?

She cannot answer, of course, for her mouth is stopped up with
mud.

I first saw him in the concourse of the Inverness Railway Station,
a tall young man leaning over his bike, trying to catch his breath.
His T-shirt was soaked with sweat so that the vertebrae underneath stuck up prominently, almost as though they were buttons,
as though he had been buttoned neatly into his skin.

'Tender buttons,' I thought, but Stein meant mushrooms, not
the backbone of a bicycle-rider. The arc of his back and wheels
of his cycle made a nice composition; I wished I were a
photographer so that I could approach him and ask if he'd mind
if I took his picture—no, don't look up, you're perfect the way
you were. But I don't take photographs, just snapshots of my
children and their children—a snapshot is quite a different
thing from a photograph. I don't carry a camera when I'm
travelling, not because I fear it might get stolen but because I
fear I might stop looking. However, once in a while I regret this

policy and now was one of those times.

The high arc of the boy's back, his stillness (except for the deep breath, in/out, in/out, in/out), the back of his neck which was tanned and freckled by the sun. He had dark red hair, the colour of an Irish setter, but were I a photographer I would have taken his photograph in black and white. In the beginning, then, he was just an aesthetic arrangement for me—like Whistler's mother.

I had been a week up in the Orkney Islands, walking and sightseeing. The weather was perfect except for one day of rain, and the Orkneys had impressed and moved me in a curious way. The whole place is a kind of museum and yet the people go about their daily lives in a completely natural way, in spite of the standing stones and Viking graves and neolithic treasures, many no doubt still to be uncovered. In the small museum at the Tomb of the Eagles I was allowed to hold in my hands the skull of a woman who died over four thousand years ago. The skull was the colour of field mushrooms, smooth and slightly cool to the touch.

She died at thirty-four, an old woman for those times. There was a deep indentation across the top of her head where a band of leather had pressed down, day after day, year after year, as she carried her loads from one place to another. I held the skull to my ear, like a shell as though I might hear her calling to me over all those centuries. Her back molars had been worn down by chewing, softening leather perhaps. The farmer's wife, who ran the museum, smiled at me. 'We are all Chalk Thompson's bairns.'

'I'm sorry?'

'An old name for Death,' she said, and took the skull from me to give to the next person in our group.

Fat sheep nibble at the grass around the headstones in the cemetery at Orphir. A farmer digs a hole to bury a cow and turns up a Viking skeleton. But it wasn't a morbid or dreary place; I wouldn't want to give the wrong impression. There was just a certain acceptance of it all that left me feeling cleansed, uplifted, more at peace than I had been in a long long time.

When I travel I wear my wedding ring and if the subject comes up I say my husband has passed on. I don't add that he passed on to a younger woman. There's no shame in being divorced these days, not like when I was growing up, but a widow is a highly respectable thing to be. I figure my husband owes me that, my little deceit. I feel safer as a widow than a divorcée; a widow, unlike a widower, isn't necessarily looking for another mate. And if someone asks, 'when did you lose your husband?' I can answer in all honesty.

I had reserved a seat on the 5:30 train from Inverness to Edinburgh just in case the train from the north was late; as a result I had plenty of time on my hands, although not quite enough to venture too far away from the city centre. I put my bag in a locker and walked around a bit, browsed in a couple of touristy shops which sold the usual tartan ties and kilts, lambswool sweaters, shortbread, whisky miniatures and silver jewellery based on Celtic designs; but I had already done my shopping in Orkney and had it sent home, so I soon tired of that. It was tea-time, but the one tea-room I really liked the look of was full up so I retraced my steps and had an indifferent tea at the Station Hotel. Nearly everything had been eaten up except for some dry cheese-and-tomato rolls and packet biscuits. I had a Scottish mother who always stopped for tea and whose love of baking would be frowned upon by any self-respecting dietitian today. We had cream scones and pancakes and shortbread (with real butter) and Dundee cake and maid of honour tarts and Victoria sandwich. Thursday was her baking day and I raced home to lick bowls and munch on pastry strips which had been sprinkled with cinnamon and sugar and baked in a hot, hot oven. My mother laughed at her excesses, blamed it on the war, even though, after she met my American father, her family had more than most. My father says she fell in love with him on the day a huge fruitcake arrived from his relatives in Massachusetts. My father was tall and skinny, like this boy with the bicycle. He could eat and eat and never gain an ounce. My mother was short and rather plain and grew stout as the years went on. At the age of fifteen, realizing that I took more after my mother's side than my Yankee father's, I gave up all the sweets. My mother laughed at me and went right on baking. She was a great hit with my boyfriends and, later, with my children. Now that she is dead I have begun to bake, with recipes from her old black-covered notebook. I take boxes of goodies to my father and I bake for various groups I belong to. No doubt, when my grandson has graduated from baby food I shall bake—I would have baked—for him too, secretly of course; his mother never touches sugar. My father teases her and sings an old song his father taught him, something about everything being 'illegal or immoral or it makes you fat.'

I looked at the station clock and went to retrieve my suitcase. When I came back the boy—the young man—was over at the fruit stand very carefully selecting fruit for the trip. He pointed here and there and made the seller laugh. I smiled because I knew exactly what he was doing. The price of fruit in Scotland always shocks me; I too am very picky here as I want to make sure I get my money's worth. We are spoiled back home; I've tried to imagine what it was like during the war, with an ounce of this and an ounce of that, one egg a week. I was only a toddler when the war ended and we left for the United States. The first time I came back I thought some miracle would happen and all my infant memories would present themselves to me like old home movies; it wasn't so. I felt comfortable in Scotland, that was the extent of it. (But not comfortable with my relatives, those stern, uncompromising Presbyterians. I stayed at a Bed and Breakfast in Edinburgh and took the bus out to visit those that were left. Two of my ancient aunties bragged that they had never been below the border. No central heating to this day and fires not lit until November.)

The young man turned quickly and saw me smiling. He paid for his purchases, stuffed them in his backpack and came over, pushing the bike with one hand. That was the first I had a good look at his face. He stood looking down at me with a cheeky grin.

'And just what are you smiling at?' he said.

Once, on a beach in Crete, a woman from the American south asked me if I liked lookin' at all those little no-hipped boys in their tiny swimsuits. She was about fifteen years older than I was, about the age I was that day in Inverness.

'No,' I said, 'not particularly.' She wiggled her painted toes.

'Well, Sugar, you got that pleasure comin' to you.'

But it wasn't like that at all, it never has been for me. I look at mouths and eyes. It's the head that's important, like the engine at the front of a train. For me, usually, the rest of the body is just pulled along by the head. And this boy's body was nothing to write home about in any case. When he was actually in motion he seemed more than loose-limbed, dangerously so, as though he needed to be re-strung. An arm or a leg might come flying off at any minute. But his eyes: his eyes were a bright, clear, cloudless blue. I felt that if his eyes were sliced open the blue colour would go all the way through, like the yolk of a hard-boiled egg, that eyes such as those could not possibly be hollow. 'Blue Spanish Eyes,' I thought, although he was as Scottish as they come.

'I was smiling at the way you chose your purchases,' I said. 'I do the same thing. I want *this* particular banana, *that* apple.'

He sat down next to me on one of the ugly plastic chairs British Rail now provides for its customers. I suppose they are easy to keep clean but I would prefer old-fashioned waiting-rooms and wooden benches. Even Waverley Station, that opulent place, has these seats which belong only at some fast-food outlet. His legs were much too long for him to sit comfortably in such chairs.

'New England,' he said, 'but with a touch of something else.' Here he launched into a clever parody of the Kennedys. 'Ask what you can do for your country,' he said. 'Hahvahd Yahd.'

'I don't talk like that,' I said, 'do I?'

'No, not really, but it's there. What else? Want to hear my New

York accent, hey youse, want to hear dat? Or my Georgia accent, won't yawl have a bit of Mama's peach pickle? You name it, I can do it.'

'Are you an actor?' I asked. He didn't seem like an actor, less self-absorbed, although he looked a bit like Gregory in *Gregory's Girl*.

'Me! An actor? Not on your life. But I can do a great Marlon Brando. Want to see Marlon Brando play Hamlet?' He rolled up the sleeve of his T-shirt and tucked away an imaginary pack of cigarettes.

'To be or not to be,' he growled. Then held the pose, head on one side.

I waited.

'That's it,' he said. 'Pretty good, hey? No, I'm not an actor, just a film junkie. Especially the old films. Especially films in the afternoon. I dropped out of school so I could go to films in the afternoon. My mother never knew until she ended up sitting next to me one afternoon. And then wasn't there hell to pay, oh my.'

'I have to go now,' I said, 'my train's just been put up on the board.'

'Edinburgh?'

'That's right.'

'I'm going as far as Stirling. Could I sit with you? I promise to be entertaining.'

'I reserved a seat,' I said, 'the seats around me might be taken.'

'We'll see about that. Just let me put my bicycle in the guard's van and I'll come find you.' He paused. 'That is, if you're agreeable?'

I'd finished all the books I'd brought with me, except a P.D. James I was really saving for the plane and some ladies magazine I had bought just for amusement. Having someone to talk to for three hours on a Sunday afternoon might be fun. Or listen to. I wasn't sure how much talking I would manage to get in. I strapped my bag onto the little wheeled cart I had vowed ten years ago I would never own. A wheeled cart seemed in the same category with Oil of Olay or even those plastic raincaps old ladies carry in their purses to protect their perms if it should rain. The boy had loped on ahead. Perhaps I would be seated and my luggage stowed away by the time he found me. I could always tell him about hitchhiking around Europe with an enormous pack when I was his age or even a little younger. It was borrowed and the base hit my spine in the wrong place. They weren't rip-stop nylon then either; they were heavy brown canvas, leather and metal. When I got to the train and was walking along the platform searching for my car, I decided to make a game out of the wheelie I was dragging behind me. Just in case he was watching. 'Come along, Shep,' I said, 'there's a good dog.' But I was settled and reading a magazine before he finally slid into the empty seat across from me.

'*The Lady*,' he said, plucking it out of my hands and flipping through the pages.

'"'I'll never forget,' says Jeanne Laidlaw, recalling her WAR-TIME CHILDHOOD." Is this what you read? "Fitted bed linens." "The Brightest Idea in Kitchen Boards." "Society for the Assistance of Ladies in Reduced Circumstances." Are you looking for a position as a nanny or a resident housekeeper in a nursing home? You don't really seem the type.'

'I bought them as a joke—to take back home. I didn't know magazines like this still existed. *Woman's Own,* sure, but not *The Lady*.'

He tossed the magazine aside and took out a pack of cards.

When someone you love tells you that it's over, when you've been married to that someone for twenty years, something terrible and permanent happens to you. It's like being in a bad car crash or an airplane crash. Even if you survive, even if you survive with no visible scars, something happens to your soul. You become frightened of things that never frightened you before—loud noises, a sudden scream, the sight of blood. You have lost a certain innocence, or perhaps the word is 'trust'. You never get over it; all you can do is get around it.

Even when he says you've done nothing wrong, that it's he who is at fault. Even when he says there's no particular other woman, just a desire to 'explore other avenues of myself.' It is probably easier if there is another woman, a name, perhaps a face. Then the hurt and anger can be localized, contained, instead of spread wide, like an oil spill. It spreads to strangers, even to this boy. What would he think of me for having a wheelie, for buying such a stupid, conservative magazine? What would he think of me when I told him I don't play cards? I watched his strong hands shuffle the pack and reshuffle. The hairs on his arms were like gold wires. I noticed then that he wore a wedding ring.

'The only game I know,' I said, 'is gin rummy. Other than children's games, snap or go-fish—games like that.'

'Just choose a card,' he said, 'any card. Memorize it and stick it back in the deck.' He smiled. His face was covered in faint freckles, as though he'd been dusted with some spice. I hesitated.

'Hurry along,' he said, 'we've not got all day.'

The city of Inverness stands at the top of the Great Glen, a geological fault that slices with a diagonal across the Highlands. When the Caledonian Canal was built in the early-nineteenth century the North Sea was connected to the Atlantic Ocean. In nature great faults are seen as challenges—at least to engineers. Things are made to link up by bridges, canals and other ingenious devices. My husband was an engineer, his heroes were—no doubt still are—Thomas Telford and Isambard Kingdom Brunel. He was 'handy', as they say over here and could fix anything. Except our marriage. Marriages wear out, he said, just like motorcars; it isn't anything you've done.

(I memorized the Creed at my mother's knee: We have left undone those things which we ought to have done and done those things that we ought not to have done and there is no health in us.)

Of course the boy picked the right card, again and again. His fingers danced above the little table which lay between us.

'You're a teacher, I'll wager,' he said.

'A professor of Art History.'

He pulled a face.

'A *professor*, is it? Good pay? Long holidays? Lots of trips to places with *objets d'art* ? The Mona Lisa. Venus de Milo, that sort of thing?'

'Are you mocking me?'

'Not really. I believe in education. Or I do now. There was a while when I was one of the lost boys—you know—Peter Pan. Didn't want to grow and face responsibility.'

He made a waterfall of the cards, and then another. A thick honey-coloured light lay over the purple hills.

'How old do you think I am?' he said.

'Twenty-five.'

He looked at me in surprise. 'Bang on.'

'I have a son the same age as you.'

'What's his name?' He held out the deck and I took another card.

'Donald,' I said, 'after his grandfather.' Those blue eyes watching me, not the cards.

'That's my name too,' he said. 'Do you think we were fated to meet?'

He gave me a smile of such incredible sweetness I could have wept. Men my age did not smile at me like that, openly, just delighting in the moment, the coincidence.

'His grandfather was a Scot,' I said.

'My Mother was a Scot—from Fife.'

'"The thane of Fife had a wife: where is she now?" You see, I remember something from all that Shakespeare at school. That's what I heard in your voice, then, an echo of Fife.'

'And you are from Glasgow,' I said, 'or thereabouts.'

He put the cards away and we began to talk, really talk, as the daylight faded and the train rattled along in the dusk. Every so often I wondered if my sons—either of them—would have talked so openly to a strange woman of my age. Students talk to me sometimes, it's true. Young people like to talk to you, Mother, my daughter said once. I wanted to tell her—even your father, when he was young.

The boy—Donald—had been married for three months; his wife taught maths at a secondary school. He bought her a bike for a wedding present and they went cycling in the Western Isles. It was brilliant, that trip, he said, rolling his *r* 's.

'Why does that make you cry?' he said, and put his hand over mine.

He went to the buffet car and got us each a drink. In the Ladies my cheeks were pink, as though I had a fever.

His grandmother died in July and he still couldn't think of her without become tearful. His grandmother! How could you not trust someone who talked so about his grandmother?

I was twice his age and yet we had both read all of Robert Louis Stevenson, most of Poe, Jack London, the Swallows and Amazons books.

'Your hair is a lovely colour,' he said.

'I help it along a bit now,' I said. It was a lovely colour on its own not long ago.'

He was studying to be an electrical engineer and every so often he was sent, by the firm, up to a place beyond Inverness. He always took his bike. On the classified pages of *The Lady* he drew diagrams, trying earnestly to explain exactly what it was he did up there. I watched his hands with their freckled backs.

'When do you leave for home?' he said, without looking up from his elaborate drawings of circuits.

'That stuff's lost on me,' I said, 'I couldn't get beyond algebra and Train A and Train B heading towards each other at different speeds—when would they crash.' I wanted him to look up, to look at me with his blue Spanish eyes, but he continued drawing.

'Next week,' I said, 'But before that I'm treating myself to a room at the North British Hotel so I can walk around Princess

Gardens looking at all the free Fringe events.'

'Ah, the pull of the city, the crowds, the grease-paint. I can understand that. But you shouldn't turn your back on the mountains so soon. Have you never explored the Grampians or the Cairngorms?'

Now he looked at me and put the pencil down.

When he suggested I get off at Kingussie and spend another day or two in the mountains I nodded and thanked him for his advice. Why not, I thought, why not? At the station he handed me down my bag and my wheeled cart, kissed me. Have you ever held your hand over a candle flame? He wished me *bon voyage*.

The taxi driver took me to a small hotel where I asked for a room at the front. Then I went upstairs, had a sweet, slow bath and changed my clothes. I sang in the bathtub: 'please please don't cry. This is just adios and not goodbye.' I sang the song all the way through and then I started again. Blue Spanish eyes, dum dum de dum de dum of Mexico. I told the landlady my son was on a cycling tour and perhaps he would join me later. I saw him from the upstairs window and ran down to meet him.

Late that night we went for a walk beyond the town. A gentle rain was falling, more like a cool web than any rain I had ever felt before. The air smelled of rain and of heather.

Then the rain stopped and he took my hand.

'See,' he said, 'even the moon is lying on her back.'

That was the first of several lovely days we spent in that wild country.

W.D. VALGARDSON

The Cave

I first came upon Sigga Anderson at her cousin's farm. I had knocked on the screen door and got no reply, so I went around to the back and there, wearing a wide-brimmed hat, a white dress and no shoes, she was picking raspberries. I must have made some slight sound, for she glanced up.

Her blond hair was curled to her shoulders. Her skin was damp and pink with the heat and her lips were red with the juice of the berries she had eaten. We stared at each other without saying anything, then she rose and held the white enamel bowl toward me. The berries were piled so high that some cascaded down and dropped to the ground.

'*Godan daginn*,' she said.

'*Godan daginn*,' I said.

'*Tala thu Islenzku?*'

'*Nay*,' I replied.

'That's too bad,' she said, in the slightly ponderous way that Icelanders have of speaking English. 'You are Valgardson. I recognize you from Einar's description.'

'Is Einar home?'

'They've all gone to the beach.'

'But not you.'

'Would you have me roasted alive? I'm not used to the sun yet.'

'And the mosquitoes?'

'They're devils.'

She put the white basin into my hand and lifted up her dress for me to look. Her legs were spotted with angry-looking lumps. Iceland does not have mosquitoes, and Icelanders who come to Canada suffer terrible reactions when they are first stung.

'Has Einar any beer in the well?' I asked. She let down her dress. 'It was a long ride on my bicycle.'

She was, I discovered, twenty, single and quick-tempered. The last did not keep me from making daily trips to Einar's. Nor was I deterred by the fact she was Gunnar Thordarson's great-granddaughter.

We went walking in the hayfields together and along the edge of the poplar bush, picking wild roses and Indian paintbrush and wild lilies. We filled buckets with berries.

More and more often, though, our trips ended at one of Einar's haystacks. At mealtimes and in the evenings, there were good-natured comments around the table about the work it took to make a good stack and how, if the tops were thrown about, the hay would not survive the rain and snow.

Until then I had not even considered marriage. As a matter of fact, I had frequently bragged that I would not marry until I was thirty and well established. Since I still had three years to go, my relationship with Sigga caused some sly comments and smiles.

By late August, I no longer cared about looking foolish. Quite confidently, I asked her to marry me. I didn't go down on bended knee. It would have been quite impractical. We had just made love and were lying on top of one of Einar's precious haystacks. It is one of those special times I remember with painful clarity.

There were three small, fluffy clouds sliding slowly westward. There was no sound except for the occasional shifting in the hay. I was laying with one arm under my head, the other around Sigga.

If I remember the incident as clearly as I think I do, I said, 'If you wanted, we could get married before school starts.'

'No.' She said it so quietly and agreeably that, at first, I took it for assent. When it finally registered that I had been refused, I rolled toward her to look into her pale green eyes.

'Sooner?'

'Not sooner. Not later.'

I felt as though my heart had stopped. I would have been angry except that I was so taken aback. 'But I love you,' I protested.

'Yes,' she agreed.

'And you love me?'

'Yes.'

With that, my heart started to beat again. Or, at least, I became aware that it was still working.

'Then why in heaven's name . . .' I had been so sure of her reply that I had already rented a small log cabin behind the school. It had a kitchen, living room and two small bedrooms. There were red shutters on the windows and a natural stone chimney. It had taken all my persuasiveness to convince the owner, who lived in Winnipeg and used it for a summer cottage, to let me have it from September until the end of June. 'I've rented Brynolver's cabin,' I blurted out.

'Good. Living there with you will be nice.'

'Then, for God's sake, let's get married.'

She let her eyes slide away from mine. 'No. I would like to live with you, but I won't marry.'

'Are you crazy?'

It was not a good thing to say. I felt her stiffen. I had momentarily forgotten that her great-grandfather had been Gunnar Thordarson and that her father was Valdi Anderson.

There are times to be silent. I lay back and studied the pale blue sky. Normally, Sigga would have curled against my side but now, although she remained with her head on my arm, her body was stiff.

'Remember the roses,' I said.

One day after she had fallen asleep, I slid down the haystack, ran to the side of the road, and using my shirt like a sack, filled it with the petals of wild roses. I returned, scattered them over her naked, golden body. When she awoke and sat up, rose petals filled her lap, clung to her hair. We made love again and the bruised petals engulfed us in their sweet scent.

'If I marry, my husband will want sons. I will have no sons.'

Earlier, the thought that I had a rival had made my head ring with jealousy. Now, I suddenly wished it were that simple.

'I'm a high school teacher. If we live together, the board will have fits.'

'I had promised myself to care for no one,' she answered quietly. 'Then you appeared with your one pant leg held in place with a bicycle clip.'

'I had promised not to marry until I was thirty and then only to a widow with a good income.'

'It was your beard and the shocked look in your eyes.' She squeezed my hand.

'This is madness,' I answered.

'If only it weren't,' she answered and began to cry.

If this were a piece of fiction, all this description would be irrelevant detail. I would follow Poe's dictum and start closer to the climax. I would organize it toward one effect and ruthlessly eliminate everything else. But it is not fiction. What matters is not plot or theme but only that you understand. To ask, for example, 'What is your motive?' of someone is to imply a simplicity about life that, except for the stupidest of people, is hopelessly inaccurate.

What was my motive in researching the lives of Sigga's great-grandfather and father? To prove that they were not crazy? To reassure Sigga that if she was to have a son, he would escape their fate? To reassure myself of the same thing? To defuse the innuendo and gossip that have persisted about this family for over seventy years? And more. Some of which I, myself, am still not clear about.

Life, unfortunately, is not as tractable as fiction. I cannot invent my characters or their lives. They already exist. I can only attempt to discover and understand.

I began by visiting people I knew. There was nothing formal about it, nothing, at first, even deliberate. I'd drop by for coffee and, after we were settled around the kitchen table, ask questions about Gunnar and Valdi.

It was unproductive. Not so much because everyone was deliberately evasive, but because each person had such small fragments of Gunnar and Valdi's lives. At times, I felt like I was collecting the parts of a shattered stained glass window, the pieces of which had been picked up by people over the years and tucked away in drawers or cupboards. Some had forgotten where they put them, others still knew where they were and, if I was lucky, would go get them to give to me. Some, because of the passage of time, had mixed them up with pieces of glass from other windows and gave me fragments that caused nothing but confusion. Some pieces were never picked up and were irretrievably lost.

If it was not for the fact that Sigga discovered and gave me a fish box full of Gunnar's diaries and letters, plus her father's correspondence, I would have given up. These records were not complete. However, to stick to my stained glass analogy, these records provided the lead in the window.

Because I'm a short story writer—W.D. Valgardson is hardly a name to conjure with, but here and there, people have read my stories—I'm very conscious that if this were fiction, I'd not begin like this, with a lot of explanation and excuse making. Instead, I'd go right to the heart of the story and I'd leave myself out of it, become an effaced narrator, or if I used the first person, it would not really be me, but a mask.

One of the first things you learn in telling a story is to condense time for dramatic effect, but how can I condense four generations? In a piece of fiction, I cast about for the right structure, the method of telling the story that will get me closest to the truth. This research and retelling in which I have been involved has nearly driven me to distraction because there is no structure except the one that life has imposed, and if there is any lesson about life, it escapes me. What I have finally resolved to do is to take the coward's way out—tell the story in a reasonably chronological fashion.

My beginning is arbitrary. I chose it because there is a major change in the lives of the main participants, but I could equally as well have begun elsewhere. In life there are no real beginnings or endings. There are so many moments where one can say, 'That's where it started,' and, in most cases, it is both true and false. Life is nothing if not untidy.

GUNNAR AND RUNA

Gunnar's family owned a good-sized farm, Hagar,[1] but the volcanic eruptions of 1875 reduced it to half its size. Just before the eruption, Gunnar had married Helga Jonsdottir. The marriage, by all accounts, was an unhappy one. Both were quick-tempered and proud. They took offence easily and were slow to give up grudges. Helga's father was, in Icelandic terms, well-to-do, and one day, when Gunnar—his family nearly reduced to penury by the destruction of their land—refused Helga something she wanted, she said she would ask her father for it. Enraged, he slapped her. She picked up a knife and, if being six months pregnant had not made her awkward, would have killed him. Instead, she left him with a cut that ran from his eye to his jaw. Sometime during the next week, with the help of a farmhand, she returned to her father's house.

Gunnar followed her and tried to force her to return home with him. Her relatives stopped him. He began to drink heavily and, at every opportunity, to abuse his wife's family with scathing verses that he recited to anyone who would listen. Then, abruptly, after his wife gave birth, Gunnar's behaviour changed. He called on her—sober, repentant, his voice gentle—gave her silver equal to the price of a cow. He no longer tried to get his wife back, but from time to time, he visited Reykjavik to see his

[1] Icelandic word for meadow. Icelandic farms were all named. The tradition was so strong it was carried to Canada.

daughter and to leave *skyr*[2] and mutton. Because of what had occurred, he would not enter his in-laws' house. Instead, he and Helga walked with the child to the home of mutual friends. This went on for two years.

Then, abruptly, Gunnar sold his farm and notified his wife that he intended to give the child part of the money from the sale. He also told her he was emigrating to North America. Two days before he was to leave, he arrived at his in-laws' front door and asked his wife if he might spend some time alone with the child. It was unlikely, as he pointed out, that he would ever see her again.

His behaviour had been so exemplary that Helga agreed. Besides, Gunnar's ship was not due to arrive for another day. They were gone all afternoon, but Helga was not overly concerned. She expected that Gunnar was going from house to house saying goodbye to his friends. However, when supper time came and passed, she began to worry. She put on her coat and went to see if she could find them.

It was too late. Gunnar and Runa were already on their way to Denmark on a small freighter. His planning was meticulous and must have been started shortly after his daughter was born.

GUNNAR AND RUNA IN WINNIPEG

Gunnar and Runa arrived in Halifax on July 23, 1878. They travelled from there to Toronto, stayed in Toronto three months and arrived in Winnipeg on October 28. Egil Fjelsted was a child at the time. He went with his father to the CPR station to meet them. He was very young and did not actually remember their arrival, but afterward he heard about it so often that he said it was as if he remembered it.[3]

October was no time to be arriving in Winnipeg. Summer construction and farm work were over. Gunnar spoke hardly any English, so most nonlabouring jobs were closed to him. He and

[2]An Icelandic yogurt.
[3]Fjelsted, Egil. Died, Betal, Gimli, Manitoba, 1968.

Runa boarded in the West End at the Fjelsteds' until Crooked Eye Oddleifson turned up.

Oddleifson was a barrel of a man, slope-shouldered, with big, shovel-like hands and one eye that turned in so much he appeared to be looking at his own nose. He hired Gunnar to help him with fishing. No one else would go. Oddleifson's camp was more isolated than most. He had a reputation for feeding his help poorly, working them hard and, if he could get away with it, not paying their wages. That Gunnar accepted the job indicated how desperate he was becoming.

He could not take Runa. Even if she could survive the hundred and fifty-mile trek in the cold, the camp was no place for a child. The two men would leave every day before dawn and stay on the ice until dark. Reluctantly, he agreed to leave her in Mrs Fjelsted's care.

GUNNAR AND ODDLEIFSON
The weather was bitter. Ten degrees below zero during the day. Thirty below at night. Oddleifson had brought a horse and a sleigh but used it only for supplies. To keep warm, they walked. Fort Garry, Gimli, Icelandic River, Mikley and, finally, all the way to the camp. They slept at stopping places along the way. Breakfast they got from the owners of the houses, but lunch and supper were bread and smoked fish they kept inside their jackets so it wouldn't freeze.

It must have been a frightening experience for a man like Gunnar, who, in Iceland, was used to staying close to his own farm. Day after day, he walked over endless miles of drifted snow. In his diary, he compares it to entering a white hell. Before they reached the camp, he became snow-blind, and Oddleifson had to tie a rope around his waist and attach it to the sleigh. Gunnar was forced to follow helplessly, sometimes walking, sometimes running, frequently falling, while, behind him, the known world retreated.

The camp was worse than he expected. It was one room

carelessly kept. Life in a fish camp was hard enough, but Oddleifson was dirty without need. What he could have done to make life more bearable, he did not do.

The two men did not get along well. Oddleifson had been described by others as insensitive, even brutal. Because of his eye, he had a strange way of turning his head to one side and hunching his shoulders. It earned him a second nickname of 'the Bull'.

Gunnar, besides being a farmer, had been a poet of some reputation. Moreover, he was well educated and sensitive. Having to live day in and day out with Oddleifson, with his gross habits and crude conversation, must have been difficult. How it would have worked out was never discovered, because three months after they began fishing together, Crooked Eye put an ice chisel through his foot. His uncleanliness did him in. The wound infected, and within a week, he died.

Now, do you see what is so maddening? It is as if everything is connected and yet nothing is connected. Do you know what I mean? If this were a piece of fiction, I could have foreshadowed, dramatized and then subtly not revealed what actually happened. You would have deduced that Gunnar, isolated, angered, actually killed Oddleifson. There would be an epiphany and you and I would share a secret understanding of men's hearts.

I can do no such thing. I can find no evidence that Gunnar stuck an ice chisel through Oddleifson's foot, rubbed it with horse shit and then waited for him to die.

Nor can I make anything of the fact Gunnar did not go for help. Given the distance and the weather, there was no point in trying to take Oddleifson in on the sleigh, even if he had permitted it. What Gunnar did do, once Oddleifson was dead, was haul his body onto the roof of the shed so that the animals could not get at it, then each day, as his work permitted, chiselled frozen ground until he had a grave.

At this point, Gunnar was faced with a choice. He could return to Winnipeg and a winter's unemployment or he could stay by himself in the camp. He had received no payment for his work and, if anything, was worse off than he had been before. He chose to stay.

Although he did not realize it, the pattern of his life was set.[4] He lived in the camp and fished fall and winter. July he spent with Runa at the Fjelsteds'. A number of times, as Runa grew older, he talked of having her come and live with him, but Mrs Fjelsted would not hear of it.

During his second year in the camp, he decided something that, at the time, seemed of no significance, and yet it ultimately affected him more than anything else he had done. His problem and his attempt to solve it was this.

During the winter, he kept his perishable food on the roof. Once the spring thaw set in, however, he had no way of keeping food fresh.

He began to search the limestone cliffs along the lake for a cave. What he hoped to find was one deep enough that if it was packed with ice and snow, would keep food frozen through the warm months. He searched for days and was on the point of giving up when he found what he was looking for—but in a most extraordinary way.

Along with being a poet, he had always been something of a mystic. Perhaps that's why events took the turn they did. He became ill, suffered nightmares and existed, for a time, in that half-asleep, half-awake mixture of reality and fantasy that leaves one uncertain of one's own sanity, for in it the familiar world shifts and changes into a quicksand of images. Finally, the fever broke and he slept soundly. During this sleep, he had a dream, and in this dream, he claims he found the entrance to the cave. The cliff appeared before him in great detail, as though it were magnified. He scrutinized the cliff, checking and rechecking all the cracks, then stopped before a place where the rock was thick

[4]There was an attempt some years later by a cousin of Oddleifson's to claim the camp as an inheritance. However, he was in Iceland, and Lake Winnipeg was a great distance away. When Gunnar heard of the claim, he only replied, 'Let him come and get it.'

with moss. There seemed to be nothing of interest there, but then the moss darkened and the rocks slanted inward.

When he woke, he remembered the dream clearly. However, he was still weak with fever and did not go out for another three days. Each night, as if it had a life of its own, the dream returned. When, at last, he was well enough to go out, the first thing he did was row a boat along the lake shore to the spot where the dream had taken him. When he came to a section of rock of which he had dreamt, it was as he remembered it. In the dream, as he had reached out to pull away the moss, he had always awakened, but now there was no waking. He felt the moss thick and moist under his fingertips; felt it tear in a long sheet. Here was a fissure that was just big enough for him to enter by angling his shoulders sideways.

He first thought it only a crack, but then, it widened. The air was cold. He went back to the beach, found a long strip of birch bark, set it afire and, using it like a torch, explored the narrow cave. Five feet from the entrance, the floor was a solid slab of ice. Where there were cracks in the ceiling, icicles hung down like stalactites. He was so excited by his discovery that in his diary, he exclaims, 'What a find! Now, I can keep food all year if I wish.'[5]

During the next winter, his only visitors were freighters who came to load his fish. He did not mind. He had brought with him a small library, and although most of his money went for Runa's support, he bought philosophical books that dealt, in one way or the other, with the existence of reality.

None fascinated him more than the theory of Bjorn Bjornson,[6] who claimed the soul never slept but inhabited bodies in two worlds and passed back and forth between them. What we call madness was not, according to this theorist, the inability to tell what was real and what was hallucination but a leakage of information from one existence to another.

[5] July 6, 1879.
[6] Bjornson, Bjorn, 1750-1797, *Souls Adrift*, Oslo, private printing, 57 pp.

There is very little description of Gunnar's appearance and no photograph. We know that toward the end of 1910 he grew a full beard. His grey hair he let grow until it reached his shoulders. He wore a beaded deerhide jacket, which he had bought from the Indians. That is known because Axel Arnason, the freighter, recorded this in a report to his sister in a letter.[7]

At first, the cave was no more than a convenience, a place to keep deer and moose meat and enough fish to supply his huskies during the spring and fall when he could not get on the water. It was only later that it became an obsession.

During the winter of 1914, Axel Arnason arrived to pick up fish. There was no one in the cabin. That, in itself, meant nothing. Gunnar could be on the lake or in the bush. Axel lit the fire and waited. No one came, and as he said in his deposition to the police,[8] after a time he became nervous. The sleigh was outside the door, but there was no sign of the dogs. There were no tracks in the snow and there had been a heavy snowfall a week before.

He went outside, kicked at a mound of snow and found a dead husky. Then another and another, all still chained to their ground pegs. In the lean-to, the horse had frozen to death standing up.

It took the police a month to get a man out to the camp. There was no rush. Gunnar was certainly dead, probably under the ice or frozen in the snowdrift. His belongings were collected and put in fish boxes and shipped to Runa.

Gunnar's Diary
—translated by Miss S. Stephanson

August 18, 1911
The cave is seventy-five feet long, ten feet high at its highest point and four feet across. Its general shape is that of a canoe with blunt ends.

[7]Icelandic collection, University of Manitoba.
[8]RCMP archives, Regina, Saskatchewan.

August 19, 1911
I returned to the cave today. This time I took a better
torch, which I fashioned from reeds and pitch. The walls
are thick with the past. It is like memory frozen in stone.
Animals and plants bleached white. I made some
sketches.

His diary, more and more, records the details of the cave. He
made a grid of string so that floor, walls, roof, were divided into
three-inch squares. Each segment he mapped. At the same time,
his recording of weather, of nets, of fish, begins to fall off.

Gradually, intertwined with his studies, grew the thesis for his
essay 'The Seasons and the Blood'. From his reading, he began
to collect every example that would prove history is cyclical and
that the future can be predicted from the past. In 1939, Runa
discovered this essay, made a copy and offered it to a number of
Scandinavian publishers; however, arriving as it did in the face
of a rapidly advancing technological age whose justification for
its excesses lay in the assumption that time is linear and all
change leads to improvement, it was rejected.

September 20, 1911
Today, I smashed through the curtain of ice at the rear
of the cave. My axe discovered a narrow slit in the rock
that I could hardly squeeze through. What is there?

What was there, he discovered, was a series of caves, a
labyrinthine honeycomb that underlay the entire area. The surface looked, from above, impervious, solid, real, but although it
supported infinite trees, marshes and animals, its solidity was
only illusion. It was a secret world discovered by dreams, a secret
world that altered his whole concept of reality.

For a time, he was satisfied to do no more than recalculate his
earlier findings, refining and rechecking his measurements of the
antechamber. On sheets of brown wrapping paper, he sketched
each fossil in detail. He began to keep track of the waxing and

waning of the ice. He planned to order finely calibrated instruments so that he could measure the annual lengthening of the stalactites.

The new entrance became a torment, a question demanding an answer. In December 1911, he was determined to block this entrance with stone. A week later, he was equally determined to squeeze through with a torch and a rope. In March he had still not committed himself, but he recorded that he had had a series of nightmares, all to do with his vacillation. Finally, at the end of May, forced into idleness by a spring thaw, he gathered five hundred feet of string, a hundred feet of stout rope, a lantern, four pitons made from ring bolts and a hand axe. He also took a dozen matches, a pound of mixed raisins and two *hardfisk*.

He drove a piton into a crevice close to the entrance, fastened the string to it, then forced his way into a small cavern that led downward to a larger cavern, which he described as big as the biggest whale.

The diary for the next two years is missing, but a letter to his daughter dated January 1914 stated that he had explored numerous caves, each one unique and full of wonders. In one there was a pool, and from it, he caught blind fish. He added that he was afraid but that he could not stop. 'As much as I have learned the secrets of the earth,' he said, 'I have learned more about myself.'

On the table the day Axel the freighter discovered the empty cabin, the dead dogs and horse, was this cryptic note:

'To the farthest depth . . .'

RUNA
By the time Gunnar had disappeared, Runa was married and had a son called Valdi. For some years, Gunnar had not come to town. The only communication between him and Runa were his infrequent letters. The result was that when he disappeared he was little missed. The few times he had visited his daughter, he had spent most of his time in his room sitting at the window and

smoking his pipe. Silence had become a habit with him. Over the years the Fjelsteds had become Runa's true family.

The boxes of Gunnar's belongings were stored in the attic of Runa's Sargeant Avenue house. There they would have stayed if it had not been for Valdi.

VALDI ANDERSON

Runa's son became a teacher and taught for a year at Hecla.

It was there that, for the first time, he heard the Fjelsteds were not his blood relatives. The shock was so great that, for time, he refused to believe what he had been told. At last, on a weekend trip to Winnipeg, he confronted his mother, who reluctantly admitted that his grandfather had been Gunnar. When he pressed her, she refused to talk about it.

'Leave it,' she cried. 'You did not know him. I did not know him. What does it matter?'

'It matters.'

'The Fjelsteds loved me.'

'What was he like?'

'I don't know.'

He was still young and filled with the anger that seethes within the young like unexplained fire. He began to shout.

'Are you ashamed of him?'

'No. It's not that.'

'Then what?'

'He lived. He died. I hardly saw him.'

'How did he die?'

'I don't know.' Runa, who was unused to confrontation, began to wring her hands. Her own early sense of abandonment, her own fears, welled up like debris that had been hidden beneath the waters of a deep lake and suddenly stirred. 'Nobody knows.'

Like his maternal grandfather, Valdi was large. Like him, too, he could take offence easily and nurse a grudge.

His mother, desperate to stop the questions, thought of the boxes under the eaves. She offered him these in return for peace.

There were three wooden fish boxes filled with letters, books, drawings and diaries. Valdi impatiently pulled loose the lids, certain that what had been hidden would now be revealed.

'I can't read this,' he said.

Everything was in Icelandic.

In spite of this defeat, he took the boxes with him. Perhaps he was afraid that his mother would burn the contents, then deny their existence. From time to time, he returned to the boxes, puzzling over the carefully executed drawings of trilobites, clam shells, a feathery leaf. The books and diaries were dry and brittle, the paper yellow, the letters as fragile as last fall's leaves.

Caught up in the rush of teaching and marriage, he was too busy to pay much attention to these relics, but still, they posed a question. It was not the kind of question that demanded an answer but the kind that nagged, the way the picture of a small, ragged child begging will nag at the conscience of the well fed.

Do you see what I mean about this task? God help me. What love will drive a man to do. There are too many characters. Everybody gets involved. Already we've got four generations. Gunnar—Runa—Valdi—Sigga. Why can I not just condense it, make it less messy? There is no unity of time or place. Aristotle, wherever you are, give God some good advice. Tell Him to get organized.

Here's Valdi so busy teaching classes, grading papers, screwing his pretty little wife from Akureyri, taking classes for his certificate, repairing the roof, that he sets aside these three bloody boxes and, now and again, late at night, looks them over, promising himself that when he gets time, he'll learn to read and write Icelandic and translate them. I keep wanting to shout 'Action. Get on with it. To hell with the picnic. To hell with going to Gimli for *Islindingadagurinn*. Never mind that damn birthday party.'

Five years passed. How's that for a transition? Bugger the details, the character development, go for the main point. Five years passed, and damned if he didn't start to take Icelandic lessons in 1944 when he got a job teaching in Winnipeg at Kelvin High School. Twice a week, he took lessons with Rev. V.J. Eylands, D.D.[9] At last—in spite of the protests of his wife, who wanted him to get rid of the papers—little by little, he began to translate.

The more he read, the more the idea of the cave took hold. He began to question every elderly person he came across who might know some part of his grandfather's story. Soon he began to seek these people out. He followed rumours. He wrote letters.

He began to dream about the cave. From the notes and diagrams, he knew it more intimately than his own house. Awake, he found it intruding upon his thoughts. When he was certain he had pinpointed the location of the cabin, he bought a boat.

On a weekend at the end of July, he drove to Pine Dock. The road began in pavement, changed to gravel and finally dwindled to one lane of mud. Beside a sagging dock, an old woman lived in an abandoned ice shed. He saw her face behind a dusty window, but she refused to answer his knock. A black goat was tethered to a tree stump. He slept in his car. Before dawn, he slid his boat into the dark water. He travelled slowly, staying close to the shore and keeping the map on his knee. The forest pressed to the very edge of the lake. When he reached his destination and shut off his motor, the silence amazed him.

He was rewarded with the remains of a log cabin. The roof had collapsed and rotted away, but the silvered walls were still standing. Grass grew thickly from the mud floor. Outside the walls, grass and moose maple filled what had been a clearing. He could, when he closed his eyes, see the ice-covered window, the frozen dogs, the snow drifting in ragged lines over the ground. He returned the next weekend with his wife and daughter. He cleared a twenty-foot circle around the cabin. The

[9]Dr Valdimar J. Eylands, an able preacher and writer. A leader in the Icelandic community.

discovery of the rusted remains of the metal pegs that had held the dogs excited him.

He did not have to teach until September, so he returned to Winnipeg, bought enough supplies to last him a month and returned by himself. Because of the cold wind off the lake, he set up his tent inside the cabin walls. A day after he arrived, he began his search. For all the details in the diary about the cave itself, the precise location was never described.

The shoreline was in ruins. Great columns of limestone had been weathered from the cliffs. Trees grew in profusion. He was not discouraged. He knew that the entrance could not be far away. A half-mile in either direction was the outside limit. A greater distance would have made transporting supplies difficult.

Clambering over the rocks was strenuous. At first, he had to rest frequently. As the days passed, he grew stronger and was able to search for hours on end. He took three rolls of film. He also had collected all the information about the area that he could find. It did not surprise him that there was no mention of caves. Knowledge, he had discovered during his academic career, looked extensive only until a specific answer was sought.

In the middle of August, he found a number of false leads, caves that disappointed him by going only a short distance before stopping. On August 25, he found a cave he thought was the one for which he was looking. On August 26, measurements demonstrated that it was not the right cave. When he was ready to give up, he found, in his grandfather's dreams, the clue he needed.

He closed his eyes and constructed for himself the cliffs as he remembered them. When he returned to the cliffs, he realized his memory had been inaccurate. Rather than continue his earlier fruitless physical search, he sat just offshore in his boat and watched the cliffs until he was certain their image was printed on his mind. Twice more he had to return, but then he lay on the grass before the log cabin and slept. In his sleep, he saw the entire cliff in every detail. A purple shadow and the slant of some rocks told him what he needed to know.

On August 30, he used a crowbar to clear the entrance. The cave was not as long as it had been, but he knew immediately that he was in the right place. His grandfather's piton he found embedded in ice.

He played his light over the entrance to the deeper caves. The walls were all highlights and shadows. Ahead was darkness and the unknown. Overwhelmed by his fear of being lost in the maze that he knew stretched before him, he resolved to return home and burn his grandfather's materials.

The next morning, he changed his mind. Instead of starting south, he entered the cave. He took with him fifteen hundred feet of blue thread to unroll as he went. The time of his leaving is known, for he wrote it down to the minute: 6:15, August 31.

Six months later, his wife returned to Iceland with Sigga. There Sigga stayed until just before we met at Einar's farm and had our summer together.

Because of her refusal to marry me, because of who we were, because of the times, our relationship did not last. I searched, during this time we had together, God help me, I searched, trying to find answers so that she need have no fears, but I could not then and cannot now make any sense out of it. No epiphany. Not for me. Not for you.

Sigga left. One day I went to work. When I came back, she was gone. A year after, I heard that she was living in Iceland. I wrote again and again but never received a reply.

I married someone else. That didn't work out either. We're separated and waiting for a divorce. I doubt if being married to anyone would have worked out. Sigga was too much in my heart. That summer we had together, drenched in passion and colour, made everyone and everything seem pale by comparison. Still, as the years passed, even Sigga faded.

Then a week ago, a letter arrived. I was from a Ragnar Williamson. He is, he says, my son. Sigga, he informs me, is dead. Cancer.

His mother was pregnant when she left here. She returned to Iceland, bore him, raised him, never married, never told him who his father was. Now, with a great deal of effort, he has tracked me down.

He is coming to visit me. He wants, above all, to learn about his family.

RUDY WIEBE

A Night in Fort Pitt
OR (IF YOU PREFER)
The Only Perfect Communists in the World

Late one November evening in the thirty-third year of the reign of Queen Victoria, a solitary horseman might have been seen riding along the hills that parallel the North Saskatchewan River. He had been riding west since before daybreak, but now long after sunset the giant sweep of the frozen river suddenly confronted him, forcing him south, or as nearly south as he could surmise from the stars that glittered occasionally, momentarily, between storm clouds. And the wind which had been threatening snow all day now roared, it seemed, with a malignant fury up the cliff down whose steep slope he could not risk his exhausted horse, though he knew that he must somewhere, somehow get across the valley if he was to find shelter at Fort Pitt, the only white settlement along three hundred miles of river between Fort Carlton and Victoria House.

The night before the rider and his small party had endured among bare poplars in the fold of a creek; when they emerged that morning onto the prairie before dawn to continue their journey, they discovered the entire sky brilliant with aurora, torn sheets of light gently glowing and leaping into blaze above them and smouldering away again. The man had stopped his horse, watched, stunned; felt himself shrink as it were into and then grow incandescent in that immense dome of brilliance until sunrise burned it into sheer light, and he became aware that his Indian guide and Métis companion had vanished into the apparently flat earth; leaving nothing but the line of their passing in the hoary grass. The quick winter afternoon was already darkening before he caught up with them in their relentless track. The radiance of aurora still informed him and he told them they had veered too far south; sunset perhaps verified his perception, for after the long day's ride they still had not encountered the river. He refused to accept another night in the open and swung onto his weary mount. His men had already unburdened theirs, preparing to weather the storm they insisted was driving up from the west in a brushy hollow. So they watched him ride west alone, the prairie so open he could inevitably be found if lost, as impatient and as superior with all necessary knowledge as every white man they had ever met, riding into darkness following stars.

And now in stinging snow the stars were lost, though it did not matter since he had found the North Saskatchewan River. Well, it did matter, because he knew that every Hudson's Bay settlement was on the north bank; he must cross over the river or he would miss Pitt, he could ride as far as he had already ridden in a month, another five hundred miles across prairie into the glacial mountains themselves and not encounter a white man. As if at the thought, his horse stopped. No urging could move it so he slid off, straightening his long legs against the ground with a groan. The horse turned its long, squarish head to him, nudged him, breaking the icicles off its nostrils against his buffalo coat and then finding the warmth of his armpit. Perhaps this hammer-headed bay from Fort Carlton could become as good a companion to him as Blackie had been—the storm shifted an instant and he realized they were on a point of cliff. Perhaps a tributary cut its way into the river here as steeply as the main river. Where was he? Even if he got down into the valley, if Fort Pitt was built half a mile back from the river in a bend like Fort Carlton, he would never find it. He sheltered his crusted eyes against the whistling snow that enclosed him: the air seemed as solid as any frozen prairie. He would walk on it easily as dreaming out into the sky. . . .

The cheekstrap of the bridle hit his frozen face when the horse moved. He felt that, his arm slid onto its neck.

> He knew he could not lose this one certain warm body also, his mittens clamped onto its stiff mane and so suddenly he was led forward and down, sideways and down, the incline almost vertical and shifting like relentless sand, but that one body was solidly with him, there, whenever they slipped they slid closer together, their six feet all one and always somehow set certainly into the side of that incline of what might be rock or frozen clay, deadly as ice, but so reliable, so trustworthy he would never let go of this horse, never leap aside even if river ice parted into water as it had when he leaped from Blackie sinking, scrambled to safety while seeing his horse sink into blackness and there was its beautiful head bursting up, its front legs, neck arched, and knees clawing ice with its deadly shod feet, trying to climb up into the bright air by sheer terror, nostrils flaring bloody and the ice smashing now again and again in ringing iron, and he turned away, sprinted for his rifle—he was an English soldier, soldiers can always offer the ultimate mercy of running for their bloody rifles—and he knelt there expert sharpshooter on the white, deceptive ice until the shots hammered back at him tripled from the cliffs and the long water ran flat again and implacably empty; on his knees, crying.

But this hammer-head bay led him so easily down . . . down five hundred feet or a thousand—instinctively he was counting steps, an officer must always carry some facts, even if they are estimated—and they scrambled out between broken boulders (or were they frozen buffalo?) and there was river ice again, certainly, hard as the cliff here and he was still clutching the horse. But with his arms and legs now, completely, and it moved with his frozen face in its mane, he could smell prairie slough hay, hear scrub oaks at Fort Garry scarlet as cardinals in October light, the chant of *Te Deum* prayed by monks in a roofless Irish ruin, and he became aware that the sting of snow had quietened: there was an upthrust darkness moving beside him, a dense blackness and he loosened one hand, reached out: it was most certainly the usual twenty-foot spruce palisade. Never anything in stone like the permanent ruins of Ireland. And a gate in the wooden wall; hanging open. Perhaps the Indians here were all dead, the gates hanging so open.

The bay followed him through that hanging gate like any dog and the storm was so abruptly quiet he felt himself breathing. High peaked roofs, gabled, around a square, he could not distinguish a light or a sound. Perhaps smallpox had discovered them all, Indian and Métis and white alike, as in Fort Carlton. Winter would keep the bodies perfectly, death already blossomed over them like spring flowers. He limped across the open square to avoid what lay at the edge of every shadow, what might move, dreadfully: a door, darkness in the centre building. He seemed to have reached the heart of something, corpses were keening all around him, at the very hoared edges of his fur cap and he wheeled around, listening. But there was only his own small breathing, nothing but the horse snoring, bent low like grass behind him. So he turned back to the door and began to pound on it. Nothing. The plank door would not budge to his fists, its cracks blacker than its wood, and he tilted forward, hands, face clutching the frame, they were all dead, O open up, *o miserere mei* . . . he heard a sound. Inside. Against his face an opening, of light, the skin of a face, a young woman's face. Impossibly beautiful.

Such materializations are possible out of the driving blackness of a prairie blizzard, lantern-light and such sudden woman's beauty as perfect as it is unbelievable? He found himself bending forward slowly, past the worn planks of the doorframe, tilting slowly into her light, his frozen cheek, his still tactile tongue . . . and felt . . . nothing. Those eyes, the black brows and exquisite nose, was it white, that skin in the golden light? Was it believable though impossible?

It is possible that when Lieutenant General, the Right Honourable Sir William Francis Butler, Knight Grand Cross of the Order of the Bath and member of the Privy Council of Ireland died in his bed in Bansha Castle, County Tipperary, on June 7, 1910, died as his daughter then wrote, 'of a recent affection of the heart . . . that was brought to a crisis by a chill', it is possible that on his deathbed thirty-nine and a half years later Sir William could still not decide: was that face he instantly loved at Fort Pitt on the North Saskatchewan River in the North-Western Territories of Canada on November 18, 1870, loved as only the truest Victorian male who believed all his life that Jesus Christ and Napoleon Bonaparte were the greatest men in all of human history could love, a latter day romantic when romanticism was still acceptable in a male if he was also practical and above all heroic, dear god, was a man who championed the innocent and detested the brutalities of war all his life while becoming one of Victoria's most honoured and decorated soldiers, a member of Field Marshal Wolseley's brilliant Officers Ring that fought for the Empire on four continents, and who dreamed for forty years of 'the Great Lone Land' as he called the Canadian prairie and never saw again and idealized every Indian person he lived near for those few months in 1870 and 1871 when they were either dying of smallpox or more or less starving despite their unselfish greedless tradition of sharing everything, which makes Indians, as he wrote then, 'the only perfect communists in the world, who, if they would only be as the Africans or the Asiatics it would be all right for them; if they would be our slaves they might live, but as they won't be that, won't toil and delve and hew for us, and will persist in hunting, fishing, and roaming over the beautiful prairie land which the Great Spirit gave them: in a word, since they will be free—we will kill them'; this Butler who on the same journey contemplated the parklands of the Saskatchewan, observed their remarkable similarity to the English downs and found it 'mortifying to an Englishman' that they were, as he so concisely put it, 'totally undeveloped': this Butler was forced over an unseeable landscape by a November blizzard to be confronted by a woman's face, her thick black braids hanging to her hips; wearing a loose nightgown.

The nightgown was probably not thin. More likely it was heavy flannel since any Hudson's Bay fort at the time (they were really nothing of forts but rather clusters of log buildings surrounded by log palisades, all of which could and did, as easily by accident as by design, burn to the ground) was badly heated by cavernous openhearth fireplaces, doubtless she wore that heavy flannel of solid red or delicate floral design which the Company traded with the Cree and which those people suspended as gift offerings to the Thunderbird on the Centre Tree of their thirst dance lodges in June. And here it would hang as gracefully, draping between braids, shoulders and arms and nipples and hips a slender revelation. And the very handsome, six-foot-two and always brave and presently very hoarfrosted Lieutenant Butler, late of her Majesty's 69th Regiment in India and the Fenian Raids in Quebec across the Canadian border from New York, and most recently renowned as Intelligence Officer of the Colonel Wolseley Red River Expedition against the Métis founder of Manitoba, Louis Riel: frozen or not, Butler must fall instantly in love.

As he stood there, erect and frozen, clamped to the handsawn plank of the doorframe, his faithful pony having discharged its final faithful duty of carrying him to safety and about to collapse in faithful exhaustion behind him, did Lieutenant Butler say, 'Madam, I very nearly gave up hope of ever reaching succour'?

And did she reply as stiffly, 'O sir, our rude abode is but little better than the storm, nevertheless . . .'?

And he, accepting her hesitation: 'Madam, if I may be so importunate . . .'?

And she, accepting his: 'O sir, of course, do come in sir, come in out of the storm'?

And did she turn to send the dark servant woman standing

behind her scurrying to the kitchen to revive the fire that was no more than embers in the hearth?

Perhaps that was how Fort Pitt, named after the great Prime Minister but doomed never to be as famous as Pittsburgh, named after his father the Great Commoner, perhaps that was how Fort Pitt offered itself to him. Or did she exclaim out of the lamplight, 'O la sir, what a storm brings you here!' and he, bursting into laughter, reply, 'What you see is mere weather, my fine wench. There will yet be greater storms than this!' Staring so closely down into the luminous whiteness of breasts her nightgown made but small attempt to contain.

Her father, Hudson's Bay Factor John Sinclair, had only a brutal litany of disease and starvation and death to offer him at Fort Pitt. He always kept the palisade gate locked—some damn Indian had tore it loose—every building locked, they were under siege and if thirty-two of sixty people at Fort Carlton was dead, including the factor, and half the McDougall missionary family at Victoria dead too, then Pitt had been saved because he wouldn't let one goddamn Indian into the place, trade or no trade, locked them all out, and he had been damn quick in summer when he first heard the smallpox spreading and he got some blood out of a Saulteaux Indian vaccinated at the mission in Prince Albert and used that to vaccinate everybody—well, damn near everybody—in Pitt and he had kept every Cree locked out, every bloody one of them: Butler could barely restrain himself. Use them, use them any way you can, use their very blood . . . but he sat at the kitchen table devouring (with perfect Army manners, of course) the mound of buffalo steak and potatoes Mary (now properly dressed, of course) served him before the pine fire blazing on the hearth—where was the mother, the inevitable Indian, at best Métis, mother? The free traders, muttered Sinclair into his rum, had destroyed the hide and fur trade anyway, what did they care about Indians, just soak the buggers in whisky, steal all they could from them today and to hell with tomorrow, so now even at Pitt, the very heart of buffalo country, the beasts were gone, not enough robes this summer to make three decent bundles and he'd have nothing at all to eat except potatoes if Big Bear, that ugly little bastard that never got sick, hadn't dragged in ten to trade and he'd risked taking them even though half of Big Bear's band was spitting blood, they caught it fighting the Peigans near the border who got it from the American Bloods, hell, they said it was the US Army deliberately infecting the Indians down there to wipe them off the face of the earth because it was costing them damn near a million dollars each to shoot them! The smallpox was sure cheaper, about as cheap as wolfers throwing strychnine all over the prairie, and about as effective. There'd soon be nothing but corpses stinking up the whole goddamn stinking North-West.

Butler looked at him carefully: Sinclair was typical enough, a poor Scot forced to spend his whole life remembering home from the other side of the world, living who knows how in what overwhelming monotony of daily life and endless, endless miserable seasons repeating themselves, too old now for even the occasional Indian woman to rouse him, and suddenly a government official appears out of the night at whom he could momentarily blurt whatever he wanted, an official not on the summer boats but riding an assignment in the dead of a deadly boring winter on orders from the Lieutenant Governor of the Territories—there was one at long last—someone who had been within breathing distance of all those invisible Hudson's Bay lords in London barely seven months before, who had often smelled the 'goddamn heather' and seen the Queen herself who had finally survived her grief for Albert and was now the emerging mother of a world empire: what poor lonely sot of a homesick Scot wouldn't seize such an opportunity to snore every pessimistic worry he had aloud into his grog?

To be starving in Pitt, Sinclair suddenly roared, is like freezing to death in Newcastle! This is buffalo country, one herd moved over these hills for seventeen days and nights in '62, over two million, there was no end of them summer or winter and he'd fed every fort from Rocky Mountain House to Vermilion and the Pas, every goddamn fur dragged out of this country and every bloody ounce of stuff dragged back into it in every bloody York boat—every fuckin' trader had Pitt pemmican in his gut and now Big Bear brings in ten jesus carcasses and he has to burn the hides and boil the fuckin' jesus christ out of the meat! But at least that old bugger knew what he was doing, telling people to leave the fort and scatter in the bush and maybe the winter would be cold enough to kill the white man's disease, though what they would live on, even their dogs and miserable horses so far gone. . . .

Butler saw Mary Sinclair turn like a flame in front of the fire. After a month of half-fried bannock and pemmican—which had all the taste of boiled shoeleather—her baked potatoes were beyond any remembered cream and butter, dear god their very aroma—and she facing solitary winter darkness, a lifetime of that incredible skin drying up in cold and mosquito-and-blackfly heat, such a shape hammered slack by year after year pregnancies. At her bend by the hearth for another rack of buffalo rib he felt his body thaw and stretch completely, his powerful legs, toes flaring so fluidly, a kind of tensile vividness she awoke in his hands hard from cold and clenched reins all day, a touch of, somehow, flesh and resistance needed; despite heavy cotton the length of her leg, her curved thigh, her quick smile past her shoulder, her extraordinary face even when seen sideways or upside-down. Her father snored, fat arms flat on the table: every night such a lullaby and every night lying somewhere innocent, somewhere in this clumsy building, every night she was here naked against cotton and he rolled in his deerskin sack on the frozen prairie, sweetest jesus why is there no comfort in the world ever *together*?

The Métis servant came sluffing down the stairs. The bed for the gentleman was warming with hot stones between buffalo robes, would he go up? It was Mary who spoke, Mary who led him up the narrow stairs through her own shadow to the door, opening it without so much as a glance: she gave him the lantern and was gone, not a gesture of her lithe body even at his stumbled goodnight, and thank you again . . . the hall was empty before he grasped her going. Wind moaned in crevices. Well, doubtless to help the Métis woman hoist her father back into bed again. He stripped quickly, blew out the light. The stones were too hot, the robes total ice; he felt his body slowly shrinking into a huddle. Be I as chaste as ice, as pure as snow, I shall not . . . he sensed a footstep and sat up: she was there, he knew. But it was several seconds before the rustle she made told him she was lifting the heavy cotton nightgown over her head.

Could he say anything when she came in beside him, he the Irishman of endless easy words, when she laughed aloud so gently at all his sweaty underwear? And she peeled it off him, chuckling again at the memory of his goodnight, did he think Pitt was a hotel and she a chambermaid? Hot stones in bed were no better than campfires: you were always roasted on one side and freezing on the other. He may have had a small hesitation,

The bed . . . is too narrow.
Wide enough for one is wide enough for two.

And her skin fit completely around him, her head warm as opening lips in the hollow of his neck. If despite twelve years of Her Majesty's army his body still did not know what to do, she doubtless helped him to that too; and perhaps his own skin and various tongues in that black room taught him something of her invisible shape.

Perhaps this happened to William Francis Butler in Fort Pitt in the North-Western Territories of Canada on the night of November 18, 1870. Perhaps, if he was *really* lucky and Mary Sinclair was, thanks to her mother (certainly not her father), one of the world's perfect communists.

There is of course another story; the one Mary Sinclair told forty years later. Before the rebellion, she said, when I was only a young girl, an English officer came to Fort Pitt. He was tall and very good looking and he talked and talked and he could talk so well I thought perhaps I could love him. He told me about his home in Ireland, he came out of the snow and storm one night like someone from a different world and then when his men arrived after him he rode on to Fort Edmonton and I could only think about him. But he came back again, and he asked me to marry him. He asked me to go live with him in the Old Country. There I was, a child of the Saskatchewan, what would I do in another country? Perhaps I cried a little, but I sent him away. And after a while I did not think about him so often.

I sent him away. That is how Mary Sinclair later told it; but not Butler. He wrote a book, and he mentions her only in the same sentence as 'buffalo steaks and potatoes'. For these in Fort Pitt, he writes, 'I had the brightest eyed little lassie, half Cree, half Scotch, in the whole North-West to wait upon me,' and he mentions this 'lassie' not at all on his return journey from Fort Edmonton at the end of December, 1870, when bitter cold and a lack of sled dogs forced him, so he writes, to wait at Fort Pitt for seven days. Did she then also with steak and potatoes wait upon him? Serve him? Such a handsome Victorian soldier wrapped in tall furs on government assignment would perhaps not have remembered that she sent him away, especially not after he discovered in Ottawa a mere four months later that all the 'excellent colonial ministers', as he calls them, had large families and that 'an army officer who married a minister's daughter might perchance be a fit and proper person to introduce the benefits of civilization to the Cree and Blackfeet Indians on the western prairies, but if he elected to remain in single cussedness in Canada he was pretty certain to find himself a black sheep among the ministerial flock of aspirants for place.' Premier John A. Macdonald's only daughter Mary was handicapped beyond any possible marriage, and the most beautiful girl on the prairies could certainly not have helped Butler be an 'aspirant for place' in lumber Ottawa so, despite letters as excellent as excellent colonial ministers could make them for his excellent service, the tall officer returned to the heart of the Empire still a lieutenant, still without a permanent government appointment, still without a steady war in which to achieve the fortune that could purchase his promotion; he could not know that soon the kingdoms of hot Africa would provide him with a quarter of a century of men he could, with his enormous organizational efficiency, help to kill. In Fort Pitt on the Saskatchewan in November and December, 1870, during cold so severe no Englishman could imagine it, a beautiful young woman 'waited upon me', as he said; sent him away, as she said.

Or is a fourth story possible? Did they dream together, narrow bed or not? Did they see those enormous herds of buffalo that once flowed along the rivers there, such a streaming of life never again seen anywhere on the surface of the earth or even in the depths of the sea? And in the darkness did they see the long, hesitant parade of the Cree chiefs approaching Treaty Number Six that ordered them thereby to cede, release, surrender, and yield up all that land forever, and behind them the one chief who would not, the chief Big Bear as the whites called him, but perhaps better translated 'Too Much' or 'More Than Enough Bear' who would ask them all how could one person give away forever what they had all forever had, who had more than enough of everything except the power to persuade his people of his defiant vision until Fort Pitt was burning, was becoming a great pillar of smoke bent over the river and the empty hills and all that flour and rancid treaty pork they had never wanted, had abhorred as soon as ever they saw it, surrounded them, rained on them, dripped black and stinking out of the very air they were forced to breathe?

> She knows that darkness alone can offer what he longs to accept. Smell and touch and the tongue in the ear, yes, taste itself, yes, yes—but not sight. Eyes for him are impossible.

The fire locked inside each palisade log, the factor's house, the spruce walls close about their narrow bed springs into light, fire lifts Fort Pitt, transforms it into air and its place, here, on this earth, is lost to any memory, the valley and the hills changed as they are already eternally changed beyond the going of the animals and some day the Hutterite farmers will break through the bristly poplars, domesticate them into wheat fields and a plough furrow along the bank of the still relentless river one day reveals a shard of blue willow china; its delicate pastoral a century's confirmation of her waiting upon him, of her serving him?

> Behind the double darkness of his clenched eyes he sees again the length of his rifle barrel and the black hair whorled behind Blackie's straining ear: the blood explodes exactly there! They had to cross today, the daily plan is irrevocable, iron shoes or not on thin ice or no ice they must cross, and his groans, his endlessly contained and most irregular, totally unplanned, tears.

They may have dreamed something together. Possibly they dreamed the scarlet riders of the police he would recommend the Canadian government establish to force English law upon the western plains, the police whose thin implacable lines would weave the red shroud of the old Queen's authority over every child of the Saskatchewan until Inspector Francis Jeffrey Dickens, the great novelist's third son who aspired to his appointment by patronage, not by excellent merit of excellent colonial service, would at Fort Pitt become the most infamous officer in the history of the world-famous force. Force indeed.

Or they dreamed again the gaunt Cree dying, scraping their pustulated legs and arms and breasts and infants' faces along the gates, the doorframes, the windows of the locked fort to force the white man's disease back upon him, to somehow smear him with his own putrefaction. And perhaps they also dreamed Big Bear walking so emaciated among his people, his magnificent voice persuading them they must scatter to the woods and the animals, that only on the solitary land would they be given the strength to destroy this invisible, this incomprehensible evil that rotted them, his words and his great scarred face proof of his lifelong power over the white man's diseases, his name certain and forever More Than Enough Bear for everything except the white man's words on the white man's paper, words that would one day endlessly whisper to him behind the thick, sweating walls of Stony Mountain Penitentiary.

Was it Big Bear who helped her say to him then: go away.

Only she could dream that. It is impossible for Lieutenant William Francis Butler to dream such a hopeless dream; even in a narrow bed in Fort Pitt, even in Mary Sinclair's warm and beautiful arms.

Biographies

MARGARET ATWOOD was born in Ottawa in 1939, educated at the University of Toronto and at Radcliffe College, Harvard University, and now lives in Toronto. Distinguished in poetry, fiction, and criticism, she is one of Canada's best-known writers, with an international reputation, and has been generous and outspoken in support of artistic, political, and social causes in Canada and abroad.

Atwood's first book of poems, *The Circle Game* (1966), won a Governor General's Award. Since then she has published eight other collections of new poems, including *The Journals of Susanna Moodie* (1970), *Power Politics* (1973), *Two-Headed Poems* (1978), and *Inter-lunar* (1984); her *Selected Poems: 1966-84* was published by Oxford University Press Canada in 1990. She is the editor of *The New Oxford Book of Canadian Verse in English* (1982) and co-editor (with Robert Weaver) of *The Oxford Book of Canadian Short Stories in English* (1986). Her novels are *The Edible Woman* (1969), *Surfacing* (1972), *Lady Oracle* (1976), *Life Before Man* (1979), *Bodily Harm* (1981), *The Handmaid's Tale* (1985), and *Cat's Eye* (1988). Both *Surfacing* and *The Handmaid's Tale* have been filmed. In criticism Atwood is the author of the influential and controversial *Survival: A Thematic Guide to Canadian Literature* (1972) and of *Second Words: Selected Critical Prose* (1982).

Margaret Atwood's short fiction has been collected in *Dancing Girls* (1977), *Murder in the Dark* (1983), and *Bluebeard's Egg* (1983). 'The Age of Lead' was first published in *Toronto Life* and will be included in a new collection of her stories, *Wilderness Tips*, to be published by McClelland & Stewart in September 1991.

NEIL BISSOONDATH was born in 1955 in Trinidad and now lives in Montreal. He comes from a literary family. His grandfather, Seepersad

Naipaul, was a journalist on the *Trinidad Guardian* for most of his working life and published a collection of short stores in Trinidad in 1943. Two of his sons became well-known writers: V.S. Naipaul and Shiva Naipaul, who died suddenly at the age of forty in August 1985.

Bissoondath immigrated to Canada in 1973, partly on the advice of his uncle, V.S. Naipaul. He studied French at York University, Toronto, and afterwards taught in a language school in that city. He has published two collections of short stories, *Digging Up the Mountains* (1985) and *On the Eve of Uncertain Tomorrows* (1990)—which includes 'Security'—and a novel, *A Casual Brutality* (1988).

DIONNE BRAND was born in Trinidad in 1953 and now lives in Toronto, where she studied at the University of Toronto and OISE. She is best known as a writer of poetry that has been published in a number of literary magazines and anthologies, including the *Penguin Book of Caribbean Verse*. Her most recent collection, *No Language Is Neutral* (1990), was published by Coach House Press. Dionne Brand's short stories have been published in *Fireweed* and the anthologies *Stories by Canadian Women* and *From Ink Lake*. Her collection *Sans Souci and Other Stories* (1988) includes 'St Mary's Estate'. She has been writer-in-residence at the Halifax City Regional Library and the University of Toronto. Her *Lives of Black Working Women in Ontario—an Oral History* is forthcoming.

BONNIE BURNARD (b. 1945) lives in Regina. Four of her stories appeared in *Coming Attractions* (1983), the annual anthology in which Oberon Press introduces new fiction writers. Other stories have been published in various literary magazines, broadcast on CBC radio, and dramatized for television. Burnard's short-story collection, *Women of Influence* (1988), was named the best first-published book in the Caribbean-Canada region for the 1989 Commonwealth Writers' Prize. It includes 'Moon Watcher', which was previously published in *Best Canadian Short Stories* (1981) and in the anthology *More Saskatchewan Gold* (1984).

TIMOTHY FINDLEY was born in Toronto in 1930. The city of his birth, two world wars, the ugly history of fascism in the twentieth century, the lives of such public figures as Ezra Pound and the Duke and

Duchess of Windsor are all obsessions with which his fictions try to come to terms.

Before becoming a writer Findley had a promising career as an actor. He played summer stock in Ontario and worked in the Stratford (Ontario) Shakespearean Festival in its first season in 1953. Then, for three years, he acted in Europe, England, and the United States, and was encouraged by, among others, Ruth Gordon and Thornton Wilder. Throughout his later career as a writer of fiction he has continued to write scripts for CBC radio and television and has also occasionally acted.

Findley's first short stories were published or broadcast when he was in his twenties; two novels, *The Last of the Crazy People* and *The Butterfly Plague*, were published in the late 1960s. *The Wars* (1977) won a Governor General's Award, and it was followed by *Famous Last Words* (1981), *Not Wanted on the Voyage* (1984), and *The Telling of Lies* (1986). Findley's short stories have been collected in *Dinner Along the Amazon* (1984) and *Stones* (1988), the title story of which has been reprinted here. His most recent book is *Inside Memory* (1990), a selection of journal entries and memoirs covering his career in the theatre, as a novelist, and as an activist on artistic issues in Canada.

CYNTHIA FLOOD (b. 1940) lives in Vancouver, where she teaches English at Langara College. For the past two decades she has been active in the women's movement and in left-wing politics. Her short stories have been published in several anthologies and a number of literary journals, including *Fireweed*, *Queen's Quarterly*, *Room of One's Own*, and *Wascana Review*. Her story 'My Father Took a Cake to France', first published in the *Malahat Review*, won the $10,000 Journey Prize and was published in the second edition of *The Journey Prize Anthology* (1980), published by McClelland & Stewart. 'A Young Girl-Typist Ran to Smolny . . .'—one of several stories about people who are deeply involved in radical politics—is from Cynthia Flood's first collection *The Animals in Their Elements* (1987).

MAVIS GALLANT was born in Montreal in 1922 and educated in seventeen different public, private, and convent schools in Canada and the United States. She worked briefly for the National Film Board and then on the Montreal *Standard*, a weekly newspaper that was a competitor of the Toronto *Star Weekly* (both newspapers are now gone). She left Montreal in 1950 and has lived in Paris ever since, though she returned to Canada in 1983-4 to be writer-in-residence at the University of Toronto.

Gallant has published two novels, *Green Water, Green Sky* (1959) and *A Fairly Good Time* (1970), and a half-dozen collections of short stories. Almost all her stories first appeared in *The New Yorker*, to which she first began contributing in 1951. Her collections are *The Other Paris* (1956), *My Heart Is Broken* (1959), *The Pegnitz Junction* (1973), *From the Fifteenth District* (1979), *Home Truths: Selected Canadian Stories* (1981), which won a Governor General's Award, and *Overhead in a Balloon: Stories of Paris* (1985), which includes 'Lena'. A selection of Gallant's stories, *The End of the World and Other Stories*, edited by Robert Weaver, was published in the New Canadian Library in 1974.

Mavis Gallant has also written distinguished non-fiction. *The New Yorker* published, in September 1968, her two-part account of the student riots in Paris in the spring of that year—'The Events in May: A Paris Notebook'—and a long essay, 'Immortal Gatito: The Gabrielle Russier Case' (June 26, 1971), about a thirty-year-old teacher of languages in Marseilles who had a love affair with a sixteen-year-old male student, and who, hounded by French society, later killed herself. These essays, with other writings, were collected in *Paris Notebooks: Essays and Reviews* (1986).

KATHERINE GOVIER was born in 1948 in Edmonton and studied at the University of Alberta, where she was encouraged as a young writer by Rudy Wiebe and Dorothy Livesay. She now lives in Toronto, where she has taught creative-writing courses at York University and is active in national writers' organizations. She has written articles and reviews for the Toronto *Globe & Mail*, the Toronto *Star*, *Saturday Night*, and *Toronto Life*, and has won several national journalism awards, but she is best known as a writer of fiction. She has published three novels, *Random Descent* (1979), *Going Through the Motions* (1982), and *Between Men* (1987). Her fourth novel, *Hearts of Flame*, will be published by Viking in the fall of 1991. Katherine Govier's short stories have been published in magazines in Canada and abroad, and her first collection, *Fables of Brunswick Avenue* (1985), appeared in the Penguin Short Fiction series. 'The King of Siam' was first published in *Encounter* (London) and is included in her second collection, *Before and After* (1989).

JANICE KULYK KEEFER, born in Toronto in 1953, has been able to combine an academic career with an impressive range of literary activities. She received her doctorate in modern English literature from the University of Sussex. She taught at the Université Sainte-Anne in Nova Scotia, where she lived for several years, and now teaches at the University of Guelph. She has published a collection of poetry, *White of the Lesser Angels* (1986), and a novel, *Constellations* (1989), but Keefer is best known for her short stories. They have been collected in *The Paris-Napoli Express* (1986), *Transfigurations* (1988), and *Travelling Ladies* (1990), which includes 'A Really Good Hotel'. She won the first prize for fiction in both the 1985 and the 1986 CBC Literary Competition. She is also the author of two critical works, *Under Eastern Eyes* (1987), a study of Maritime fiction, which was nominated for a Governor General's Award, and *Reading Mavis Gallant* (1989).

NORMAN LEVINE was born in 1923 and grew up in Ottawa's Lower Town. He served in the RCAF during the Second World War and afterwards studied at McGill University. He went to England in the late 1950s and lived there—for much of the time in St Ives, Cornwall—until his return to Canada in 1980. He now lives in Toronto. He has been a full-time writer for most of his adult life.

Levine published a collection of poetry, *The Tight-Rope Walker*, in 1950, and a war novel, *The Angled Road*, two years later. In the mid-1950s he began to work on a book combining autobiographical material with an investigation of Canadian society from the underside, in the manner of Henry Miller and George Orwell: *Canada Made Me*, published in England and the United States in 1958. There was no Canadian edition until 1979.

Levine published a second novel, *From a Seaside Town*, in 1970. But he is best known, as a writer of fiction, for his short stories. Among his collections are *One Way Ticket* (1961), *Thin Ice* (1979), and *Champagne Barn* (1984). Many of his stories have been broadcast by the CBC and the BBC and have been translated and published throughout Europe. 'Something Happened Here' has been broadcast by the CBC and published in *Encounter* (England), and is included in the most recent German collection of Levine's short fiction. It is the title story in his latest collection, published in 1991.

DANIEL DAVID MOSES was born in 1952 on a farm on the Six Nations lands along the Grand River in southwestern Ontario, and as he grew up he was very much influenced by the Iroquoian religious and political systems. He graduated in Fine Arts from York University, Toronto, and earned an MA from the University of British Columbia, where in 1977 he won the Creative Writing Department's prize for drama. In 1979 he returned to Toronto, where he worked at a number of jobs until, in 1986, he began to devote all his time to writing, producing poetry, short fiction, and plays. He has published two poetry collections, *Delicate Bodies* (1978) and *The White Line* (1990). His play *Coyote City* received a production by Native Earth Performing Arts, Toronto, in May 1988, and its sequel, *Big Buck City*, was workshopped at the Theatre Passe Muraille the following month and will be produced in 1991. 'King of the Raft' first appeared in Issue 16 (1987) of *Canadian Fiction Magazine*, devoted to native writers and edited by Thomas King.

ALICE MUNRO (b. 1931) lives in Clinton in southwestern Ontario, not far from Lake Huron or from another town, Wingham, where she was born and grew up. Most of her stories are set in fictitious towns that clearly belong to this part of Ontario—'Alice Munro country'.

She began writing stories while she was a student at the University of Western Ontario, and her early fiction was published in *Queen's Quarterly*, *The Canadian Forum*, *Chatelaine*, *The Montrealer*, and *The Tamarack Review*. Her first collection of stories, *Dance of the Happy Shades* (1968), won a Governor General's Award (she has won three Governor General's Awards for fiction); her first, and only, novel, *Lives of Girls and Women* (1971), won the Canadian Booksellers' Award in 1972. Five more collections of her stories have been published: *Something I've Been Meaning to Tell You* (1974), *Who Do You Think You Are?* (1978), *The Moons of Jupiter* (1982), *The Progress of Love* (1986), and *Friend of My Youth* (1990). 'Meneseteung', like most of Alice Munro's recent stories, first appeared in *The New Yorker*, and is included in *Friend of My Youth*.

Several of Munro's stories have been dramatized for television. 'Boys and Girls', a production of Atlantis Films, Toronto, won an Academy Award in 1984. Alice Munro was the first Canadian winner, in 1978, of the Canada-Australia Prize, and she received the Molson Prize in 1991.

DIANE SCHOEMPERLEN was born in 1954 in Thunder Bay, Ontario. She graduated from Lakehead University there and lived for the next ten years in Canmore, Alberta, working at various jobs, including bank teller and avalanche researcher. She now lives in Kingston, where she teaches creative writing at St Lawrence College and in the summer at the Kingston School of Writing, Queen's University. Schoemperlen has published four books of short fiction: *Double Exposures* (1984), *Frogs and Other Stories* (1986), *Hockey Night in Canada* (1987), and *The Man of My Dreams* (1990). In 1986 *Frogs and Other Stories* won the Writers' Guild of Alberta Award for Excellence in Short Fiction, and the title story from *Hockey Night in Canada* has been made into a 30-minute television play.

'Red Plaid Shirt' was first published in *Saturday Night* and is included in *The Man of My Dreams*.

CAROL SHIELDS (née Carol Warner) was born in Oak Park, Illinois, in 1935, and was educated in Indiana and at the University of Ottawa. Married to Douglas Shields, a professor of civil engineering, and the mother of five children, she has taught at the Universities of Ottawa, British Columbia, and Manitoba, and lives in Winnipeg.

Shields has had a wide-ranging literary career. Beginning in the early 1970s she has published poetry, short stories, literary criticism— her MA thesis, later published as a monograph, was about Susanna Moodie—and novels, and has written plays for radio and the stage. Her first novel, *Small Ceremonies* (1976), won the Canadian Authors' Association Award for the best novel of the year. Her other novels are *The Box Garden* (1977), *Happenstance* (1980), *A Fairly Conventional Woman* (1982), and *Swann: A Mystery* (1987). A new novel, *Bodies of Water*, will be published in 1992. A Carol Shields Issue of the magazine *Room of One's Own* appeared in 1989, and she was given the Marian Engel Award in 1990.

Sheilds' stories have been collected in *Various Miracles* (1985) and *The Orange Fish* (1985), which contains 'Milk Bread Beer Ice', first published in *Saturday Night*.

AUDREY THOMAS was born in 1935 in Binghamton, NY, and educated at Smith College in Massachusetts and St Andrew's University in Scotland. She and her former husband immigrated to Canada in 1959 and in the mid-1960s spent three years in Ghana. The United States, Canada, West Africa, and Scotland have all provided settings for her fiction. In recent years she has combined her writing with periods of teaching at the University of Victoria, the University of British Columbia, the Centre of Canadian Studies at the University of Edinburgh, and Concordia University in Montreal. She won the Canada-Australia Literary Prize for 1989 and will spend some time in Australia early in 1991. The magazine *Room of One's Own* published an Audrey Thomas Issue in 1986.

Thomas's fiction has been almost equally balanced between novels and collections of short stories. The novels include *Mrs Blood* (1970), *Songs My Mother Taught Me* (1973), *Blown Figures* (1974), and *Intertidal Life* (1984). Her first collection of stories was *Ten Green Bottles* (1967), followed by *Ladies & Escorts* (1977), *Real Mothers* (1981) in the New Canadian Library, *Goodbye Harold, Good Luck* (1986), and *The Wild Blue Yonder* (1990), from which 'Blue Spanish Eyes' is taken.

W.D. VALGARDSON (b. 1939) grew up in Gimli, a town in the Interlake District not far from Winnipeg, whose inhabitants are mostly of Icelandic descent. He was educated at United College in Winnipeg, the University of Manitoba, and the University of Iowa, where he was enrolled in the influential Writers' Workshop. Valgardson has published four collections of stories: *Bloodflowers* (1973), *God is Not a Fish Inspector* (1975), *Red Dust* (1978), and *What Can't Be Changed Shouldn't Be Mourned* (1990). Many of his stories have been translated and published in Russia, East Germany, and the Ukraine. He is also the author of two books of poetry, *In the Gutting Shed* (1978) and *The Carpenter of Dreams* (1986), and of a novel, *Gentle Sinners*, which won the 'Books in Canada' First Novel Award for 1980. *Gentle Sinners* and several of Valgardson's short stories have been filmed for television, and he has written a number of radio plays for the CBC. He lives in Victoria, B.C., and teaches in the Creative Writing Department of the University of Victoria. 'The Cave' was first published in the magazine *Border Crossings* and is included in *What Can't Be Changed Shouldn't Be Mourned*.

RUDY WIEBE was born in 1934 near Fairholme, Saskatchewan, and attended a Mennonite High School in Coaldale, Alberta. He studied at the University of Alberta, where he now teaches Canadian literature and creative writing, and the University of Tubingen in Germany. In addition to his full-time teaching career, Wiebe has been a prolific and ambitious writer. He has published a half-dozen novels and two books of short stories. Two of the novels—*Peace Shall Destroy Many* (1962) and *The Blue Mountains of China* (1970)—are concerned with the Mennonite experience in the New World. *First and Vital Candle* (1966) is about Indian and Eskimo life in the North. Both *The Temptations of Big Bear* (1973), winner of a Governor General's Award, and *The Scorched-Wood People* (1977) are about the nineteenth-century rebellions of the Indians and Métis in the Canadian Northwest. *The Mad Trapper* (1980) is about Albert Johnson (who shot a Mountie and was hunted down and killed in a dramatic chase through the North), who had already been the subject of an essay by Wiebe and a short story.

Wiebe's short stories have been collected in *Where Is the Voice Coming From?* (1974) and *The Angel of the Tar Sands and Other Stories* (1982). The story in this anthology, 'A Night in Fort Pitt . . .', was first published in *Saturday Night*.